AF334525

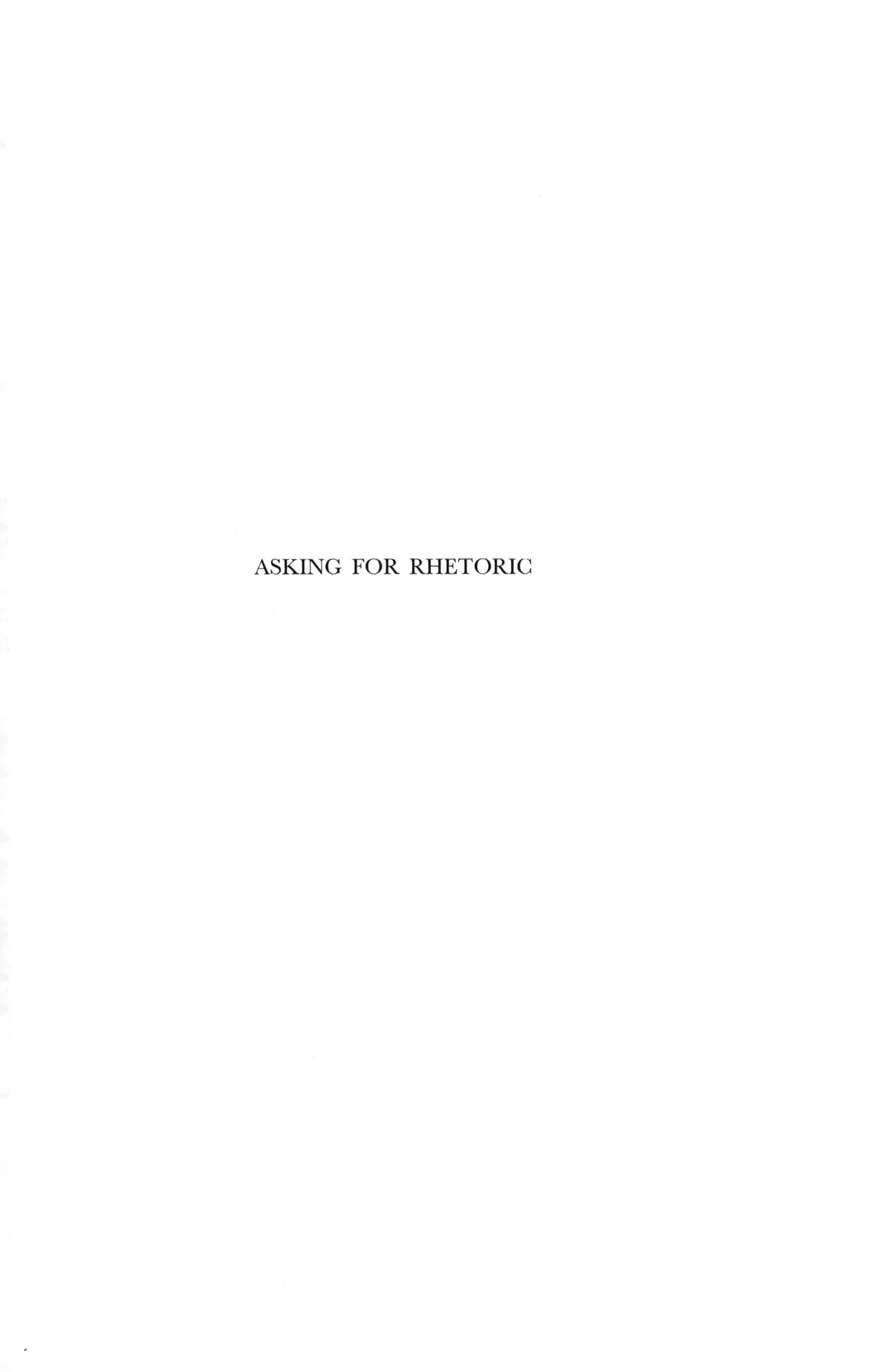

ASKING FOR RHETORIC

BIBLICAL INTERPRETATION SERIES

Editors

R. ALAN CULPEPPER
ROLF RENTDORF
ELLEN VAN WOLDE

VOLUME 73

ASKING FOR RHETORIC

The Hebrew Bible's Protean Interrogative

KENNETH M. CRAIG, JR.

BRILL ACADEMIC PUBLISHERS, INC.
BOSTON • LEIDEN
2005

Library of Congress Cataloging-in-Publication Data

Craig, Kenneth M., 1960–
Asking for rhetoric: the Hebrew Bible's protean interrogative / by Kenneth M. Craig, Jr.
p. cm — (Biblical interpretation series; v. 73)
Includes bibliographical references and index.
ISBN 0–391–04231–9
1. Bible. O.T.—Criticism, interpretation, etc. 2. Questioning in the Bible. 3. Rhetoric in the Bible. I. Title. II. Series.

BS1171.3.C73 2005
221.6'6—dc22

2004027245

ISSN 0928–0731
ISBN 0–391–04231–9

PRINTED IN THE UNITED STATES OF AMERICA

To

Alexandra and Luke

CONTENTS

TABLES

PREFACE

Research for this monograph was made possible in part by various grants. I am grateful to the Andrew W. Mellon Foundation Trust and the Appalachian College Association for fellowships I received in 1997 and 1998, to the Catholic Biblical Association for the CBA Young Scholar's Fellowship I received in 1995, and to Lees-McRae College for providing travel money to professional conferences.

Earlier forms of three chapters appeared in journals, and I am grateful to editors who have granted me permission to incorporate revisions in this book: *Journal for the Study of the Old Testament* 86 (1999): 107–28 (chapter 3); *Catholic Biblical Quarterly* 56 (1994): 221–39 (chapter 4); *Semeia* 63 (1993): 159–76 (chapter 9). An earlier form of chapter 11 was first published in *Forming Prophetic Literature. Essays on Isaiah and the Twelve in Honor of John D. W. Watts* (Sheffield: Sheffield Academic Press, 1996), 224–44. Preliminary drafts of some chapters were also presented at meetings of the Society of Biblical Literature and the American Academy of Religion, and I am grateful for the insightful remarks from members of both societies (see note 1 in chapter 1).

To my colleagues in the Humanities Division at Lees-McRae College I am greatly indebted for many illuminating comments and debates. I particularly benefited from frequent exchanges of ideas with Rachel McClure, whose insightful questions and many conversations have taught me more about theology than I learned in graduate school, and also with Michael Vines and Alison Gulley, whose ostensibly different research interests more than once proved relevant to mine. I should also like to single out John Keener, chair of our division, and Jim Watts, at Syracuse University. Both read my work in the face of a recalcitrant subject and an equally recalcitrant manuscript. They have helped me more than I can say. Correspondence and conversation with Jack Sasson (Vanderbilt Divinity School) and Phyllis Trible (Wake Forest University Divinity School) proved helpful at an early stage. I should also like to thank Dwaine Greene (Campbell University), Burke Long (Bowdoin College), Robert Polzin (Carleton University), and Evelyn Thibeaux (Georgetown University) for their interest and comments on early chapter drafts. For the weakness and imperfections that remain I am responsible. Another group of readers, who are every bit as important as the preceding but who must here remain an anonymous band, are the many Lees-McRae College students who over the past several years have studied with me the texts explored herein. They revealed in their unencumbered readings unexpected facets of texts I had turned over in my mind many times before.

Research would not have been possible without two libraries and their keepers, at the University of North Carolina at Chapel Hill and at Lees-McRae College. Patti Bowers, Faye Williams, and Ramona Hayes at the latter were always helpful and efficient when I needed assistance. The software developers and support staff at Nota Bene also helped by simplifying the task of writing. The greatest source of support has come from my wife, Niki, and our children, Alexandra and Luke, for they give my life meaning.

Most translations of scripture are my own. On occasion, I follow the New Revised Standard Version.

ABBREVIATIONS

AB	Anchor Bible
ABD	*Anchor Bible Dictionary*, ed. David Noel Freedman, New York, 1992
AJSL	*American Journal of Semitic Languages*
ANET	*Ancient Near Eastern Texts Relating to the Old Testament*, 3rd edition, ed. J. B. Pritchard, Princeton, 1969
Ant.	Josephus, *Jewish Antiquities*
ASOR	American Schools of Oriental Research
BTrans	*The Bible Translator*
Bib	*Biblica*
BWANT	Beiträge zur Wissenschaft vom Alten und Neuen Testament
CBC	Cambridge Bible Commentary on the New English Bible
CBQ	*Catholic Biblical Quarterly*
EI	*Eretz Israel*
ETL	*Ephemerides Theologicae Lovanienses*
GKC	*Gesenius' Hebrew Grammar*, 28th edition, ed. E. Kautzsch, trans. A. E. Cowley, Oxford, 1910
G^L	Greek text, Lucianic recension
GNB	Good News Bible
HAR	*Hebrew Annual Review*
HS	*Hebrew Studies*
HTIBS	Historical Texts and Interpreters in Biblical Scholarship
HUCA	*Hebrew Union College Annual*
ICC	International Critical Commentary
impf.	imperfect
inf. abs.	infinitive absolute
Int	*Interpretation*
JB	Jerusalem Bible
JBL	*Journal of Biblical Literature*
JBQ	*Jewish Biblical Quarterly*
JETS	*Journal of the Evangelical Theological Society*
JSOT	*Journal for the Study of the Old Testament*
JSOTSup	Journal for the Study of the Old Testament Supplement Series
JTS	*Journal of Theological Studies*

KJV	King James Version
LXX	Septuagint
MT	Massoretic Text
n.	note
NAB	New American Bible
NASB	New American Standard Bible
NCBC	New Century Bible Commentary
NEB	New English Bible
ni.	niphal
NICOT	New International Commentary on the Old Testament
NIV	New International Version
NJB	New Jerusalem Bible
NKJV	New King James Version
NRSV	New Revised Standard Version
OLP	*Orientalia lovaniensia periodica*
OTL	Old Testament Library
pf.	perfect
pl.	plural
REB	Revised English Bible
RHPR	*Revue d'histoire et de philosophie religieuses*
Proof	*Prooftexts*
Sam Pent	Samaritan Pentateuch
Sem	*Semeia*
sg.	singular
TDOT	*Theological Dictionary of the Old Testament*, ed. G. J. Botterweck, H. Ringgren, and H. J. Fabry; trans. J. T. Willis, G. W. Bromiley, and D. E. Green; Grand Rapids, 1974–
TS	*Theological Studies*
Vg	Vulgate
VT	*Vetus Testamentum*
VTSup	Vetus Testamentum Supplements
WBC	Word Biblical Commentary
ZAW	*Zeitschrift für die alttestamentliche Wissenschaft*

CHAPTER ONE

WHAT IS A QUESTION?

"David said, 'What have I done now? It was only a question.' "

—1 Samuel 17:29 (NRSV)

"Abner! Will you not answer?"

—1 Samuel 26:14 (NRSV)

"[Saul's] character zone is filled with doubt and uncertainty. Surrounded by a dubious aura, Saul is the epitome of a questionable choice. . . . our introduction to him . . . is one who . . . continually asks questions."

—Robert Polzin, *Samuel and the Deuteronomist*

The invocation of a question, an utterance in interrogative form, represents a special literary phenomenon.[1] A question is an opening that seeks to be closed, and its rhetorical play derives from how it

[1] My first attempt at surveying the myriad contours of questions began when I reflected on the book of Jonah's concluding interrogative in *A Poetics of Jonah: Art in the Service of Ideology* (Columbia, S.C.: University of South Carolina Press, 1993) 8, 17–18, 29–30, 60–70, 141–142, 157–158. Five subsequent papers laid the foundation for the present study. "Asking for Rhetoric: Invoking and Fielding Questions in Eden," presented to members of the "Reading, Rhetoric, and Hebrew Bible Section" of the national Society of Biblical Literature meeting in Chicago on November 21, 1994 (chapter 2); "Yhwh, Cain, and their Rhetorical Interchange," presented to members of the "Hebrew Scriptures / Old Testament Section" of the regional meeting of the Society of Biblical Literature in Gainesville, Florida, on March 11, 1995 (chapter 3); "Asking for Rhetoric: Rhetorical Questions in the Deuteronomistic History," presented to members of the "Reading, Rhetoric, and Hebrew Bible Section" of the national Society of Biblical Literature meeting in Kansas City on November 24, 1991 (chapters 1 and 4); "Rhetoric and the Character(ization) of God in 2 Samuel 7," presented to members of the "Reading, Rhetoric, and Hebrew Bible Section" of the national Society of Biblical Literature meeting in San Francisco on November 22, 1992 (chapter 9); and "What's the Literary Connection and other Trifling Issues Raised by Haggai-Zechariah 1–8,"

disposes its energies: how it invites opening, how it imposes closure. Questions are not innocent. They solicit replies while presupposing a range of acceptable responses. Proof is found in the Bible's very first question, when the serpent asks the woman, "Did God say?" "Every question is a seeking," Heidegger reminds us. "Every seeking gets guided beforehand by what is sought."[2] The journey from opening to closure reveals that questions not only mean something; they *do* something. The effectiveness of interrogatives depends not only on meaning—and the propositions they contain—but on the way they are uttered and received, that is, upon their illocutionary force. Questioners may ask, beg, solicit, demand, or lament, and the character, motives, and desires of petitioners are often indicated by tone. Questioners also expect answers, explanations, agreement, promise, reason, or solution, and the responses they receive may indicate the character and aims of the respondents as well. A quick look at two questions from the Deuteronomistic history reveals that meaning and illocutionary force are, in fact, interdependent phenomena. When Eli asks Hannah, "How long will you make a drunken spectacle of yourself?" (1 Sam 1:14), he not only reveals his limited perspective but also his desire to assert power over her. When David confronts Uriah, who has been summoned from the battlefield and asks how Joab and the people are doing and how the war is going (2 Sam 11:7), he, too, is playing the power game: his questions are a front, an attempt to cover over his thoughts with words.[3]

Questions frequently appear in biblical narrative. Characters invoke more than one hundred forty interrogatives in 1 Samuel, and a single chapter, 2 Samuel 19, contains more than twenty syntactical questions. In one of the most famous interchanges of the Bible, Yhwh and Cain invoke six interrogatives in a short narrative space (Gen 4:6–10), and their rhetorical interchange is only one example of the Hebrew Bible's deceptively simple art. In all these and other instances,

---

presented to members of the "Formation of the Book of the Twelve Consultation" of the national Society of Biblical Literature meeting in New Orleans on November 23, 1996 (chapter 11).

[2] Martin Heidegger, *Being and Time*, trans. John McQuarrie and Edward Robinson (New York: Harper, 1962), 24.

[3] David will later ask Uriah why he does not go down to his house. The reader senses the irony of Uriah's response as his refusal is stated twice—on the first occasion as a rhetorical question, and as an oath the second time. Both the question and the oath are emphatic devices (2 Sam 11:10–11).

questions function as part of overall syntactic, compositional, and stylistic plot designs where characterization is often achieved not only in the asking of questions but also in the fielding of them.

It is generally held that questions may be placed in one of two categories. (We will soon challenge this traditional understanding.) Characters sometimes ask for information; at other times they invoke questions for rhetorical flourish. The *information-seeker* is a question that people in both the real and the narrative worlds ask routinely when seeking details, motivations, data, explanations, and so forth. For example, when the Danites look for territory to claim as their own, they send five spies to explore the land around the hill country at Ephraim (Judg 18:1–2). While at Micah's house, the spies recognize (נכר)[4] the voice of a young Levite and desire to learn more. They ask him three questions: "Who brought you here? What are you doing in this place? What is your business here?" (v 3). The answer to this question series contains welcome news for the spies: this man is a priest, one who is able to address questions to—and, one assumes, get answers from—God (vv 5–6). A *rhetorical question*, the second type, is any utterance that invokes the conditions of an interrogative but serves some further figurative purpose, either assertive or expressive—as for example when David laments, "But now he is dead, why should I fast? Can I bring him back to life again?" (2 Sam 12:23). When Yhwh says to Cain, "Where is your brother Abel?," Cain takes Yhwh's question to be of the information-seeking type and responds by saying, "I do not know; am I my brother's keeper?" (Gen 4:9). Both Cain and Yhwh have asked questions, yet both are concerned with more than the literal meaning of words.

The reason so-called rhetorical questions are not asked for the sake of acquiring information is because the answer derives from a self-evident assumption that both the speaker and addressee share, one which is not open to debate or discussion. Yet, sometimes, when a rhetorical question is invoked, characters express contrasting points of view. One such example is found in 2 Sam 19:22, where Abishai

[4] The Hebrew is ambiguous. J. Alberto Soggin concludes that "they must therefore have known him well" (*Judges: A Commentary*, OTL [Philadelphia: Westminster, 1981], 272). John Gray determines that "they either recognised the dialect as of Judah near their home country, or the voice of the individual, which is less likely, or they may simply have heard him at the service and recognised a priest" (*Joshua, Judges, Ruth*, NCBC [Grand Rapids: Eerdmans, 1986], 343).

addresses David and asks, "For this, shall not Shimei be put to death because he cursed the anointed one of Yhwh?" David quickly rebuffs Abishai with three of his own rhetorical questions (v 23). The syntactical arrangement of Abishai's question fulfills diverse functions, and its persuasive force derives from the implied assumptions that cursing and throwing stones at David and his servants and siding with Absalom (see 2 Sam 16:5–7) should not be overlooked. Shimei deserves to be punished, and his extravagant obeisance before David (2 Sam 19:19–20) should not obviate his previous actions. Abishai thus informs David of his position, but even more, he tries to persuade him.

In this example, Abishai's rhetorical question requires a double transformation to arrive at meaning. First, the addressee is invited to alter the valence of the question (transforming it from negative to positive): "Yes, Shimei *should* by punished for cursing Yhwh's anointed." Second, the question requires an alteration of grammatical structure. David eventually transforms the interrogative to a declarative statement—"[Shimei] shall not die"—but even before he speaks these words, his emotionally charged questions reveal that the conclusion he reaches (i.e., that Shimei shall not die) precedes his recorded verbal response. That is, while the reported order is of David's three rhetorical questions (v 22) preceding his concluding statement (v 23), the actual sequence is: conclusion reached (stated in v 23) prior to the three rhetorical questions (v 22). Both the valence and alteration of grammatical structure require the addressee (and the audience) to rephrase the original sentence in order to arrive at the functional meaning of the question. "Shall not Shimei be put to death for this because he cursed Yhwh's anointed?" is transformed by the addressee-audience into something like, "Because Shimei has cursed David who has been chosen by Yhwh, Shimei deserves to die." As in real life, characters in literature perform this double transformation routinely, some might say mechanically, and in matters of communication and interpretation everything hinges on making the connections.

This conversation between Shimei and David (four questions in two verses) allows for a generalization: often the purpose of so-called rhetorical questions is to cajole, convince, berate, affirm, denounce—in short, to change—the addressee. And another component must be considered, because dialogue is not only heard, but overheard. Writers use a number of techniques to involve the audience, and such questions certainly draw those listening into the story. The author may change or exploit any or all members of the speaker-addressee-audience triangle by invoking a question.

The present study proceeds from two presuppositions: (a) the Bible's interrogatives have many and various rhetorical implications, and (b) the traditional division of questions into two basic types does not do justice to their protean forms. In short, the two traditional categories obfuscate the rich variety of rhetorical devices which the authors of the Hebrew Bible use with great effect. All questions—even those that appear to be merely repeated—have much to do with both the representational and the persuasive functions of language, and the traditional assumption that interrogatives either seek explanation or attempt to persuade is certainly a narrow view. Questions serve diverse functions: they involve addressees; they may call attention to discrepancies in power; they may allow the speaker to be ironic or satiric; they may promulgate ambiguity and vagueness. Other preliminary issues set the tone for this study, which seeks to move beyond the traditional understanding of interrogatives: Who hears questions? Who answers questions? Do any characters mistake a rhetorical question for an information-seeker? What focusing techniques emerge? What about discontinuities in language, representation, and communication?

And what about answers? Questions can be answered with a summary formula (כזה וכזה, "thus and such," Judg 18:4); at other times readers are left to wonder if questions are answered at all (Josh 7:25; Judg 8:1; 1 Sam 4:3). Elsewhere—in 1 Sam 14:37 and 28:6, for example—it is clear that Yhwh does not respond verbally to Saul's inquiry. This silent treatment contrasts with answers that David receives from Yhwh. The narrator reports in 1 Sam 23:2, "David inquired of Yhwh, 'Shall I go and attack these Philistines?' Yhwh said to David, 'Go and attack the Philistines and save Keilah.'" Later, just after David delivers his famous eulogy over Saul and Jonathan, the narrator once again gives the impression that David's questions are answered without pause: "After this David inquired of Yhwh, 'Shall I go up into any of the cities of Judah?' Yhwh said to him, 'Go up.' David said, 'To which shall I go up?' He said, 'To Hebron'" (2 Sam 2:1).

Another preliminary issue is the role of duplicated questions. Both the performative status and role of quoted speech depend upon unique reality models which vary from one context to another. This is certainly true of non-interrogative statements. David's remark "I have sinned" (2 Sam 12:13) is not identical to Saul's twice-spoken confession "I have sinned" (1 Sam 15:24, 30), because of the actions which precede and follow the utterances. David confesses in the very first recorded words he speaks after Nathan reveals Yhwh's disappointment in the "anointed" one (2 Sam 12:7). Saul, the first "anointed" king of Israel (1 Sam 15:17), confesses that he has sinned, but only after attempting to cover over his actions with a series of lies. In addition, Saul's attempts to persuade Samuel to believe that it was the people who caused him to sin contrasts with David's unqualified confession (2 Sam 12:13).[5] Such statements are identical only when extracted from their narrative context. The same holds for questions. When Elijah spends the night at a cave at Horeb, the word of Yhwh comes to him saying, "What are you doing here, Elijah?" (1 Kgs 19:9). Elijah's quoted response reveals that this prophet's devotion to Yhwh contrasts with the Israelites who have forsaken the covenant, destroyed the altars, and killed all the prophets except for Elijah. The question "What are you doing here, Elijah?" will soon be repeated verbatim, and the prophet will respond with words identical to his earlier answer (vv 13–14). The intervening actions, however, bring the second question-answer series to a different level. In a scene reminiscent of Moses on or near the mountain (Exod 33:17–23), Elijah is summoned to stand before Yhwh (v 11), where he witnesses a mighty wind powerful enough to break mountains and split rocks, an earthquake, a fire, and the famous "still small voice."[6] Unlike the first question-answer series, the second sequence is conveyed and interpreted in light of the first. The duplicated complaint reveals that not even the mighty show can energize this prophet. The enervated Elijah does not recommit to the prophetic office. In fact, Elijah's forecasted anointing of Hazael, Jehu, and Elisha never takes place.[7]

Another example illustrates the contextual function of duplicated questions. Ahaziah worships Baal, just like his father Ahab. The story

---

[5] Saul's explanation, "I have sinned . . . because I feared the people and obeyed their voice" (v 24) is not supported by events described in the enactment scene. In fact, we are first told that *Saul* took Agag (1 Sam 15:8; cf. v 9). The monument which Saul erects "for himself" reinforces the reader's suspicion when Saul blames the people (vv 12, 15, 21).

[6] Or, something like "gentle small breeze." קוֹל דְּמָמָה דַקָּה is difficult to translate. The possible renderings are conveniently summarized and discussed by Richard D. Nelson, *First and Second Kings* (Atlanta: John Knox Press, 1987), 123–25. The other elements are familiar signs of a theophany; cf. Exod 19:16, 18; Judg 5:4–5; Ps 18:7–14 and 29:3–9; Hab 3:4–6.

[7] It is Elisha who announces that Hazael will be king (2 Kgs 8:13), and it is Elisha who anoints Jehu (2 Kgs 9:1–3). Elijah throws his mantle over Elisha (1 Kgs 19:19), which no doubt reflects the fact that prophetic authority could be conveyed by contact with a prophet's mantle (cf. John Gray, *I & II Kings*, OTL [2nd ed.; Philadelphia: Westminster, 1970] 411), but this action also shows an enervated Elijah.

from 2 Kgs 1 treats the violation of the first commandment, Yhwh's initial charge to the people, "You shall have no other gods before me" (Exod 20:3; Deut 5:7). Ahaziah sends messengers to Ekron, a Philistine town twenty-two miles west of Jerusalem, to seek out Baalzebub ("Baal the Fly"). By sending messengers this distance to one of the Philistine cities, Ahaziah leaves no doubt that he imagines Baalzebub, rather than Yhwh, to be the lord of life. The stage is set for another challenging confrontation with Elijah. Three times in the opening chapter of 2 Kings the same rhetorical question is invoked. Three characters, speaking in three different settings, ask, "Is it because there is no God in Israel?" The question is shadowed by the threefold duplicated ominous prophetic word: "Therefore you shall not leave the bed to which you have gone—but you shall certainly die." These words are intended for the king, but we first hear them when the messenger of Yhwh transmits them to Elijah (v 3). On the second occasion they are conveyed to the king by his messengers who hear them from Elijah (v 6). Finally, Elijah himself communicates them to the king. Such repetition focuses attention on the prophecy itself, and the threefold duplication is enhanced by the stylistic device of the rhetorical question "Is it because there is no God in Israel?"

In the face of David's retreat from Jerusalem and Absalom's advance on the capital city, the narrator provides details of five different royal encounters: with Ittai the Gittite (2 Sam 15:19–22), Abiathar and Zadok (15:24–29), Hushai the Archite (15:32–37), Ziba (16:1–4), and Shimei (16:5–13). While David's future does not look bright—"the hearts of the Israelites have gone after Absalom" (15:13)—we do learn about support that still exists, as well as something about the considerable strength of David's character in the midst of mounting pressure and ubiquitous conflict. A quick glance at a fragment of conversation in one of these encounters sets the stage for the present study of the Hebrew Bible's protean interrogative forms.

While fleeing from Jerusalem, David receives word that Ahithophel has joined Absalom in the rebellion. Placing matters in God's hands, David prays, asking God to turn Ahithophel's counsel to foolishness (15:31). With torn garments and dirt on his head, Hushai arrives. David sends him back to Jerusalem after advising him to pretend to defect to Absalom. David says to Hushai:

> And if you return to the city say to Absalom:
> Your servant, I, O king, will be. Just as your father's servant I formerly have been, so now I will be your servant (15:34).

Hushai, friend of David, returns to Jerusalem just as Absalom is entering it, and transforms the projected speech of David. Hushai now says to Absalom:

> And furthermore whom (למי) should I serve? Should it not (הלוא) be his son? As I have served your father, so I will serve you (16:19).

With persuasion on his mind, Hushai makes David's words more convincing in the retelling. He opens with a (non-projected) rhetorical question, which he himself answers. His comparison is similar to David's original statement. While both speakers make a comparison ("as"), Hushai shifts from the nominal "servant" to a more forthright, compelling verbal comparison: "as I served in the past, so I will serve in the future." Hushai thus works from David's outline, and Hushai's new speech reflects his good sense as well as Absalom's personality as viewed by Hushai, who no doubt recognizes that Absalom is swayed by flattery. Yet Hushai, careful to conceal fawning, exercises restraint. Some features of his speech are also found in the subsequent advice he gives Absalom (17:7–13): negation, bipartite structure, rhetorical devices, and adulation. The parallels in speech reflect significant aspects of Hushai's disposition.

In the chapters that follow, I attempt to illustrate what I mean by the protean contours of the Bible's various question forms. In chapter 2 I focus on the compositional design and the use of the five interrogatives invoked in Eden (Gen 2:16–3:13). Attention is given to mediated discourse, changes in language, and the impact of (mis)quotation on characterization. The focus in chapter 3 is on the sequel scene outside the garden (Gen 4:1–16), where Cain and Yhwh invoke six interrogatives. Their rhetorical interchange is explored, along with the modulations to and from dialogue. Consideration shifts in chapter 4 to the functional role of two questions that Saul asks Yhwh, questions which Yhwh "does not answer" according to 1 Sam 14:37 and 28:6. These two verses form an *inclusio* (a narrative frame), and the multiple effects of a king groping for answers and the role of silence are discussed as part of the motif of Saul's loss of power. These questions answered with silence illustrate best, I believe, the relationship between asking and power. Ice-cold silence leaves no room for dialogue. The focus in chapter 5 is also on questions that appear as part of another, more complex frame. The famous celebratory song "Saul has killed his thousands, and David his ten thousands" is reported on three distinct occasions.

A concentration of questions linked to one another in a chain implies a distinct rhetorical strategy. In the following three chapters, sequential questions are examined. In chapter 6 I trace the parallel plot pattern in two chapters from 1 Samuel, 24 and 26, before considering how rhetorical points are scored in the question chains of chapter 26. The close relationship of questions and rhetoric is discussed in chapter 7. Here, the focus shifts to 2 Sam 19:32–44, where Barzillai and David converse (vv 32–41) before the Judahites and Israelites speak in collective dialogue (vv 42–44). Sequential interrogatives are prominent in both conversation scenes. A third instance of sequential questions is taken up in chapter 8. The scene is 1 Sam 20. More than one rhetorical flourish can be found in the midst of the question series which propels this famous sham archery session, where Jonathan befriends David even as he conspires against his father.

In chapter 9 attention turns to the multiple ways that God's character is drawn in 2 Sam 7. The contours of speech, a preponderance of dialogue, the blending of perspectives, and the invocation of questions all combine to convey God's psychological and ideological point of view. Questions sometimes serve a duplicitous purpose. Chapter 10 explores the crafty questions in 1 Kgs 1:11–31, a scene where Nathan and Bathsheba achieve their political goals as they conspire against the ailing King David. In an effort to secure Solomon's place on the throne, Nathan proposes a plan whereby the old king will circumvent the scheming Adonijah and his supporters. Duplicity reigns. Their goal is accomplished through dialogue seasoned with interrogatives. In chapter 11 four interrogative types are isolated. I ask if the frequent invocation of questions in the prophetic books of Haggai and Zechariah is evidence of a distinct rhetorical pattern and an indication of literary affinity.

The questions surveyed herein remind us of the representational function of language, of persuasion, of the establishment of power, and of the exercise of authority—or, in a word, of rhetoric. In relation to form and content in biblical narrative, it is the creative synthesis of the specific formulation within a pericope that makes for distinct compositions. Persuasion becomes possible by means of invention, argumentation, control of emotion, treatment of subject matter, and most especially the exercise of power, which establishes and then alters narrative situations. Power may be displayed in the tone of asking, as, for example, in Goliath's question of David, "Am I a dog that you come to me with sticks?" (1 Sam 17:43), or with answers, such as Gideon's response to the angel, "But sir, if Yhwh is with us, why then has all this happened to us? And where are all [of God's] wonderful deeds?" (Judg 6:13). Possibilities abound.

In his essay on Homer and the Bible, Erich Auerbach addressed the biblical writers' concern with reality and concluded that "the Bible's claim to truth . . . is tyrannical—it excludes all other claims."[8] Tacit in my argument in the chapters that follow is an assumption that biblical writers' diverse accents on "truth" allow for a greater degree of play and maneuvering along the way from opening to closure than Auerbach alleged. These accents are most apparent and interesting when questions are invoked.

[8] Erich Auerbach, *Mimesis: The Representation of Reality in Western Literature*, trans. Willard R. Trask (Princeton: Princeton University Press, 1974), 14.

CHAPTER TWO

FIELDING QUESTIONS IN EDEN (GENESIS 2:16–3:13)

The speeches of the woman, serpent, man, and Yhwh Elohim—the four dialogists in Eden—are mediated discourse, filtered to us through the norms, intentions, and rhetoric of the narrator. In biblical narrative, the storytelling agent incorporates character utterances into an overall syntactic, compositional, and stylistic design, and, since modulating into dialogue is *always* an option, the words of characters are never totally independent. They always lie within the narrator's frame. Even when silent, the narrator speaks through voices of his or her own devising, and we who listen in must confront the possibility of an ironic mediating agent behind the speakers. The garden story thus unfolds as a network of competing voices, an interaction of speakers and points of view, and the interplay of various levels of cognition pits characters against two audiences, one outside and another within the story itself. The audience outside may have access both to original speech events and to their repetitions. Since characters are recipients of words spoken by other characters, recontextualization takes on great importance in this story, and a text like the garden story shows us that characters themselves also appropriate the words of others. Like the audience outside, they too may have access to one or more speech events that are recontextualized.

Paraphrase is, of course, to be expected in quotation, and any reproduction of another's speech produces changes—intentional or not—in meaning. Even so-called verbatim duplication of speech, which can be verified in passages such as Exod 32:1 and 32:23, is not the same as original speech. The setting into which subsequent quotations appear differs from the original context. The frame affects the inset. And, of course, not all duplicated speech masquerades as verbatim repetition. A paraphraser, like the serpent, uses God's words to accomplish his own crafty purpose. In this story, where the serpent is but one skilled paraphraser, the audience hears the words which one speaker reproduces and also the context into which one (mis)speaks. Changes in language thus emerge against a backdrop of context and total voice.

I propose to highlight the mediated discourse and the web of perspectives in Eden by focusing on the use of the interrogative, a prominent rhetorical feature of the story. The dialogue in Eden often unfolds by means of questions. Two of the four dialogists invoke a total of five interrogatives.[1] The command (2:16–17) and the five questions that issue from it (3:1, 9, 11[2x], 13) are listed in Table 1. Since the author of this text provides both original speech and its subsequent misquotations, we have an opportunity to trace the dialogue while considering the impact of misquotation on characterization.[2] In the series of questions in Eden, Yhwh Elohim addresses the man, woman, and serpent, but asks and receives verbal responses—feeble as they are—only from the human couple. These questions are vocal acts that call for responses from the addressees, and the way in which they are posed often dictates the terms of the answer: "Did God say," the serpent begins as he opens his conversation with the woman. The asking implies a certain type of response.

The man and woman have several options when confronted with questions in Gen 3, and, from the standpoint of reception, the variety in response may be referred to as fielding questions. Fielding is different from answering because it encompasses more than simple verbal responses. As in real life, an addressee may respond verbally or with cold silence. The response might be straightforwardly honest or duplicitous. The addressee might ask a return question of the questioner, and this return question might seek more information or deny the validity of the original question outright.

---

[1] In the sequel scene outside the garden, Yhwh also initiates a trial by means of questions. Cain and Yhwh Elohim invoke six interrogatives in the scene (4:6[2x], 7, 9[2x], 10). I trace the mediated discourse, points of view, modulations to and from dialogue, and compositional design in the next chapter.

[2] Designs similar to the ones traced in this paper might be explored in Exod 32. Note the following quotation from the enactment scene: "Aaron said to them, 'Take off the gold rings that are on the ears of your wives, your sons, and your daughters, and bring them to me.' So all the people took off the gold rings from their ears, and brought them to Aaron. He took the gold from them, formed it in a mold, and cast an image of a calf" (vv 2–4a). But in the hearing of Moses (v 24), Aaron explains, "So I said to them, 'Whoever has gold, take it off'; so they gave it to me, and I threw it into the fire, and out came this calf!"

Table 1

The command (Gen 2:16–17): And Yhwh Elohim commanded the man, From every/any tree of the garden you may freely eat; but from the tree of the knowledge of good and evil you shall not eat from it, for in the day that you eat of it you shall surely die.

ויצו יהוה אלהים על־האדם לאמר מכל עץ־הגן אכל תאכל:
ומעץ הדעת טוב ורע לא תאכל ממנו כי ביום אכלך ממנו מות תמות:

Question #1 in narrative context (Gen 3:1): And the serpent was more crafty than any other creature of the field that Yhwh Elohim had made. And he said unto the woman, Did Elohim really say you (pl.) shall not eat from every/any tree of the garden?

והנחש היה ערום מכל חית השדה אשר עשה יהוה אלהים
ויאמר אל־האשה אף כי־אמר אלהים לא תאכלו מכל עץ הגן:

Response (Gen 3:2–3): And the woman said to the serpent, From the fruit of the trees of the garden we may eat. But from the fruit of the tree that is in the middle of the garden, Elohim said you shall not eat from it, nor shall you touch it, lest you die.

ותאמר האשה אל־הנחש מפרי עץ־הגן נאכל:
ומפרי העץ אשר בתוך־הגן אמר אלהים לא תאכלו ממנו ולא תגעו בו פן־תמתון:

Question #2 in narrative context (Gen 3:9): And Yhwh Elohim called unto the man and said to him, Where are you?

ויקרא יהוה אלהים אל־האדם ויאמר לו איכה:

Response (Gen 3:10): And he said, Your sound I heard in the garden, and I was afraid because I was naked. And I hid myself.

ויאמר את־קלך שמעתי בגן ואירא כי־עירם אנכי ואחבא:

Questions #3–#4 (Gen 3:11): And he said, Who told you that you were naked? From the tree that I commanded you not to eat from, have you eaten?

ויאמר מי הגיד לך כי עירם אתה המן־העץ אשר צויתיך לבלתי אכל־ממנו אכלת:

Response (Gen 3:12): And the man said, The woman whom you gave (to be) with me, she gave me from the tree and I ate.

ויאמר האדם האשה אשר נתתה עמדי הוא נתנה־לי מן־העץ ואכל:

Question #5 (Gen 3:13a): And Yhwh Elohim said to the woman, What is this you have done?

ויאמר יהוה אלהים לאשה מה־זאת עשית

Response (Gen 3:13b): And the woman said, The serpent tricked me and I ate.

ותאמר האשה הנחש השיאני ואכל:

The Command: Prelude to Questions

Characterization of the man and woman in the garden narrative is achieved as they are addressed by a disembodied divine voice. The series of five questions which appear in Gen 3:1, 9, 11[2x], and 13 issues from Yhwh Elohim's first words addressed to the man in 2:16–17:

> And Yhwh Elohim commanded the man, From every/any tree of the garden you may freely eat; but from the tree of the knowledge of good and evil you shall not eat from it, for in the day that you eat of it you shall surely die.

The words are spoken in an unspecified place in the garden, and the absence of representational detail calls attention to the speech event itself. Indeed, the characters in Eden often develop as words are addressed to them with little attention to appearance, traits, or motivations, and the impressions we form come in large measure from the words characters speak and misspeak.

The man is addressed as the "you" of Yhwh Elohim's utterance, and the narrator reports the speech by means of a performative verb, "command." This divine command contains a permission and a prohibition, both important types of performative speech.

> You may freely eat.
> You shall not eat.

The command is remarkable for the freedom it gives, and, at the grammatical and phonological levels, is marked by repetition. The writer employs the infinitive absolute with imperfect construction to emphasize the point that the man may *freely* eat (אכל תאכל) and has a wide range of options: "from every/any tree" (מכל עץ). Within this ample compass there is but one prohibition: against eating from the tree of the knowledge of good and evil, expressed in the emphatic form לא (rather than אל) as in the decalogue (cf. Exod 20:3–17; Deut 5:7–21). Emphasis by repetition continues as the divine voice speaks again by means of the infinitive absolute imperfect construction: violation will certainly lead to death (מות תמות). This small-scale grammatical and phonological repetition will be modified throughout the scene as characters speak and misspeak. The command and/or penalty uttered by Yhwh Elohim in 2:16–17 will appear in altered form in 3:1 when the serpent speaks ("Did God say . . ."), in 3:3 when the woman speaks ("but God said . . ."), and in 3:17 when God speaks ("about which I commanded you, saying . . ."). Three times the original words are recontextualized to suit the particular goals and objectives of the three dialogists.

The First Question

Free to shape those of us listening in, the narrator sets the stage for misquotation before delegating speech to the dialogists. Prior to shifting to so-called direct quotation, the narrator highlights the serpent, a unique animal. He is described as a creature made by God, more "clever" (עָרוּם) than the others, or even more "cunning,"[3] a word highlighted by its close proximity to the phonologically similar "naked" (עֲרוּמִּים) from the previous verse. The cleverness of the serpent contrasts with the couple's unashamed innocence. The man and woman are united by their nakedness, a fact stressed by the narrator: they are both unashamed (2:25). It is this crafty serpent who now threatens their unity. After they violate the prohibition, the author returns to this image: the eyes of both are opened and they realize they are naked. This awareness serves to initiate the process of separation, a process that begins with God's questions posed first to the man and then to the woman, and then culminating in singular indictments.

The narrator's report in 3:1 that the serpent was more "clever" is displayed on two fronts. First, the narrator reports that the serpent chooses to speak to the woman, who happens to be one step removed from the divine utterance against eating from the tree. That is, she was not present when it was first uttered in 2:16–17. Second, the eight-word speech itself in 3:1 reveals a clever mind at work. The serpent immediately seizes the opportunity to distort the woman's understanding of prohibition. Dialogue between the two opens with what appears to be a simple question, "Did Elohim really say (אף כי־אמר אלהים) you shall not eat from every/any tree in the garden?"

[3] "Shrewd" and "subtle" are also in the semantic field. As slippery as the serpent, the Hebrew word appears nowhere else in Genesis, but shows up several times in Proverbs, where it denotes a virtue worth cultivating (Prov 12:16, 13:16, 14:8). Misused, it becomes a source of "unsuccessful intrigue/craftiness" (Job 5:12; cf. Exod 21:14, Josh 9:4). Thus, outside Genesis the term is ambivalent; it may denote a desirable or undesirable trait.

Divine speech, the serpent shows us, is not beyond misappropriation. His first words, אף כי־אמר אלהים, are noteworthy not only because of the interrogative-declarative debate they have sparked among scholars,[4] but for other reasons as well. While introducing God's speech, the serpent changes the original performative verb from "command" to "say." What was first commanded is now merely spoken. The woman will duplicate the word she has just heard from the serpent (3:3), and God's return to the verb of introduction (צוה) in 3:17 will, at that stage, be a critique of the earlier uses of אמר. The serpent uses the bare appellation "Elohim" in contrast to the narrator's full designation "Yhwh Elohim," which appeared as recently as 3:1b and which shows up often in the surrounding narrative. Indeed, in the conversation between the serpent and the woman, the name "Yhwh" never appears.[5] If the tetragrammaton denotes God's caring relationship with the people,[6] the serpent's use of the

---

[4] No consensus has been reached on the translation of אף כי־אמר. E. A. Speiser (*Genesis* [AB 1; Garden City, N.Y.: Doubleday, 1964], 23), J. T. Walsh ("Genesis 2:4b-3:24: A Synchronic Approach," *JBL* 96 [1977], 164), and V. P. Hamilton (*The Book of Genesis: Chapters 1–17* [NICOT; Grand Rapids, Mich.: Eerdmans, 1990], 186, 188–89) have argued that the clause does not carry interrogative force and hence should be translated along the lines of "Indeed! To think that . . . !" (Walsh). J. A. Skinner (*A Critical and Exegetical Commentary on the Book of Genesis* [ICC; 2d. ed.; Edinburgh: T. & T. Clark, 1930], 73) adopts a middle ground position: "a half-interrogative, half-reflective exclamation," which he translates as "Ay, and so God has said!" (cited by Hamilton, *The Book of Genesis*, 186). G. W. Savran (*Telling and Retelling: Quotation in Biblical Narrative* [Bloomington and Indianapolis: Indiana University Press, 1988], 63), Claus Westermann (*Genesis 1–11: A Commentary* [Minneapolis: Augsburg, 1984], 239), R. W. L. Moberly ("Did the Serpent Get it Right?" *JTS* 39 [1988], 5–6), and G. J. Wenham (*Genesis 1–15* [WBC 1; Waco: Word Books, 1987], 45, 73) all translate the sentence as an interrogative. Virtual unanimity exists in modern English Bible translations. The GNB, JB, KJV, NAB, NASB, NIV, NJB, NKJV, NRSV, REB, and RSV all render the phrase as an interrogative.

Elsewhere in the Bible, אף כי never carries interrogative force. In addition, the clause is consistently used exclusively in the second half of an argument. (Cf. Deut 3:21; 1 Sam 14:30, 21:6, 23:3; 2 Sam 4:11, 16:11; 1 Kgs 8:27; 2 Kgs 5:13; Ezek 14:21, 15:5, 23:40; Hab 2:5; Job 9:14, 15:16, 25:6, 35:14; Prov 15:11, 17:7, 19:7 and 10, 21:27; Neh 9:18; 2 Chr 6:18, 32:15.) Only in Gen 3:1 do the words introduce a thought. Since the text does not imply that the serpent has commented previously—and for the reasons outlined by Moberly, Savran, Wenham, and Westermann—the traditional question is retained here.

[5] Claus Westermann's observation (*Genesis 1–11*, 239) that the serpent speaks only of Elohim because the name Yhwh denotes relations between humans and God might be investigated in a more comprehensive fashion than is possible here. The narrator reports in Num 22:23 that Balaam's donkey saw the angel of Yhwh, and in 22:28 it is Yhwh who opens the donkey's mouth. Given such clues outside Genesis, why would this crafty and skilled paraphraser not know the name?

[6] Westermann, *Genesis 1–11*, 239.

bare term "Elohim" sets a tone for what he hopes to convince the woman of—that her creator is *un*caring. Focusing our attention on the shift in point of view from the narrator to serpent, we in the audience witness the recontextualization from "command" to "say" and from "Yhwh Elohim" to "Elohim."

Other changes have occurred. The reference to eating now appears in the plural (תאכלו), and this verbal form may suggest that the serpent regards the woman as the spokesperson for the human couple.[7] The use of plural verbal forms is intriguing. Throughout his dialogue with the woman, the serpent consistently addresses her using second-person plural masculine verbal forms and suffixes: "Did God say, 'You shall not eat'" (תאכלו); "you will not die" (תמתון); "when you eat (אכלכם) of it your eyes (עיניכם) will be opened, and you will be (הייתם) like God" (vv 2, 4–5). For her part, the woman had also included the man in her response: "we may eat" (v 2). Bone of bone and flesh of flesh from the man's point of view, they are united once more by the serpent in speech. Indeed, the perspectives of the man ("bone of my bones," 2:23), the narrator ("they become one flesh," 2:24), the serpent ("you [pl.] shall not eat?," 3:1), and the woman ("we may eat," 3:2) are aligned before the eating in 3:6.

On the surface, the serpent's duplication of many words suggests faithfulness to God's original speech ("every/any," "eat," "tree," "garden"), but, of course, the serpent misspeaks as he recontextualizes along crafty lines. He avoids referring to the tree of knowledge, and discreetly avoids any reference to God's generous permission. He neatly reverses what God had previously said by inverting the two clauses and shifting the negative injunction. That is, God's words "from every/any tree of the garden you may freely eat" are now, in the mouth of the serpent, "you shall not eat from every/any tree of the garden." He takes advantage of the negative injunction in God's original speech ("you shall not eat from the tree of the knowledge of good and evil") and assigns it instead to "every tree of the garden." The serpent's phrase לא תאכלו reverses the divine command אכל תאכל of 2:16, and God's generous permission has been omitted altogether.

By distorting God's words the serpent shows us his craftiness. His did-God-say question simply cannot be answered with one word.

[7] Cf. Phyllis Trible, *God and the Rhetoric of Sexuality* (Philadelphia: Fortress, 1978), 108–109.

The serpent implies that God has forbidden one or more trees (true) *and* all trees (false). As Phyllis Trible remarks, "It is a difficult question. Phrased in a cunning way, it cannot be answered by a simple yes or no, since God prohibited eating from one tree but not from every tree."[8] By misrepresenting the original permission and overstating the conditions of the prohibition, the serpent seeks to plant the idea in the woman's mind that the prohibition is unfair. Inset by the narrator's frame, the serpent's interrogative begins a process of moving the woman from answering the elusive question, to doubting God's truthfulness, to desiring the forbidden fruit, to ultimately desiring to be God-like, knowing good and evil.

The Woman Responds

By misquoting, the serpent intends with his question to force the woman to explain and clarify anew. He succeeds in putting her on the defensive.

> From the fruit of the trees of the garden we may eat. But from the tree that is in the middle of the garden, Elohim said you shall not eat from it, nor shall you touch it, lest you die (3:2–3).

The woman was not present at the time of the original permission and prohibition, and the author never informs us how she learns of Yhwh's directives. We are left to infer that the man conveys the message to her.[9] Although absent when God spoke to the man, she has internalized (some of?) the divine words so that she can speak for the couple. She initially quotes God indirectly ("from the fruit of the trees of the garden we may eat, but from the tree that is in the middle of the garden"), but then shifts to a more direct form of quotation ("Elohim said, 'You shall not eat from it, nor shall you touch it, lest you die'"). Form and content yield meaning, and the very shape of her response, marked by indirections in speech, is one clue that changes in perception have begun.

The woman begins by correcting the serpent. The command, she argues, is not too harsh. They are free to eat from any tree of the garden except one, and the prohibition is made for good reason: it

---

[8] Trible, *God and the Rhetoric of Sexuality*, 108–9. Cf. Savran, *Telling and Retelling*, 63–64.

[9] Trible (*God and the Rhetoric of Sexuality*, 72–143) offers a different perspective. Many commentators avoid the issue of when and how the woman learns of God's permission and prohibition altogether.

keeps them from dying.[10] But while defending God's directive, the woman uses language that, from the perspective of the audience, is new. "The tree of the knowledge of good and evil" is now "the tree that is in the middle of the garden," a change that may simply identify the tree in question by location. (Or are we to assume that she does not know the name of the tree? The phrase, "in the middle of the garden" in 2:9, appears to be more closely associated with the tree of life than the tree of knowledge.) In a departure from the narrator's full designation, "Yhwh Elohim" (2:16), she uses the serpent's word, "Elohim." She reaffirms God's permission to eat—something the serpent had omitted—but the verb נאכל ("we may eat") is less intense than God's original emphatic form אכל תאכל ("you may freely eat"). The woman dilutes, quite possibly unwittingly, God's original words in other ways as well: she does not refer to "every/any" tree, and the original death sentence, "for in the day that you eat of it you shall surely die" (מות תמות), is now simply "lest you die" (פן־תמתון). Still, from the reader's side, lexical and thematic dilutions are accompanied by expansions. The woman adds the words "fruit" and "middle of the garden," and she has, perhaps for good reason, read too much into the prohibition "do not eat." It is now "do not (even) touch."[11] In her attempt to correct the serpent, she unwittingly—quite possibly influenced by the man whom we infer spoke to her—follows his tack: she exaggerates.

The Serpent Responds

Omissions and embellishments appearing in the woman's speech provide the crafty serpent another door of opportunity. The woman's paraphrase of פן־תמתון for מות תמות offers the point of departure in his next speech. He now twists her words—and Yhwh Elohim's—to turn God into a liar. God had initially said מות תמות (infinitive absolute with imperfect in 2:17), which the woman (or man) changed to פן־תמתון (conjunction with imperfect in 3:3). The serpent now

[10] As Westermann (*Genesis 1–11*, 239) remarks, "they are provided for and at the same time protected from danger."

[11] Now all five senses in the story have appeared: smell, 2:7; sight, 2:9; taste, 2:9; and hearing, 2:16 (Trible, *God and the Rhetoric of Sexuality*, 112 n. 36). The woman increases the scope of God's prohibition; she appears to know that touching may lead to eating. In her wisdom, she "builds a fence around the Torah," a procedure the rabbis will later develop to protect the law (Trible, *God and the Rhetoric of Sexuality*, 110).

returns (v 4) to God's original emphatic construction (infinitive absolute with imperfect), but negates it (לא) outright: "You will not die." He succeeded in opening a door with his initial provocative did-God-say question to the woman. In this next round he shifts from the interrogative to the declarative mode as he claims access to God's mind: "God knows that when you eat of it your eyes will be opened, and you will be like God, knowing good and evil."

At v 5 the report of dialogue between the woman and serpent ends; the serpent has accomplished his objectives. The narrator resumes by describing how both the man and woman violate the prohibition: she eats, she gives to her husband who has been with her,[12] he eats. The point of view has moved from the serpent to the woman and then finally to the narrator, who confirms that the woman perceives (ראה) the truth of the serpent's statement. Beginning with v 5, attention shifts from speech to the sense of seeing (ראה), a sense that denotes perception. The serpent first informs the woman that her eyes will be opened if *they* (not *she*) eat the fruit from the tree (v 5). She sees that the tree is good for food, a delight to the eyes (v 6). After both she and the man violate the prohibition by tasting the fruit, the narrator confirms that the eyes of both are opened: they see their nakedness for the first time (v 7). Immediately and with a touch of irony, the narrator reports that they wish not to be seen. From this altered state of consciousness, the narrator continues by shifting our attention from sight to sound. God appears merely as a sound of footsteps as they hear the sound of Yhwh Elohim walking in the garden. While they see their nakedness (v 7), they relate to God only through the sense of hearing (vv 8–10).

---

[12] Biblical Hebrew does not employ the pluperfect tense per se, but the narrator may in fact be indicating here that the man has been with her all along, a point that seems all the more obvious in the light of recent studies on the Bible's art of chronological displacement. Cf., for example, M. Sternberg, "Time and Space in Biblical (Hi)story Telling: The Grand Chronology," *The Book and the Text and Literary Theory* (ed. R. Schwartz; Oxford: Basil Blackwell, 1990), 81–145, and Craig, *A Poetics of Jonah*, 5–7, 14, 28, 33, 44, 135–36, 148.

The phrase "and she gave also to her man who was with her" could be conveyed perfectly well without the prepositional qualifier. How else could she give it? Joel Rosenberg ("The Garden Story Forward and Backward: The Non-Narrative Dimension of Gen 2–3," *Prooftexts* 1 [1981], 13) has made the astute observation that, when faced with God's anger, the man states, "the woman whom you gave (to be) with me" (עמדי), even though the preposition לי ("to me") "presumably would have made more sense." The translators of the REB, the NEB, and the GNB omit the word עמה ("with her") in v 6 altogether!

The Second Question

The man and woman attempt to hide, but God finds them and invokes another interrogative: Where-are-you?[13] This question, one word in the Hebrew, is profound. With it God draws the man out of hiding and exposes his guilt. The word points to a disruption that has entered the picture. It also anticipates a chain of events that will culminate in punishment and expulsion from Eden. The function of this interrogative is similar to the serpent's first question to the woman: both open the door for more conversation, clarification, and justification. As the man responds (vv 9–12), he exposes the alienation of the couple from God and from each other. But it is the narrator who first hints at the alienated state of the man and woman.[14] Even before Yhwh Elohim's speech is quoted in v 9, the narrator reports "and Yhwh Elohim called *to the man* and said *to him* . . ."

In conversation with the woman, the serpent had referred to the woman and man as if they were indeed bone of bone and flesh of flesh: "Did God say, 'You (pl.) shall not eat?' " But now God separates the couple in speech. Alan Hauser has shown how the use of the second-person singular ending in this direct address grammatically underscores the alienation between the man and woman.[15] They are no longer one. The where-are-you question sets in motion a new perspective on the situation: after their mutual hiding, the man and woman act and speak as individuals. The plural verb forms prominent in vv 1–8 are absent in vv 9–13.

The narrator's description of God's approach and the man and woman's withdrawal into hiding in v 8 is followed by the man's account of this approach and withdrawal in v 10. This scene of enactment and verbal report is carefully constructed. The rhetorical strategy of characterization through misquotation in the previous scenes now moves to characterization through a shift in point of view. Forms of three words—קול ("voice"), גן ("garden"), and שמע ("hear")—are reflected in the narrator's and man's point of view in

[13] H. Rouillard ("Les feintes questions divines dans la Bible," *VT* 34 [1984], 237) identifies this question as a "pretense question" which leads to an accusation, in contrast to others the deity asks when soliciting new information (Gen 16:8, 18:9).

[14] Cf. this pattern in 3:1.

[15] Alan Hauser, "Genesis 2–3: The Theme of Intimacy and Alienation," *Art and Meaning: Rhetoric in Biblical Literature* JSOTSup 19 (ed. D. J. A. Clines, D. Gunn, and A. J. Hauser; Sheffield: Sheffield Academic Press, 1982), 29.

the two verses. Both agree on location, in the garden (בגן), but the man's perception of his inner world (hearing) and outer world (hiding) have been altered. The narrator's report that "they heard" the sound of Yhwh Elohim is now, from the man's point of view, the singular verbal form "I heard." His reference to hiding is also reminiscent of the narrator's earlier report ("the man and woman hid themselves"), but the man now calls attention to his isolation: "I hid myself." The man never spoke his "I" to God before eating, but in his defense and admission of guilt, he asserts himself four times in v 10 ("I heard," "I was afraid," "I was naked," "I hid myself") and three times in v 12 ("with me," "gave me," "I ate"). The cumulative effect of the man's language calls attention to his new condition of weakness, guilt, and solitude, and the tone of God's interrogation leaves no doubt that the individual is held responsible for his action, an idea that will be repeated in God's conversation with the woman in 3:13 and with Cain in 4:9–12.

The Man Responds

As if anticipating the famous shifting-the-blame scene, the man redirects the dialogue. Perhaps taking his cue from the serpent,[16] he works to turn the conversation to what happened immediately after his transgression. To the question "where are you" the man does not answer "I am here," but explains instead *why* he is hiding: "Your sound I heard in the garden, and I was afraid because I was naked. And I hid myself" (3:10).

While the question was introduced with the interrogative "where," both speaker and addressee understand that location is not the issue. Yhwh Elohim's where-are-you is fielded as "what have you been up to?" To the one-word question, the man responds with a seven-word answer, using words, much like his garments, to cover his thoughts. Is it his nakedness or his assumption that it disqualifies him from meeting God that causes him to hide? He has his fig leaves with him (v 7)! The man's response contains two clauses found in the initial report of v 8 (sound heard in the garden, and hiding). Sandwiched between the hearing and hiding is his admission of fear which he

[16] A textual clue links the man with the woman and serpent in dialogue (see n. 12 above).

claims is brought on by his awareness of nakedness. The narrator has twice reported the couple's nakedness (2:25, 3:7), but the reference to fear is a new element in the plot. The introductory word, "your sound," abbreviates the narrator's "the sound of Yhwh Elohim," and the emphasis in this unusual word order is on the "sound" itself. It is, one might assume, man's fear of God approaching (note the narrator's attention to this detail in v 8) that causes him to flee into hiding. Thus the man misspeaks as he talks of his nakedness and unwittingly reveals what he most wishes to hide: he now understands the world as a place where some things can be revealed but where others must be concealed.

The Third and Fourth Questions

God's next two questions convey the image of an informed detective who prods the guilty one into confession: "And he said, Who told you that you were naked? From the tree that I commanded you not to eat from, have you eaten?" Only on this occasion in the garden does God interrogate by means of two consecutive interrogatives. With them Yhwh Elohim abandons the pretense of ignorance. The first question asks about knowledge; the second about disobedience. They are not, however, unrelated. With both questions God attempts to draw one piece of information out of the man: by what means he has acquired this new state of consciousness. With the first question God uses the man's own word, "naked," to push him into admitting the source of his guilt and shame. But rather than pausing for an answer, Yhwh Elohim piles on another question, and this have-you-eaten-from-the-tree thrust anticipates an answer about the source of the man's knowledge. It looks back in time to the command of 2:17 ("from the tree of the knowledge of good and evil you shall not eat from it") and is the climax of the narrative. Attention is drawn in this involved word order to the duplicated word "eat." The root אכל had been used three times in v 6 to describe the act, and the double appearance now in v 11 focuses the act even more sharply. Repetition of words from one context to another works to integrate the scenes.

We noted above that the serpent changed God's command (צוה) to God's speech (אמר). Now, through speech, the narrator aligns God's perspective with his own: "from the tree that I *commanded* you not to eat, have you eaten?" The asking has moved full circle. The man responds, of course, by shifting the blame in two directions. It is not only the woman who gave him fruit, but the woman whom God gave to be with the man, that he implicates. The man attempts not only to exonerate himself; the real problem, he implies, lies elsewhere. With the fourth question God has allowed the man to convict himself, a strategy now applied to the woman by means of yet another question.

The Fifth Question

The woman, who eats first, is questioned last, and the interrogative is the final one invoked in Eden: "What is this you have done?" When speaking to the man, God led up to the have-you-eaten question with two preliminary interrogatives: "Where are you?" and "Who told you that you were naked?" But with the woman, God immediately asks a question that implies guilt, and from this point on Yhwh Elohim's speech will be given over to an explanation of the consequences of disobedience (vv 14–19). Based on the information the man conveyed in v 12, God's question is rhetorical and the tone is that of shock and disgust.[17] The woman was the principal speaker in dialogue with the serpent. Now after Yhwh Elohim's accusatory question, she speaks only three words in v 13. Perhaps taking her cue from the man, the woman shifts the blame: "the-serpent tricked-me and-I-ate." Both she and the man take refuge behind a descriptive statement that assigns blame elsewhere: "the woman whom you gave to be with me"/"the serpent tricked me." Though both she and the man admit to eating at the end of their respective responses, the defendants respond differently in crucial ways. The man shifts the blame to the woman and God; the woman blames only the serpent. He first speaks his "I" in weakness and guilt ("I heard," "I was afraid," "I was naked," "I hid"), then says "and-I-ate." Her first and only "I" is an admission of guilt. Phyllis Trible has observed that the woman's answer is different from the man's in four ways.

[17] To capture the tone of God's question, Alan Hauser ("Genesis 2–3," 31) drawing from Umberto Cassuto, *A Commentary on the Book of Genesis: Part 1; From Adam to Noah (Genesis 1–6:8)* (trans. I. Abrahams; Jerusalem: Magnes, 1961], 158), translates it as "How could you do such a horrible thing?"

> First, she does not blame God. She does not say, for example, "The serpent whom you made to dwell in the garden with me" (cf. 3:1). Second, she does not implicate her companion, for weal or for woe. She speaks only for and about herself. "The serpent beguiled me" (not "us"), she says, although in conversation with this animal she had used plural pronouns that included the man. Third, the woman's answer differs in its reference to the serpent as the tempter who deceived, beguiled, and seduced—all nuances of the Hebrew verb *nś'*, but not of the verb *ntn* ("give"), which the man used to characterize the actions of the woman and of God. Fourth, the woman confesses more quickly than did the man. After two words, which blame the serpent, she accepts responsibility: "and-I-ate."[18]

In conversation with the serpent, the woman spoke as if she and the man were indeed bone of bone and flesh of flesh: "we may eat." We observed above that the man's speech suggested a new alienated state. As he spoke, he isolated them from each other: "I heard," "I was afraid." The woman speaks fewer words, but continues to call attention to their alienated state.

Summary

The garden plot, organized around tightly woven dialogue, has moved from creation, permission, prohibition, continued creation, jubilation, conversation, contemplation, violation, confrontation, to qualified acknowledgment of guilt. In the course of time, questions beget questions in this narrative, and at the end of the story we might find ourselves asking a few of our own: Why is the serpent more clever than any other wild creature? How does he learn of the prohibition, which was uttered before he was created (2:9, 3:1)? Why does the serpent tempt the woman to eat the fruit? Isn't the serpent right: wisdom, highly valued elsewhere in the Bible, is to be desired? We are told quite explicitly why the woman eats (3:6), but what motivates the man? What are their thoughts as they hide among the trees, concealing themselves from Yhwh Elohim? While questions remain, the story reaches its conclusion through speech and counterspeech, quotation and misquotation, with at least one point unambiguously clear: misspeaking, often manifest as verifiable deception, emerges as a major tool for characterization in Eden.

---

[18] Trible, *God and the Rhetoric of Sexuality*, 119–20.

The lexical similarity in these brief speeches and counterspeeches suggests more than a casual relationship among the five interrogatives and the narrative thread that connects the talking, eating, discovering, hearing, and hiding. The elements discussed above combine to show a man and woman separated from each other and alienated from God. In response to Yhwh Elohim's crucial question posed to both the man and woman ("Have you eaten?"/"What have you done?"), the couple is portrayed, once again, as one, united in their qualified admission of guilt. Both say the one crucial word "and-I-ate."[19] The man and woman are therefore ultimately alike in their disobedience, but this union they do not recognize. The eating they have in common ironically alienates them from each other. Never uttering his "we," the man betrays the woman, and after admitting to eating, both the man and woman are portrayed as speechless in Eden. The tit-for-tat dialogue in 3:1–13 (serpent-woman-serpent-Yhwh Elohim-man-Elohim-man-Yhwh Elohim-woman) is finally contrasted with a long speech of Yhwh Elohim in vv 14–19 who sentences individually the serpent, the woman, and the man.

The dialogue in Eden has been constructed around five questions that penetrate communicative barriers and bring to light what is hidden. The emergence of suppressed language and knowledge constitutes the central feature of the garden story, and the theme will emerge time and again in Genesis (Cain and Abel, Abraham and Sarah in Egypt, Sarah and Hagar, Judah and Tamar, Jacob and Esau, Shechem and Dinah, and Joseph and his brothers). The couple's hiding is followed by striking questions that point to the deceit and in some cases the lie that sustains such deception. The pattern highlights the breakdown of communication and understanding as one of the deepest concerns in Eden.

[19] While the story set in Eden shows some interesting parallels with the subsequent one set outside Eden (see Alan Hauser, "Linguistic and Thematic Links between Genesis 4:1–16 and Genesis 2–3," *JETS* 23 [1980], 297–305), the qualified admission of guilt distinguishes the first story from the second. After murdering his brother, Cain never admits guilt. Indeed, his lie and supercilious question asked of God—"I do not know. Am I my brother's keeper?"—suggest a contemptuous attitude quite different from that of his mother and father.

CHAPTER THREE

FIELDING QUESTIONS OUTSIDE EDEN (GENESIS 4:1–16)

The story of Cain and Abel incorporates competing voices and points of view in a world where the narrator presents characters as recipients of the words of others. The dialogue unfolds at numerous moments in narrative time by means of questions, and the speeches of Eve, Cain, and Yhwh are mediated to us, once again, in a carefully constructed overall syntactic, compositional, and stylistic design. This mediated discourse and the web of perspectives in Gen 4:1–16 can be highlighted by focusing on the questions that are invoked (see Tablc 2).

Table 2

The Offerings

[3]ויהי מקץ ימים ויבא קין מפרי האדמה מנחה ליהוה [4]והבל הביא גם־הוא מבכרות
צאנו ומחלבהן וישע יהוה אל־הבל ואל־מנחתו [5]ואל־קין ואל־מנחתו לא שעה ויחר
לקין מאד ויפלו פניו

[3]And it was at the end of some time, and Cain brought from the fruit of the ground an offering to Yhwh. [4]And Abel, he also brought from the firstlings of his flock and from their fat portions, and Yhwh gazed at Abel and at his offering. [5]But at Cain and his offering, Yhwh did not gaze. And Cain burned (with anger) greatly, and his face fell.

The Questions (I)

[6]ויאמר יהוה אל־קין למה חרה לך ולמה נפלו פניך [7]הלוא אם־תיטיב שאת ואם לא תיטיב
לפתח חטאת רבץ ואליך תשוקתו ואתה תמשל־בו

[6]And Yhwh said to Cain, Why do you burn with anger? And why has your face fallen? [7]Is it not the case that if you do well, you will be lifted up, and if you do not do well, at the door sin is stretched out and unto you its desire is? But you must master it.

Table 2 (*cont.*)

The Crime

8 ויאמר קין אל־הבל אחיו ויהי בהיותם בשדה ויקם קין אל־הבל אחיו ויהרגהו

[8]And Cain spoke to Abel his brother. And it was when they were in the field and Cain rose up against Abel his brother, and he killed him.

The Questions (II)

9 ויאמר יהוה אל־קין אי הבל אחיך ויאמר לא ידעתי השמר אחי אנכי 10 ויאמר מה עשית
קול דמי אחיך צעקים אלי מן־האדמה

[9]And Yhwh said to Cain, Where is Abel your brother? And he said, I do not know. Am I a keeper of my brother? [10]And he said, What have you done? The voice of your brother's blood is crying out to me from the ground.

Two of the three dialogists invoke six interrogatives. Most questions originate with Yhwh. Yhwh asks Cain three questions in vv 6–7; the narrator does not report a verbal response from Cain. Yhwh asks Cain a question in v 9a; Cain lies (v 9b), then invokes a haughty rhetorical question of his own. Yhwh returns with a pointed two-word question. The final interrogative obviously seeks confession, but Yhwh continues with an accusation. When the questions end, the scene moves from charge and countercharge by questions to sentencing, and the scene's accusation-sentencing pattern recalls events narrated in chapter 3: the "where are you," "who told you," "have you eaten" series was followed by "cursed are you among all animals," "I will greatly increase your pangs in childbearing," and "by the sweat of your face you shall eat bread" (3:9–19). This sequence and other structural similarities may suggest more than an insignificant relationship between the stories inside and outside Eden. In the words of Alan Hauser, "it would appear that numerous key elements in the stories have been deliberately paralleled in order to lead the reader to relate major motifs in one account to major motifs in the other."[1] We will consider a few of the similarities and differences in rhetorical strategies in the interrogative-rhetorical interchanges of Genesis 3 and 4, while focusing on Yhwh, Cain, and their rhetorical interchange outside Eden.

[1] Hauser, "Linguistic and Thematic Links," 298.

The Narrator's Introduction

Chapter 4 of Genesis opens with the narrator's introduction of the children born to the man and Eve. Indeed, the narrator dominates through most of this scene and gives up his storytelling privilege only once. Eve's speech of three words (קניתי איש את־יהוה) is the only recorded dialogue.

> [1]And the man knew Eve, his wife, and she conceived and bore Cain. And she said, I have acquired a man with Yhwh. [2]And next she bore his brother Abel. And Abel was a keeper of flocks, while Cain worked the ground. [3]And it was at the end of some time, and Cain brought from the fruit of the ground an offering to Yhwh. [4]And Abel, he also brought from the firstlings of his flock and from their fat portions, and Yhwh gazed at Abel and at his offering. [5]But at Cain and his offering, Yhwh did not gaze. And Cain burned [with anger] greatly, and his face fell.

The initial word, האדם, stands out for several reasons. First, the subject is here placed before the predicate. A departure from expected word order, "the man" is emphasized. Second, while the son is called איש by his mother subsequently in v 1, the man is not referred to as איש, the masculine nominative form of his counterpart, אישה, who is mentioned in the verse. Third, the use of האדם thus serves to link this new chapter with the action of the preceding chapters.[2] And fourth, the word serves a proleptic function as part of a narrative frame. Cain, we learn at the end of v 2, works the ground (אדמה), and this is where the action in 4:1–16 unfolds (vv 2, 3, 10, 11, 12, 14).

The mother of all living, Eve gives birth to Cain, then to Abel. The narrator presents the events in true chronological sequence through three verbal forms that convey sexual intimacy, conception, and birth. But in Eve's voice, the birth is expressed through the new single verb קניתי ("I-have-acquired") and modifier את־יהוה ("with-Yhwh"). The first hint of discord can be traced to these laconic descriptions of birth. In the next verse we learn that Eve bears Abel, but the references to intercourse and conception are omitted, and we are not told that this second child is acquired "with Yhwh." Joy over the firstborn is proverbial among the Hebrews (Jer 20:15), but the

---

[2] (ה)אדם: 1:26, 27; 2:5, 7 (2x), 8, 15, 16, 18, 19 (2x), 20, 21, 22 (2x), 23, 25; 3:8, 9, 12, 20, 22, 24. (ה)אדמה: 1:25; 2:5, 6, 7, 9, 19; 3:17, 19, 23.

narrator conveys more than this euphoria. Children of the same parents, the narrator begins to lay a foundation for discord. Cain's name קין is phonologically related to the word קניתי that his mother speaks. His arrival is heralded ("I have acquired") by what we might infer to be a mother's radiant tone. On the other hand, the name of the second born, הבל, conveys the idea that life is brief.[3] As is often the case in biblical Hebrew, the name anticipates the fate of the individual, but in this instance the arrangement of the brothers' names also has implications at the level of plot. In vv 1–2 Cain surrounds Abel in narrative space: קין → הבל : הבל ← קין.

The introduction of Abel also departs from the word order of the preceding verse. In v 1 we learn that the man has sex with Eve, his wife. (This appositional construct reflects the original Hebrew.) She next gives birth to brother Abel whose name is *preceded* by the familial reference, and while *she* gives birth, her son's character is linked not to her identity but to his: "she bore his brother Abel." This shift in form anticipates in small part the anger that surfaces in the scene (which in turn leads to murder, then to denial), and the fraternal relationship will be repeated throughout: Cain addresses Abel his brother, Cain rises against Abel his brother, Yhwh asks Cain about his brother's whereabouts, Cain responds that he does not keep his brother, the blood that cries out is that of a brother, and the ground receives the blood of a brother.

In a subsequent passage that displays some affinity with Gen 4:1–16, Esau is described as "a skillful hunter, a man of the field," whereas his twin brother is "a quiet man, living in tents" (25:27). In this scene, Rebekah gives birth to Esau and then to "his brother (אחיו) Jacob" (v 26). After this nuanced introduction, the theme of sibling opposition also develops, but in contrast to Gen 4, the parents reemerge in the unfolding plot. The change in plot dynamics is highlighted by a linguistic change from brother-brother to mother-son in 27:15. In an attempt to dupe Jacob, the narrator indicates, Rebekah takes garments *from her elder son* (בנה הגדל) Esau and puts them on *her younger son* (בנה הקטן) Jacob (cf. also 27:18–29, 41–42).

At Gen 4:3 the narrative shifts completely from mother and father

[3] The word appears occasionally in prophetic literature (Isa 30:7, 57:13; Jer 10:3, 10:15, 16:19; Zech 10:2), and frequently in Wisdom literature (Job 7:16, 9:29, 21:34, 27:12, 35:16; Prov 21:6; and Eccl 1:2 [3x], 14; 2:1, 11, 15, 17, 19, 21, 23, 26; 3:19; 4:4, 7, 8, 16; 5:9; 6:2, 9, 11; 7:6; 8:10, 14 [2x]; 11:8, 10; 12:8 [2x]).

to the next generation, to brother and brother. With the one verb ויהי the narrative moves from a birth scene to a description of the adult-life professions of both sons. Abel is a shepherd, Cain a farmer. Though the occupations of the brothers are delineated, we may infer that the keeper of grazing animals and the farmer both depend upon the *ground* for their livelihood. This combined imagery of animals, plants, and ground complements descriptions from the previous three chapters. The soil links brother to brother, children to parents, and humanity to creator: Humanity is charged with dominion over the living creatures in the initial story of creation (1:26, 28), and Cain's working the ground (4:2) corresponds to the narrative frame surrounding the story of the garden of Eden (2:5 and 3:23). God creates the animals of every kind, including cattle and everything that creeps upon the ground (1:25). At a time when a stream would rise and water the whole face of the ground (2:6) before there was anyone to till the ground (2:5), God formed man from the ground (2:7). Indeed, it is out of the ground (2:9) that Yhwh Elohim caused every tree to grow, including the tree of life and the tree of the knowledge of good and evil. The narrator returns to the idea in 2:19: out of the ground Yhwh Elohim formed every animal of the field and every bird of the air. After the man disobeys God's injunction, the ground is cursed (2:17) and he is told that he shall return to it (2:19), to the place from which he came. And finally, Yhwh Elohim expels the man from the garden of Eden to work the ground from which he was formed (3:23). An important site in chapters 2 and 3 and a frame in 4:1–2, the ground is the locus of action in the drama that unfolds.

The Offerings

Both brothers present offerings, and the sequence is marked by correspondence and subtle disparity. Six Hebrew words are used to describe the actions of each brother, and the same verbal root (בוא) introduces the execution:

ויבא קין מפרי האדמה מנחה ליהוה
והבל הביא גם־הוא מבכרות צאנו ומחלבהן

The origin of Cain's gift is highlighted by its unusual syntactic position. Objects usually precede their modifiers in Hebrew, and in the construction "and brought Cain from the fruit of the ground an offering," the fruit from the ground is emphasized. The narrator's reference to Abel also bringing (גם־הוא) suggests equivalence, but the explicit reference to an offering is lacking and his gift is "from the firstlings and their fat portions." While we expect the brothers to offer from their holdings, what are we to make of the narrator's subtle distinctions? From Abel's side, two expressions in the Bible's idiom underscore that his offering was of the best kind: of the firstlings and of their fat portions. Such double emphasis—the firstlings are the best of the flock[4] and their fat portions are their best parts[5]—underscores Abel's desire to gratify Yhwh. With respect to Cain's offering, Gunkel concludes from context ("Zusammenhang") that the fruit is obviously the best of all ("natürlich das Beste davon").[6] Many modern commentators take a similar view.[7] On the other hand, rabbinic exegetes maintain that Cain offered the poorest quality produce.[8] But does the text allow either of these extreme views? The narrator states simply that Cain offered *from the fruit of the ground.* Thus, the brothers' offerings are distinct, but are they diametrically opposed? Abel chooses the finest offering in his possession; Cain apparently chooses the first at hand. Cassuto seems to get it right when he writes, "Abel endeavored to perform his religious duty ideally, whereas Cain was content merely to discharge this duty."[9]

To the giver-gift sequence is added God's polar responses. Yhwh gazes at (that is, has regard for) Abel and his offering, but does not gaze at (and hence has no regard for) Cain or his offering. Acceptance and nonacceptance is directed at both givers and the gifts, and the motif of favor for the second born, abundant in the Genesis narrative, is introduced here. Different conjectures have been given to explain Yhwh's opposing responses: as a result of the man's sin, the earth was cursed (Gen 3:17), so the offering of fruit of the ground did not find favor; animal sacrifices are worth more than vegetable offerings; farming keeps one rooted in a specific location, whereas

[4] According to ancient practice, first fruits and firstborn belong to the deity (Exod 34:19). Israel, the nation, is described as God's firstborn (Exod 4:22; cf. 13:2, 11–13).

[5] With animal sacrifices, the fat was burned (Lev 3:16–17; Deut 32:38).

[6] H. Gunkel, *Genesis* (8th ed.; Göttingen: Vandenhoeck & Ruprecht, 1969), 42.

[7] G. J. Wenham (*Genesis 1–15*, xix, 103) has observed that Keil, Delitzsch, Speiser, and Kidner agree implicitly with Gunkel's position.

[8] J. P. Lewis, "The Offering of Abel (Gen 4:4): A History of Interpretation," *JSOT* 37 (1994), 491.

[9] Cassuto, *A Commentary*, 205. Gunkel goes too far in his assertion: "Damit sagt die Erzählung: Yahve liebt den Schafhirten und das Fleischopfer, aber er will nichts wissen von dem Bauern und dem Opfer von Früchten" (*Genesis*, 43).

God prefers shepherding because it is peripatetic in nature, allowing one to come into contact with the world.[10] But if our understanding of the different disposition of the two givers is correct, such theories miss the point. Yhwh's regard and disregard for the oblations is shaped by the attitude of the ones presenting the offerings. The action undoubtedly anticipates the idea expressed in Exod 33:19: "I [Yhwh] will be gracious to whom I will be gracious, and I will show mercy on whom I will show mercy."

The text is once again characterized by parallel expressions that are both similar:

אל־הבל ואל־מנחתו
ואל־קין ואל־מנחתו

and contrasting:

(impf.) ישע
(pf.) לא שעה

The names of the brothers appeared in vv 1–2 in a chiastic pattern. This design is repeated now in vv 3–5. The structure itself anticipates the action; Cain surrounds Abel again in the narrator's description of events:

Cain brings.
Abel brings.
Abel's gift elicits Yhwh's gaze.
Cain's gift does not elicit Yhwh's gaze.

קין → הבל : הבל ← קין.

The double symmetry, Cain-Abel-Abel-Cain (vv 1–2 and 3–5a), ends at v 5b as the narrator focuses on Cain's response to God's lack of regard for the offering. Discussions about how Cain learns of Yhwh's attitude are numerous. According to Theodotion and late haggadic Midrashim, Abel's offering was consumed by fire, while Cain's was spared. Skinner and Jacob discover a hint in the Bible—but where?—that Yhwh became manifest to the two brothers. Gunkel assumes that a sign was given in the sacrifices themselves. Brock-Utne suggests that Yhwh bestowed blessings and fertility on Abel's animals, but not on Cain's field.[11] The text, however, seems unconcerned with

[10] Hamilton (*The Book of Genesis*, 223–25) discusses these possibilities in more depth.

[11] See the discussions by Gunkel, *Genesis*, 43; Cassuto, *A Commentary*, 207; and Wenham, *Genesis 1–15*, 103.

how Yhwh's approval was revealed. The narrator, interested in Cain's attitude, moves quickly from describing God's reaction to portraying the older brother's inner and outer world: his anger is great; his countenance falls.[12] Given the Bible's economy of detail, the description of "great" anger stands out. Cain is infuriated.

Interrogatives Outside Eden (I)

After introducing the speaker and addressee in v 6, the narrator renders Yhwh's speech to the older brother. Narration gives way to quoted speech, and in contrast to the initial scene, this quotation is a long didactic speech.

> [6]And Yhwh said to Cain, Why do you burn [with anger]? And why has your face fallen? [7]Is it not the case that if you do well, you will be lifted up, and if you do not do well, at the door sin is stretched out and unto you its desire is? But you must master it.

The narrator has reported Cain's reaction to God's disfavor by revealing the elder brother's mind before disclosing any overt action on his part, and the ensuing dialogue between Yhwh and a person represents a new mode of exchange. In the garden, Yhwh initiated speech through a prohibition. Outside Eden, Yhwh's speech is not represented until *after* the narrator reports Cain's disposition. Yhwh's utterance thus assumes a new form.

---

[12] The association of the fallen face with depression is known in the literature of the ancient Near East and is further illustrated in the Assyrian recension of *The Epic of Gilgamesh* (Tablet X), where Siduri, the ale-wife, and the despondent Gilgamesh converse:

> "[(Why) should there be woe] in *thy* belly,
> Thy face be like [that of a wayfarer from afar],
> [With] cold and heat be seared thy countenance,
> [As in quest of a wind-puff] thou roamest over the steppe?"
> [Gilgamesh says to her, to the ale-wife]:
> "[O ale-wife, why should my cheeks not be so wasted, So sunken my face],
> [So sad my heart, so worn my features]?
> [(Why) should there not be woe in my belly],
> [My face not be like that of a wayfarer from afar],
> [Not be so seared my countenance with cold and heat],
> [And in quest of a wind-puff should I not roam over the steppe]?"

J. B. Pritchard, ed., *Ancient Near Eastern Texts Relating to the Old Testament* (Princeton: Princeton University Press, 1969[3]), 90–91, ll. 42–52.

The chiasm in the previous scene, Cain-Abel-Abel-Cain, ended with a description of Cain. In this scene (vv 6–7), the spotlight lingers on Cain as Yhwh speaks at length and probes with questions and answers. God, who had no regard for Cain and his offering, now inquires about the elder brother's outward expression and inner feelings: Why are you angry? Why has your countenance fallen? These two questions each consist of three words in the Hebrew, and attention is drawn to the parallel lines through the interrogative למה ("why") that introduces both lines:

למה חרה לך
ולמה נפלו פניך

The narrator's words used to describe Cain's thoughts and expression now appear in Yhwh's speech to Cain, and this duplication has caused geneticists such as Westermann to conclude that the language of v 6 is "foreign," "unoriginal," "artificial," and "mechanical":

> In v 6 God puts a question to Cain, and in v 7 he adds an explanation. The structure of the verses has the effect of a foreign body on the context. One must reckon with the possibility that this piece does not belong to the original. It is notable that the sentences in vv 6–7 consist for the most part of repetitions, resuming words and phrases from elsewhere: v 6 repeats 5b, turning the same word into a question. The second part of v 7 resumes a phrase from 3:16 word for word but gives it a different meaning. All that is original is the first part of v 7 which seems to consist of two separate sentences which have subsequently joined together. . . . The closing words [of v 7] are taken from 3:16: "Its desire is for you, but you must master it." H. Ewald has already observed correctly that the quotation of the words from 3:16 in 4:7 is artificial and mechanical whereas the trial and the sentence of Gen 4 echo Gen 3 naturally and organically.[13]

But is this duplication of words in v 6 "artificial" or "mechanical"? Or should we instead understand the viewpoints of Yhwh and the narrator as closely aligned? They speak the same words: "burn (with anger)," "fallen," "face," and perceived through the lens of composite artistry, Yhwh and the narrator are indeed allied in the implied author's ideological narrative design. Yet the duplication of words is not mere repetition; the words reappear in a new semantic context. Yhwh's למה questions reveal a state of alienation. The first, "Why

[13] C. Westermann, *Genesis 1–11*, 298–300.

are you hot with anger?," is spoken after the narrator's report of God's lack of regard for Cain and his offering. Out of context the question might convey a sense of sympathy on the part of the speaker, but in context the divine question reveals the distance separating their points of view. The follow-up, "Why has your face fallen?," moves from Cain's inner world to his external reaction, and the shift constitutes a refusal to open a genuine intersubjective dialogue whereby Cain might gain an opportunity for questioning the favor of one offering over another.

Yhwh allows no time for answers to the first two questions about anger and a fallen countenance. Instead, the divine voice offers general advice to mollify Cain in the form of another question. The duplication of word stems from vv 5b–6 ("burn with anger," "fallen," "face") is now followed by a complex Hebrew construction: "is it not the case" and two if-clauses, "if you do well" and "if you do not do well." A new and contrasting image appears. It is possible that Cain's fallen countenance will be lifted up; the choice clearly lies with him: "if (אם) you do well, you will be lifted up." Through repetition and a departure from expected Hebrew word order, Cain's responsibility is stressed through second-person pronouns: "unto you its desire is and you must master it."

Yhwh's concern with Cain doing well is evident in this third interrogative, a rhetorical question whose answer is implied in the asking: Yes, Cain, if you do well your countenance will be lifted up. In one sense God's third question is like the serpent's provocative question in 3:1. Both questioners appear to know the answers to the questions they invoke. But while the serpent intended to move the couple toward disobedience, God means to move Cain away from sin that is close at hand.

In the garden story, the man and woman violated the prohibition, despite God's warning not to eat of the tree of knowledge of good and evil. Now God warns Cain that he must struggle against sinning, but, like mother and father, he will not master it. God concludes the speech with a warning statement and an injunction: "If you do not do well, at the door sin is stretched out and unto you its desire is. But you must master it." The word "sin" appears at the center of Yhwh's statement in v 7 and it is surrounded by one-word descriptors: לפתח ("at-the-door") and רבץ ("is-stretched-out"). Problems with the Hebrew word "stretched-out" have often been noted. Westermann articulates the view of many when he argues that the "sentence [in v 7] . . . is incomprehensible. . . . All explanations or attempts at emendation of the text have failed." And also, "it can be taken as certain . . . that vv 6–7 in their present form did not belong to the ancient narrative of Cain and Abel."[14] But exegetes of this text tend to overlook the propitious image of sin stretched out in this verse. Robbed of his life, Abel will himself soon be stretched out on the ground (v 10). In this scene characterized by narrative economy, with only a few words the narrator is able to convey a sense of movement at almost every turn: Cain's countenance falls (v 5); Yhwh inquires about the fallen countenance (v 6) and encourages Cain that he might be lifted up (v 7); Cain soon rises up (v 8) and kills his brother, who falls to the ground. And at the center of the drama is a proleptic image of sin stretched out at the door (v 7).

The Crime

> [8]And Cain spoke (אמר) to Abel his brother. And it was when they were in the field and Cain rose up against Abel his brother, and he killed him.

The second scene opens with a reference to Cain's conversation with Abel, which is followed by an account of murder. As in the real world, addressees have several options: assenting verbal response, dissenting verbal response, ambiguous verbal response, as well as a nonverbal response (i.e., silence). Hugh White discounts this point when he writes that "no communication has actually occurred."[15] To Yhwh's three questions and the injunction to master sin at the end of scene 1,

[14] Westermann, *Genesis 1–11*, 299, 301. The views of others are similar. "Die ganze Stelle bleibt auch hierbei schwierig. Der Text ist offenbar stärker verderbt" (Gunkel, *Genesis*, 44). "The text is corrupt; if its meaning is, as Skinner (*Genesis*, pp. 106–7) suggests, that the cause of Cain's dissatisfaction lies within himself, the verse, together with vs. 6, may be an addition seeking to answer the question left unanswered in vs. 5*a*" (C. A. Simpson, "The Book of Genesis," in G. Buttrick, ed., *The Interpreter's Bible*, 1 [Nashville: Abingdon, 1952], 518). "Unfortunately, the statement is in part really obscure. The *s'et*, 'lift up,' in v 7a can in our opinion be understood neither in the sense of forgiveness nor of the presentation or acceptance of the sacrifice; rather, one must relate it to the *panim*, 'face' (in contrast to the *napal*, 'fall,' in v 6b): 'If you do well, there is lifting up,' i.e., 'you can freely lift up your face'" (G. von Rad, *Genesis: A Commentary* [OTL; Philadelphia: Westminster, rev. ed., 1972], 105). "'The most obscure verse in Genesis' (Procksch). Because of its grammatical improprieties and its unusual terminology, commentators are forced to choose between emendation and positing a rare meaning for רבץ 'crouching'. To compound the problems, other words are of uncertain meaning" (Wenham, *Genesis 1–15*, 104).

[15] H. White, *Narration and Discourse in the Book of Genesis* (Cambridge: Cambridge University Press, 1991), 160.

Cain responds verbally not to Yhwh but to his brother. The content of the conversation is, however, not recorded in the massoretic text. In contrast, just before Abraham takes the knife to kill his son (Gen 22:10), Isaac inquires of his father and his speech is rendered: "the fire and the wood are here, but where is the lamb for a burnt offering?" (22:7) What are we to make of the fact that the Hebrew text does not render Cain's speech?

The problem in Gen 4:8 turns on the word אמר ("said"). In contrast to דבר ("spoke"), אמר is used with quoted speech as its object. Westermann is quite emphatic: "Because of the univocal way in which ויאמר is used it is impossible that אמר can mean: 'Cain spoke to his brother Abel' (=conversed with him)."[16] The old versions settle the matter by attributing words to Cain. Variations on Cain's request "let us go out into the field" appear in the Samaritan Pentateuch, LXX, and Vulgate, but the divergences among the recensions and translations suggest a shared trend of inserting words rather than a common original reading:

Sam Pent	נלכה השדה	"let us go into the field"
LXX	διέλθωμεν εἰς τὸ πεδίον	"let us go out into the plain"
Vg	egrediamur foras	"let us go out of doors."[17]

How then is the sentence to be understood? One option is to substitute a word with similar spelling to אמר: שמר "watched" (Böttcher, Kuenen, Olshausen, Knobel); יָמֶר "strove" (Gunkel); יִמַּר "become bitter" (also Gunkel).[18] With support in Arabic for understanding אמר in the sense of "fixing a place for meeting" instead of the traditional signification of "speaking," Cassuto argues against emendation. He translates, "Cain arranged to meet Abel his brother, and when they were in the field, in the place that he had appointed for this meeting, Cain rose up."[19]

One finds passages in the Hebrew Bible that shed some light on this problem. Gen 22:7, Hos 13:2, Ps 71:10, Esth 1:18, and 2 Chr 32:24 give us reason to question Westermann's view that אמר must have an object:

[16] Westermann, *Genesis 1–11*, 302.

[17] Cf. also Syriac, "let us go down into the valley;" Targum Pseudo-Jonathan, "come, let us both go out into the field;" Fragmentary (Jerusalem) Targum, "come, let us both go towards the field;" Peshitta, "let us go into the open field."

[18] These sources are cited by Westermann, *Genesis 1–11*, 302, and Cassuto, *Commentary*, 214–15.

[19] Cassuto, *Commentary*, 215.

(a) Gen 22:7: ויאמר יזחק אל־אברהם אביו ויאמר אבי
Translation: "And Isaac spoke (אמר) to Abraham his father and said (אמר), My father."

(b) Hos 13:2: להם הם אמרים זבחי אדם
Translation: "Those/they who sacrifice people speak to them [their idols]."
N.B.: This translation is found in the Anchor Bible and the New Interpreter's Bible commentaries.[20] Modern translations often render the verb in the passive voice: "it is said (i.e., spoken) of them" (KJV, NAS, NEB, NIV NKJV, REB).

(c) Ps 71:10: כי אמרו אויבי לי
Translation: "for my foes talk to me"
N.B.: Once again אמר is not followed by rendered speech. This translation is found *inter alia* in *Psalms 51–100* of the Word Biblical Commentary. Marvin Tate points out that although Dahood argues for understanding אמר as "to see" (from Ugaritic *'mr*), the idea of "talking about one" is appropriate for the context.[21]

(d) Esth 1:18: והיום הזה תאמרנה שרות פטס־ומדי אשר שמעו את־דבר המלכה לכל שרי המלך
Translation: "And this day the noble women of Persia and Media who have heard of the queen's actions will be speaking to all the king's nobles."

(e) 2 Chr 32:24: ויאמר לו ומופת נתן לו
Translation: "And [Yhwh] answered/spoke to him and gave him a sign."
N.B.: This translation is representative of the KJV, NAB, NAS, NKJV, NRSV, RSV, Anchor Bible, and Old Testament Library commentaries.[22]

When we take into account the notion that biblical Hebrew does indeed appear to use אמר without an object (i.e., "spoke" and contra

---

[20] F. I. Andersen and D. N. Freedman, *Hosea: A New Translation with Introduction and Commentary* (AB 24; Garden City, N.Y.: Doubleday, 1980), 624, 632. G. A. Yee, "The Book of Hosea. Introduction, Commentary, and Reflections," in L. E. Keck (ed.), *The New Interpreter's Bible*, VII (Nashville: Abingdon, 1996), 288.

[21] M. E. Tate, *Psalms 51–100* (WBC 20; Dallas: Word, 1990), 207, 209.

[22] J. M. Myers, *II Chronicles* (AB 13; Garden City, N.Y.: Doubleday, 1965), 191. S. Japhet, *I & II Chronicles: A Commentary* (OTL; Louisville: Westminster/John Knox, 1993), 975.

Westermann) on at least five occasions, we conclude that the author has created a sense of mystery, wittingly or unwittingly, by not rendering the speech itself. Cain spoke, but what did he say? In retrospect, an invitation to the field seems likely (hence the versions). The point that the story makes quite unambiguously is that Cain does not master the sin which is close at hand. He rises, then kills his brother, and the narrator's report of Cain's "rising up" looks back to v 7 where Yhwh spoke of Cain's countenance being lifted up if he did well. But his ascent now is, of course, in direct opposition to the forecasted doing well. His rising up against (אל) his brother also corresponds to the narrator's report that he spoke to (אל) his brother.

ויאמר קין אל־הבל אחיו
ויקם קין אל־הבל אחיו

To mark the repetition, אל (lit. "to") occurs after rising up instead of the expected על ("upon," "against"), and the duplication of the preposition further emphasizes *Abel his brother*. The man who lies dead is a brother![23] Thus in v 8 the narrator twice mentions the fraternal relationship: Cain speaks to Abel his brother and rises up against Abel his brother. Repetition on both small and large scales is a hallmark of biblical narrative. The writers duplicate words, images, and ideas for effect, but in this scene the harping on kinship is superredundant. The chapter opens with a reference to Eve bearing Abel who is not called her son, but brother of Cain (v 2). Immediately after v 8, Yhwh returns to interrogate Cain and asks, "Where is Abel your brother?" to which Cain promptly responds, "Am I a keeper of my brother?" Then Yhwh hears Cain's brother's blood crying from the ground (v 10). The attention to kinship, brother against brother, augments the portentous quality of this capital offense.

The murder takes place in the field (cf. 2 Sam 14:6), an important site both for Cain, a tiller of the ground, and Abel, a keeper of animals that graze. What appears by modern standards to be a rudimentary account of events is in fact an example of the Hebrew

[23] The motif of fratricide occurs often in world literature. Gunkel (*Genesis*, 44) cites Osiris and Seth, the brothers of 2 Sam 14:6, the Phoenicians Hypsuranios and Usoos, Romulus and Remus, and Eteocles and Polyneices, and concludes that the motif must have stirred the literary imagination in various cultures: those who should love each other the most become engaged in a totally destructive struggle.

Bible's deceptively simple art. While the "ground" was referenced before (vv 2, 3) and will be again (vv 10, 11, 12, 14), the mention of "field" (שדה) occurs only here in v 8. In contrast to his mother and father who eat under the cover of the tree and then hide, Cain's sinning takes place in the open, and the narrator never hints that he retreats spatially or psychologically before or during the interrogation scene (cf. 3:8–10). Based on the reference to the field, the parents, mentioned in the scene's introduction, now appear to be beyond the sight and hearing of the sons. Indeed, Deut 22:27 explains the rationale for abrogating the death penalty against the woman who cries out in the *field* (שדה) where there is *no one* to hear her.

The supreme act of violence is narrated with excruciating brevity. The murder is conveyed with the final word in the verse, ויהרגהו, and-he-killed-him. The single word is remarkable because it conveys only the cold-blooded fact that one man has taken another's life. The narrator shows no interest in physical conflict as Cain opposes Abel, and the absence of detail leaves open the possibility that the attacker struck from behind. But there is no mention of a murder weapon (stone or hands?). There is no record of a struggle, no speech, not even a sound. In a scene packed with repetition and questions, Abel, we might infer, has no time to escape or even to ask why. A theme of separation was introduced at the very beginning of Genesis, with the articulation of the universe from the silence. Light was separated from darkness (1:4), the waters above from the waters below (1:7), then the waters from the dry land (1:9), the seventh day from the first six (2:1–3), man from the earth (2:7), woman from man (2:21–22), and man and woman from the garden and immortality (2:19b, 22–24). Now a brother is separated in death from his brother. Robbed of his voice, Abel falls to the ground. The deed done, the action moves quickly to a scene of interrogation.

Interrogatives Outside Eden (II)

9And Yhwh said to Cain, Where is Abel your brother? And he said, I do not know. Am I a keeper of my brother? 10And he said, What have you done? The voice of your brother's blood is crying out to me from the ground.

In this quick interchange, Yhwh asks a fourth question of Cain who this time responds with a statement and question of his own. God's probing, "Where is Abel your brother," is, of course, rhetorical.[24] Indeed, we soon learn that God knows where Abel is—"the voice of your brother's blood cries out to me." Yhwh's question may imply that Cain has fled from his brother. It corresponds to the interrogative, "Where are you," in Gen 3:9. Both "where" questions invite the guilty to acknowledge responsibility for their deeds. They also convey a sense of community. The man does not live in isolation. God questions him. The brother does not live alone either. The question, "Where is Abel your brother?," presumes that the two men exist in relationship to each other, whether it be in harmony or enmity.

God's reminder that Abel is Cain's brother is, of course, unnecessary, and Cain cannot escape the fact himself when he retorts, "Am I a keeper of my brother?" As with the man in 3:9, Yhwh's deceptive question brings forth a response from the addressee that reflects his perception of the deity as powerful, yet limited. But in contrast to his parents, Cain never hides from the divine presence. He sought identification with God through his sacrifice, he murdered in the field, and he now addresses God in the open.

The verbal form ידע ("know") was used in the opening verse as a euphemism for sexual intimacy. The word reappears now in Cain's speech as he seeks to deny knowledge. The change from figurative to literal form coincides with other changes as well. While the first "knowing" results in conception and birth ("with Yhwh," no less), the subsequent "knowing" is abrogated (לא ידעתי) by Cain. This subterfuge is in fact a denial of the truth: He does, of course, know where his brother's corpse is, but he does not want to respond to the question put to him. Cain reveals in his lie and arrogant rhetorical question a preoccupation with self. A pronominal first-person form appears no less than in three of the five words of his response: *I*-do-not know. Am-*I* a-keeper-of *my*-brother? The declaration of no knowledge is clearly evasive, and in his followup he goes further than his parents who responded to questions in chapter 3. Syntax and context reveal a sarcastic tone. His answer is not simply a truculent statement, "I am not my brother's keeper." Nor is it an information-

[24] Savran (*Telling and Retelling*, 65) surveys the Torah and the Deuteronomistic History and finds this verse and only four others where a speaker asks a question whose answer is already known (Gen 3:9–10, 42:7; 2 Sam 20:9; 2 Kgs 5:25).

seeking question. The insidious question is rhetorical: I know but I am pretending not to know in an effort to force you, God, to admit the absurdity of your position. God asked the man where he was in 3:9. The man answered that he was afraid because of his nakedness, though the context suggested fear brought on by disobedience (3:7, 10). Throughout the interrogation scene in Eden, the man and woman responded to God's questions evasively, even deceitfully, as they shirked responsibility. As in Gen 3, the protagonist's portrayal in chapter 4 is accomplished through his own words, but Cain emerges in a much more negative light than his parents. They never counterattacked by addressing a cynical question to God.

At certain moments, the narrator conveys images with a single word. As we observed, the subject, verb, and object of the murder are conveyed with one Hebrew word, ויהרגהו. For his part, Cain utters only five Hebrew words in the entire episode (i.e., in v 9). But even here, he overspeaks. With his own words Cain compounds the crime by turning the important moral consideration into mere ploy. Rather than letting his response remain a single statement of ignorance, Cain attempts to gain the upper hand in conversation with an offhand counterquestion. Perhaps it would have been best to stop with the lie; the followup shows him on the defensive, and his impertinent question suggests his guilt.

The word שמר means "one who watches over," "protects," or "keeps safe." Abel was a keeper of sheep, and שמר is a term for shepherds (Exod 22:6, 9; 1 Sam 17:20). Cain's retort can be paraphrased, "Am I a shepherd of the shepherd (or: a keeper of the keeper)?" When Cain informs his audience that he sees no responsibility for "keeping" his brother, he implies that he may be capable of its opposite. With respect to interpretation, much hinges on this word. P. A. Riemann has discussed שמר and the context in which it is used.[25] His observations may be summarized in the following manner:

1. Does the word ever express positively one person's obligation toward another? That is, based on its usage elsewhere in the Hebrew Bible is it used in Gen 4:9 to convey the notion that one is responsible to know the whereabouts of the person one is keeping? The question can be answered rather easily. שֹׁמֵר is a participial form of a verb that is found more than four hundred fifty times in the

[25] P. A. Riemann, "Am I My Brother's Keeper?" *Int* 24 (1970), 482–91.

Hebrew Bible. None of these occurrences imply that a person's keeping another is a covenantal norm or social obligation.[26]

2. "Keeper" is a strong word, both in English and the original Hebrew. It means not only to preserve and sustain, but also to control, regulate, or exercise authority over. God is certainly portrayed in the Bible as a sustainer of the created order. The psalmist proclaims, "Yhwh is your keeper, Yhwh is your shade at your right hand," (121:5) and rejoices at the thought: "He will not let your foot be moved; he who keeps you will not slumber. He who keeps Israel will neither slumber nor sleep" (121:3–4). This verb is often used to describe God's relationship to Israel. Moses' prayer for the people of Israel is that Yhwh bless them and keep them (Num 6:24), and in Gen 28:15, God promises Jacob to "keep" him wherever he goes.

3. But what about men and women? Are they appointed to be keepers of one another? Riemann writes, "Flocks have keepers, zoos have keepers, bees have keepers, prisons have keepers. . . . Is there perhaps in Proverbs a saying, 'The wise man keepeth his brother, but the fool refuseth to be kept?' Or in the Psalms, 'Blessed is the man who keeps his brother?' No, there are no such references, or anything like them. Humanity is enjoined to remember those in need, to provide for the poor, to guard the rights of the weak—indeed, to love one's neighbor as self. But *keeping* another person is too strong an expression."[27]

4. The question then clearly expects a negative answer. Cain is not to be his brother's keeper. Riemann concludes,

> What I am urging, in brief, is that the narrator simply assumes that you will agree with Cain that he is *not* charged with the responsibility for being his brother's keeper. I go beyond the intention of the narrator when I enlarge upon this point. I do so only because it is from this very text (and this text alone—there is no other which could be used) that we have so often charged each other with the responsibility for making ourselves our brother's keeper. And this, I submit, is at the very least a great pity, for it is the last thing we really need to be encouraged to do since we are so naturally inclined to do it anyway. Either we ignore our fellow in his need, or we appoint ourselves his keeper.[28]

[26] Ibid., 483.
[27] Ibid., 488.
[28] Ibid., 489.

To his offhand lie, Cain has added a counterquestion, a familiar defensive move, as he attempts to seize the initiative in dialogue, and Riemann is correct: the Bible does not charge humans to "keep" others.[29] But he misses the point that Cain *over*states his responsibility toward Abel in order to deny *all* responsibility. It is certainly the case that one is not to look after a brother constantly, to control or exercise authority over, but a brother is expected to assist in times of trouble. Cain might not have expected to "keep" Abel, but as his brother he certainly should have been ready to redeem, to avenge his blood should he be murdered (Num 35:19–21). Evasive and indifferent, Cain's angry counterquestion is thus very much like the rhetorical questions of Jacob and Joseph, who ask if they stand in place of God in Gen 30:2 and 50:19. These questions attempt to dismiss the point raised while denying all responsibility.

In the garden of Eden story, God's questions of the man and woman became increasingly more pointed:

> Where are you?
> Who told you that you were naked?
> Have you eaten of the tree of which I commanded you not to eat?
> What is this that you have done? (3:9, 11, 13)

With language that evokes the perplexity of the event itself, God's final question of Cain probes, accuses, and reverberates as never before. With respect to the plot, the murder in v 8 is the climax of action, but the narrator has portrayed the event so laconically that the weight of the story is shifted to the sentence. Yhwh answers Cain's lie by confronting him: "What have you done? Listen; your brother's blood is crying out to me from the ground!" God hears the voice, even if no human ear does. It is not a vain cry—someone out there hears it—and it will later echo in the voices of other victims of injustice.[30] The cry (זעק) is the desperate plea of one without food (Gen 41:55), of one who senses that death is imminent

[29] For a view that contrasts with Riemann's, see F. Landy, "Humour as a Tool for Biblical Exegesis," in Y. T. Radday and A. Brenner, eds., *On Humour and the Comic in the Hebrew Bible* (Bible and Literature Series, 23; Sheffield: Almond, 1990), 106: "The first point is that according to the ethics of the Torah, and indeed of any human society, he *is* his brother's keeper."

[30] Westermann (*Genesis 1–11*, 305) makes this point and also observes that the most important word in this verse is אלי, "to me."

(Exod 14:10), or of a woman who is being raped (Deut 22:24, 27). The prophets will also assert that God hears such desperate cries for help (Isa 19:20).

God's role has shifted from interrogator to indignant prosecutor. Only two words in the Hebrew, this final question (and the accusation that follows) silence Cain. The drama is heightened by the narrator, who for the first time drops Yhwh's name from the speech introduction formula.[31] In fervent and profound exasperation, Cain stands condemned not because he denies that he is his brother's keeper, but because he is Cain's murderer.

In the interrogation scenes of chapters 3 and 4, God opens both trials with questions, but eventually abandons the pretense of ignorance to reveal the extent of knowledge about wrongdoings. In the accusation scene outside Eden, God returns to the idea that the slain victim is none other than a brother and introduces the startling idea that the dead man's blood is crying out. Rather than allowing Cain the option of a verbal response to the question about the deed, the narrator portrays Yhwh answering with six Hebrew words, קול דמי אחיך צעקים אלי מן־האדמה ("the-voice-of the-blood-of your-brother is-crying-out to-me from-the-ground"). Abel's voice, which is nowhere quoted in Gen 4, has reached God from the ground (האדמה), a place that in this story is symbolically loaded. Cain, a tiller of the ground (v 2), brought an offering from the fruit of the ground (v 3). It is האדמה, we observed above, that links brother to brother, children to parents, humanity to creator.

Metaphors, a hallmark of Hebrew poetry, appear here in prose narrative. With vivid images, metaphorical language illuminates something in a new and surprising way and adds considerable emotional charge to bare facts. Since God will not come to physically search for the body, the blood on the ground has acquired a voice which cries out. A biblical parallel for attributing a voice to blood is found in Job 16:18, and the words are virtually a compressed theology of Israel's criminal and cultic law. Blood is synonymous with life itself (Lev 17:11). According to the biblical view, blood and life belong to God. Murder goes far beyond the human sphere because taking another's life is an attack on God's right of possession. Spilled blood cannot be hidden under ground (Isa 26:21).

[31] The narrator three times gives us the names of the speaker and addressee (vv 6, 8, 9), but drops them when Cain speaks in v 9b and Yhwh in v 10. The omission draws attention to the speaking characters.

Aftermath

> [11]And now you are cursed from the ground which has opened its mouth to take the blood of your brother from your hand. [12]When you work the ground it shall no longer give its strength to you. A vagabond [lit.: trembler] and a wanderer you shall be on the earth. [13]And Cain said to Yhwh, Greater is my punishment than I can bear [lit.: lift up]. [14]Behold, you have driven me today away from the ground and from your face. I shall be hidden and I shall be a vagabond [lit.: trembler] and a wanderer on the earth, and all who find me will kill me. [15]And Yhwh said to him, Not so.[32] For anyone who kills Cain, a sevenfold vengeance shall be taken. And Yhwh put on Cain a mark so that no one who came upon him would strike him. [16]And Cain went out from the presence of Yhwh and settled in the land of Wandering, east of Eden.

Attention shifts to the consequences of the deed in the final scene, which is characterized by reversals in form and plot dynamics: Questions are no longer invoked; Cain is passive; Yhwh assumes a more active role by delivering a sentence. If people cannot or will not avenge, Yhwh will (cf. the story of Naboth in 1 Kgs 21). The man Cain is cursed, and attention is drawn to the word ארור by "attah" sounds that surround it (אתה + עתה). In Eden, the serpent was cursed, but not the man or woman. The curse in 4:11 itself elaborates upon the preceding action. The ground, which received the blood of Abel from the hand of Cain, will no longer yield any strength to the farmer. It had been cursed in the preceding drama (3:17), but, while for Adam the curse upon the ground was intended to make it difficult for farming, Cain is here cursed *from* the ground.[33] He cultivated the ground, offered fruits from the ground, and spilled his brother's blood upon the ground. And the blood cries from the ground which now refuses to give up its fruit to Cain.

If Cain remains here, he will starve and in this way become "a wanderer and a fugitive."[34] In powerful diction Cain cries out in pain as he declares that his punishment is more than he can bear. He laments that outside the land, he will be hidden (סתר) away from Yhwh's face. (Underlying the lament is the idea that whoever departs from Yhwh's realm enters lands where other powers rule [1 Sam 26:19; Jon 1:3]). In the aftermath, one discovers that the cries of

[32] Reading לא כן with LXX, Symmachus, Syriac, Theodotion, Vg, and Peshitta for MT לכן.

[33] Westermann (*Genesis 1–11*, 307) concludes that the curse upon Cain amounts to exile or expulsion from the human community.

the murdered (v 10) and the murderer (v 15) are both heard by Yhwh, who offers the murderer a mark of protection. The final divine action protects Cain from being the target of an assassin. An outcast because of the curse, he is nonetheless protected from falling victim to any malicious act on the part of another in this primeval world. With protection from murder, Cain leaves the field and the presence of Yhwh.

The rhetorical interchange outside Eden is a fine illustration of the Hebrew Bible's deceptively simple art. Characterization is achieved through questioning and counterquestioning in the syntactic, compositional, and stylistic design of the plot. In retrospect, the six interrogatives of Gen 4 share some parallels with the questioning pattern in Gen 3. Cain ultimately emerges in a more negative light than his parents by means of a number of characterization strategies: the harping on the fraternal relationship and other repetitions, correspondence and disparity in the offering sequence, the arrangement of names, the alliance of the narrator and Yhwh, variations in expected word order, the final shift from interrogation to prosecution, and the protean responses to the questions themselves.

CHAPTER FOUR

QUESTIONS ANSWERED WITH SILENCE AND LITERARY FRAMES (1 SAMUEL 14:37 AND 28:6)

Two Questions Answered with Silence

1 Samuel 14:37

In a scene from 1 Sam 14, Saul reveals his desire to surprise the Philistines. He says, "Let us go down . . . by night and despoil them until the morning light; let us not leave one of them." The people give the king a blank check ("Do whatever seems good to you"), and at this point in the narrative the priest interrupts and suggests that they first "draw near to God" (v 36) before proceeding.[1] Several modern translations are correct in understanding the initial conjunction as an *adversive vav* ("*but* the priest said"),[2] because a discrepancy between Saul's impulsive desire to attack the Philistines and the priest who urges caution is suggested by a number of contextual clues. Indeed, the priest's advice reveals what the king has apparently forgotten. The narrator had previously reported that Yhwh gave Israel victory earlier that day (v 23). At the time when Saul was made king at Gilgal, he announced that Yhwh (i.e., not kings) is the one who delivers Israel. "Yhwh has brought deliverance," Saul boldly proclaims in 11:13, but by chapter 14 the king is portrayed as one who is too anxious to assume responsibility, one who is too eager to assert power, and one who perceives the battle on a much too personal level: "Cursed be anyone who eats food before it is evening and I have been avenged on my enemies," says Saul in 14:24. The priest thus offers practical advice in v 36 to this king who is about to plunge headlong into battle. When the narrator continues by introducing Saul's questions to Yhwh, "and Saul inquired of God" (v 37), the reader may infer that Saul inquired *as a result* of this reminder.[3]

---

[1] In this chapter, a number of passages are cited from the Hebrew Bible without reference to a specific book. In such cases, the reference is to 1 Samuel.

[2] JB, NAB, NEB, NIV, NJB, and NRSV.

[3] The NAB, NEB, NIV, and NRSV highlight this point by translating the phrase as "so Saul asked/inquired of God."

Earlier, Saul had taken the initiative in directing the priest in matters related to battle maneuvers (vv 18–19), but now Saul's inquiry is nothing more than an afterthought.

So Saul asks God, "Shall I go down after the Philistines? Will you give them into the hand of Israel?" The narrator then reports that Yhwh does not answer Saul (v 37). At first glance, it might appear that a question that is ignored should be classified as an unanswered question. But silence *is* an answer, and questions that an addressee hears and chooses not to respond to verbally may be more accurately described as *questions answered with silence*. As in real life, silence after a question in the Bible signals anything from aloofness to anger, and a number of issues related to this kind of answer support the theme of Saul's loss of power. Two verses later, the narrator reveals that the people[4] are also unwilling—though, we know, not unable (see vv 28–30)—to answer the king (v 39). By the time that Jonathan appears before his father, Saul, apparently tired of the silence, demands information from his son. Because of the context, Saul's imperative addressed to Jonathan ("Tell me what you have done" [v 43] instead of the inquiring route of "What have you done?")[5] has a significant impact on characterization. While it is not unusual for a king to give orders, the combined images of a commander-in-chief issuing a roll call (v 17), frequently ordering his troops (vv 36–42), devising a trial by lot (vv 41–42), and asking questions that are rebuffed with silence (v 37, and subsequently at 28:6), all work together to reveal a desperate, virtually powerless king.

Immediately after the report that Yhwh "did not answer [Saul] that day" (v 37), the king sets out to solve the puzzle of God's silent response. In the course of devising an answer, Saul pronounces an oath: "For as Yhwh lives, who saves Israel, even if it is my son Jonathan, he shall surely die!" (v 39). J. P. Fokkelman has called attention to the king's "language of force,"[6] and indeed, this one in a position of high authority is compelled to pronounce no less than

---

[4] The narrator emphasizes the point by means of repetition: "and no one, out of all the people, answered (him)."

[5] This question had in fact been addressed to Saul in 13:11!

[6] J. P. Fokkelman, *Narrative Art and Poetry in the Books of Samuel* (3 vols.; *King David: II Sam. 9–20 & 1 Kings 1–2*, vol. 1; *The Crossing Fates: I Sam. 13–31 & II Sam. 1*, vol. 2; *Throne & City: II Sam. 2–8 & 21–24*, vol. 3; Assen/Maastricht: Van Gorcum, 1981–1990), vol. 2, 75.

three oaths in a short narrative space (vv 24, 39, 44).[7] His misfortune with this kind of forceful language contrasts with yet another oath that the people will soon declare. Their oath, "As Yhwh lives, not one hair of [Jonathan's] head shall fall to the ground; for he has worked with God today" (v 45), reveals that it is the king's son whom the people now respect. Their words, the only oath the people utter in the entire chapter and the last quoted speech in the scene, have a silencing effect on Saul.

The answer that Saul produces concerning God's silent response does not generate closure. In fact, his procedure for finding the answer may cause us to ask a whole series of questions that have been well formulated by Peter Miscall:

> Why does [Saul] assume that the lack of response is due to "this sin"? Why does he automatically pronounce the death penalty upon the sinner? . . . When he says "this sin," does he have some transgression in mind, particularly one related to his previous oath? Why does he not relate it to the army's eating flesh with the blood in it, since the latter is a sin against the Lord? Why does he not ask the army what sins have been committed? If Saul has a specific sin in mind, the lot-casting could be superfluous. Finally, why does Jonathan's name come so readily to his lips in his initial acclamation?[8]

One might supplement these questions by asking if this story—which describes the army sinning, the king seeking the sinner(s), and a lottery that singles out Jonathan—is suggesting more about Saul, Jonathan (has he sinned?), God, and possibly the lottery system itself than might be apparent at first glance. Answers to such questions may be found by focusing precisely on what is (and is not) implied in Saul's statement "let us find out how this sin has arisen today" (v 38). Previously, Saul learned that the troops had been "sinning against Yhwh (חטאים ליהוה) by eating with the blood" (v 33). It is worth noting in passing that it was Saul himself who had prohibited the people from eating (v 24), an action that no doubt explains their subsequent lack of energy (v 31). Members of Saul's army—hungry because their commander will not let them eat until he is avenged of his enemies—hastily slaughter the animals and violate Yhwh's prohibition against eating animals with the blood (v 32). In what appears

[7] In addition, the narrator in v 27 and a soldier in v 28 refer to the oath.

[8] Peter Miscall, *1 Samuel: A Literary Reading* (Bloomington: Indiana University Press, 1986), 96.

to be an attempt to stop the sinning, Saul instructs the troops to bring the animals and to slaughter them "here" (not "on the ground" as before, v 32).[9] He adds that they should not sin (any more) against Yhwh (ולא תחטאו ליהוה) by eating with the blood. The narrator then reports that *all* the people complied with Saul's instruction (v 34). The word חטא reappears, however, just after Yhwh answers the king with silence. This time Saul refers to "this sin" (החטאת הזאת), instead of to any sin against Yhwh (ליהוה) as before. In English, the change from "a sin against Yhwh" to "this sin" may not imply a major shift in thought, but in Hebrew this variation in language could imply that "the sin" mentioned in v 38 refers exclusively to the transgression of the ban against eating that Saul had previously announced. K. Koch has traced the usages of חטא in its various Semitic contexts. He writes: "in the early historical books, חטא means to commit an offense against someone with whom one stands in an institutionalized community relationship. The substantives refer to antisocial conduct directed against a person. . . . Such conduct includes . . . rebellion against one's king." Koch also points out that the word may have carried a "metaphorical" meaning as well as the more well-known "concrete" meaning of "miss (a mark)."[10] "Sinning" against a king is, in fact, mentioned in the Old Testament. David will later ask Jonathan, "What is my sin (חטאתי) against your father?" (20:1), and Shimei will confess that he has "sinned" (חטאתי) against David (2 Sam 19:21).

This contextual and extratextual evidence suggests that the reference to sin in v 38 is to nothing other than the violation of the oath. If this interpretation is correct, we may conclude that Saul has less to lose from his bold proclamation ("If this injustice [ἀδικία] is in me or Jonathan my son, O Yhwh, God of Israel give Urim")[11] than he

---

[9] P. Kyle McCarter, Jr. (*I Samuel* [AB 8; Garden City, N.Y.: Doubleday, 1980], 249) notes that "the stone permits the blood to drain from the meat. This could not be done when the animals were slaughtered 'on the ground' (v 32)."

[10] K. Koch, "חטא," *TDOT* 4, 311. The Semitic languages all share the root ḥṭ'. Arabic (haṭi'a), for example, is rendered "make a mistake," and Akkadian derivatives carry the meanings of "faulty," "guilty," "sinner," "fault," "damage," "guilt," and "sin" (Koch, 310).

[11] The long expression (v 41)—"Why have you not answered your servant today? If this injustice is in me or Jonathan my son, O Yhwh, God of Israel give Urim. But if this injustice is in your people Israel"—is found in the LXX, but not in the MT. The long expression may have been lost in MT by homoioteleuton ("Israel" to "Israel"). See E. Noort, "Eine weitere Kurzbemerkung zu 1. Samuel XIV 41," *VT* 21 (1971), 112–16.

implies. *His* life will not be on the line. After Yhwh answers Saul's questions with silence, the picture that emerges is of a duplicitous king all too eager to assign blame to anyone other than himself, and this portrait of a man unable or unwilling to examine his own actions—why the ban in the first place?—proves to be proleptic. In the next chapter Saul will attempt to cover over his own mistakes by blaming the people (and not himself) on several occasions (15:15, 21) for disobeying Yhwh's command to utterly destroy the Amalekites.

Characterization by analogy, observed previously in Saul's oaths vs. the oath of the people, is achieved from a number of other angles as well. The attempt to find the one who has "sinned" by means of the lots, for example, contrasts with the casting-of-lots ceremony that had determined that Saul would be the first king of Israel in 10:17–27. In the first lot-casting scene, Samuel summoned the people and then charged them to present themselves before Yhwh by tribe and by clan (vv 17–19). The tribes appear, presumably some are then eliminated, and Benjamin is taken by lot (v 20). The process of elimination (from tribe to family, from family to individual) continues until Saul is taken by lot. This multiple-stage (and presumably intricate) process contrasts with Saul's invoking the lots in chapter 14. The second lot-casting ceremony is not only quicker—a two-stage sequence—but Saul's words, "Even if it is my son Jonathan, he shall surely die" (v 39), give the scene a decidedly predetermined quality.

The sequence of questions and silence followed by Saul's attempt to isolate the "sinner" (14:37–42) may remind the reader of Jonathan's previous action in the chapter. Jonathan, who also desires to discern Yhwh's will, reveals a plan to his armor-bearer whereby they will fight against the Philistines, but only if the enemy says, "Come up to us" (v 10). The answer that Jonathan receives in v 12 serves as a "sign" (אות), and it contrasts with the silent response that Saul receives from God in v 37. Jonathan merely hopes for a sign—"it may be that Yhwh will act for us" (v 6). Saul, after being rebuffed, insists on some explanation for God's silence. Jonathan has occasion to affirm his belief that Yhwh is in control during the process: "for nothing can hinder Yhwh from saving by many or by few" (v 6). Saul, distressed by the answer of silence, hastily attempts to restore the threatened relationship. Thus Jonathan's confidence in God is contrasted with Saul's desperate religiosity. The narrator had set the stage of a king deprived of information at the very beginning of the chapter. Jonathan commands his armor-bearer to accompany him to the Philistine garrison on the other side. The reader has no reason to assume that Saul is part of the conversation, but, as if to make clear that Saul is in the dark, the narrator reports: "[Jonathan] did not tell his father" (v 1). The narrator reinforces the clandestine nature of Jonathan's wanderings by reporting in v 3 that "the people did not know that Jonathan had gone."

Saul's loss of power is also suggested by an analogy other than the sign (given to Jonathan) vs. questions answered with silence (given to Saul). Both father and son are accompanied by others in chapter 14. Saul has an impressive retinue. His troops number "about six hundred" in v 2 and "about ten thousand" in v 23; he is accompanied by Ahijah the priest (v 3) who carries the ark (v 18) and perhaps the sacred lots;[12] Saul has lookouts stationed at Gibeah (v 16) as well as his own group of leaders (v 38) and an assembly whom he rallies for battle (v 20). In contrast to this show of force, Jonathan is accompanied by one young armor-bearer (v 6), a far cry from the "one thousand" who accompanied him in the previous chapter (13:2). The difference is all the more striking when one focuses on the results of Jonathan's victory. He and his armor-bearer kill about twenty soldiers (v 14), and create a "panic in the camp, in the field, and among all the people [so that] the garrison and even the raiders trembled" (v 15). Saul, with all his military might, is able to cause great confusion (v 20), which causes the Philistines to flee (v 22). But the scene is narrated with less attention to details, and we are not told that Saul's forces killed a single Philistine.

One final contrast may be noted. The questions answered with silence in chapter 14 and the accompanying action do signal rejection, and this turn of events is also narrated in the surrounding chapters. Yet chapters 13 and 15 convey Saul's loss of power in a strikingly different fashion. In chapter 14 the picture of a king losing power is suggested from a number of angles: Samuel, the one who rebukes Saul on many occasions, never appears in the chapter; Jonathan outperforms his father on the battlefield; Saul is deprived of information about Jonathan; and Saul's questions addressed to Yhwh are answered with silence. Yet the word "rejection" or similar expressions (cf. 13:13–14 and 15:26) never appear in chapter 14; it is divine silence that supports the theme. The image of a king deprived of facts and answers to his own questions thus signals a distinctive rhetorical strategy.

---

[12] According to the LXX, Ahijah carries the ephod.

1 Samuel 28:6

Toward the end of the Deuteronomistic Historian's story of Saul's reign, Yhwh answers Saul with silence once again (28:6). Since 14:37 and 28:6 are the only two verses in the History where the narrator tells us explicitly that Yhwh answers an individual's question with silence,[13] we may conjecture that the respective stories in chapters 14 and 28 form an *inclusio* or narrative frame. Both chapters portray Saul as the one who receives such an answer, and they also portray him as the one who attempts to force the issue at hand. As before, the theme of Saul's decline is supported by other evidence along with the question answered with silence, and in an effort to support the idea that they comprise a narrative frame, these other similarities of the chapters will be isolated. Both of these chapters: (a) contain a number of questions;[14] (b) include a description of war with the Philistines as an occasion for the story; (c) portray one of the central characters who is famished; and (d) contain language of oaths and bans. Of these four shared features, questions and the answers they generate serve the most complex and rich rhetorical function.

In chapter 28 each of the principal human characters invokes several interrogatives within the small narrative space of vv 6–16. Saul asks four questions (vv 6, 13, 14, 15), the woman asks three (vv 9, 11, 12), and Samuel invokes interrogatives on two occasions (vv 15, 16). As in chapter 14, the unfolding plot derives in large part from the multiple effects of knowledge or the lack of it, and much of the action and reaction of characters can be explained by the questions and answers that appear. Close attention to the sequence of events and the questions that are invoked reveals that the biblical artist works through what by modern standards may appear to be rudimentary means. This artist's skill and rich imagination produce subtle changes in language that have a dramatic impact on characterization.

The Initial Question (v 6)

The first reference to a question in chapter 28 is reported by the narrator. The content of Saul's inquiry to God is not shared with the reader ("and Saul inquired of Yhwh, but Yhwh did not answer

[13] Though see 1 Sam 8:18 (a prediction); 2 Sam 22:42 (plural).

[14] 14:19 (indirectly), 37 (2x), 41 (LXX), 45, and 28:6, 9, 11, 12, 13, 14, 15, 16.

him"). This lack of detail serves to generate suspense, and the mysterious aura created by the withholding on the narrator's part will be reinforced as the story unfolds (with words like "at night," "an old man," "What is his appearance?"). Does Saul want to know if Israel can defeat the Philistines? Or does he merely need instruction about how to proceed (as he will later indicate to Samuel in v 15)? At the phonological level, the narrator draws attention to the event by producing two words in succession that are remarkably similar in sound. The subject, "Saul" (שׁאול), immediately follows the predicate, "inquired" (ישׁאל). This near duplication in sound is not required in the Hebrew since Saul was the subject in the preceding verse.[15]

This report of asking is less specific in 28:6 than it was in 14:37, yet the answering is described in a more detailed fashion. The silent response in 28:6 is highlighted by the narrator who emphasizes *acceptable* means whereby one might receive an answer from Yhwh: Saul does not receive an answer "by dreams, or by Urim, or by prophets." The ancestors (Gen 28:10–17), Job (Job 33:15–18), and kings (1 Kgs 3:5) all acquired wisdom through dreams. The mention of Urim[16] is reminiscent of the trial by lots described in the first part of the frame (14:40–42) where Jonathan was taken by the lots. In chapter 14 the sacred lots provided Saul with an answer, but they also provided the people an opportunity to overrule the response; in fact, they called Saul's inquiry to the Urim into question: "As Yhwh lives, not one hair of [Jonathan's] head shall fall to the ground; for he has worked with God today" (14:45). The mention of the Urim in chapter 28 also recalls 23:6, where Saul lost his opportunity of getting divine messages as Abiathar the priest absconded with the ephod to David.[17] The explicit reference to prophets in this second answer of silence from Yhwh (28:6) will gain its true rhetorical force as the scene unfolds: Samuel, the "trustworthy prophet of Yhwh" (3:20), will soon be summoned from the land of the dead. The narrator makes it clear in 28:6 (and had certainly suggested in chapter 14) that all doors appear to be shut as Saul seeks an answer this time.

---

[15] A similar phenomenon may be observed in 14:37, where the proper name שׁאול immediately follows the verb ישׁאל. In 14:37, however, a different subject, "priest," is found in the preceding clause (v 36).

[16] The Urim is usually mentioned with the Thummim, though see Num 27:21.

[17] The ephod was a priestly garment to which was attached an oracle pouch for the Urim and Thummim.

Yet after being rebuffed with silence, Saul sets out once again in v 7 to acquire information. This time he does not respond to Yhwh's lack of an answer by assuming sin (as he did previously, 14:38). Working from the assumption that the deceased have access to information about God's plans, Saul commands his servants to find a woman who can conjure up spirits from the dead. As before in chapter 14, Saul's own religiosity inhibits him as he seeks a response from God. In forcing the answer this time, Saul inquires through a woman who had survived the systematic expulsion that he himself had previously ordered. The narrator's statement in v 3 regarding the casting out of mediums and wizards from the land, innocuously inserted (out of its chronological place) in the midst of battle details (28:1–5), now comes to have explosive implications: Saul's desire to contact the woman is not only foolhardy and capricious, but is also unlawful. The Old Testament repeatedly insists on the illegitimacy of consulting mediums or wizards. In Deut 18:10–12 such practice as divining by the dead is described as "abhorrent to Yhwh," and raising the spirit of a prophet by such magic is especially odious. It is utterly absurd to believe that Yhwh can be forced to reply through unlawful means (Lev 19:31).[18]

While seeking (בקש) a medium is certainly illegal, the narrator appears to have more in mind in this description. Since chapter 18 Saul has been seeking David, and now at the end of his life under the cover of night and with the full knowledge that his action is prohibited, he seeks a medium. The Chronicler will later reduce the episode at Endor to two verses but will preserve this important detail by remembering Saul as one who "consulted a medium, seeking guidance, but did not seek guidance from Yhwh" (1 Chr 10:13–14). The reader has ample opportunity to catch the irony that Saul is both lawmaker and lawbreaker, and because of the Bible's numerous prohibitions against sorcery, this violation is much more serious than Jonathan's "infringement" earlier (14.27).

In seeking an answer this time, Saul disguises himself; he chooses to cover over (or to step out of) his clothes before going to the woman.[19] The changing-clothes motif of v 8 is found in several places

---

[18] Cf. also Exod 22:18; Lev 20:6, 27; 2 Kgs 21:6, and Isa 8.19.

[19] It is significant that Saul goes to (הלך) her to find the answer. The image of a king *going to* a medium is certainly startling; Saul heads for the witch probably because it would be too embarrassing to have her walk to him.

of the Hebrew Bible. For example, in an attempt to consolidate power, Jeroboam instructs his wife to disguise herself and go to the prophet Ahijah whose "eyes were dim because of his age" (1 Kgs 14:2–4).[20] In contrast to this scene, Saul acts in chapter 28 without any coaxing; the decision to disguise himself before approaching the medium is his and his alone. By removing (or covering over) his royal clothes, Saul is symbolically signalling the end of his own reign as king. He denies his own identity and future in words and actions. The clothes motif also functioned symbolically in the story of Saul's decline on a previous occasion. After Saul disobeys the command to utterly destroy the Amalekites by sparing Agag, Yhwh speaks to Samuel privately and says, "I regret that I made Saul king, for he has turned back from following me, and has not carried out my commands" (15:11). When Samuel confronts Saul subsequently, the king responds with words that are misleading at best.[21] Samuel again tells Saul that Yhwh has rejected him from being king over Israel (15:26). When Samuel turns to walk away, Saul[22] grabs the hem of his robe in a final plea for mercy. When the fabric gives way, the prophet turns the action into a symbolic act. The torn garment becomes a symbol of the kingdom that has been stripped from Saul. Samuel says, "Yhwh has torn the kingdom of Israel from you this very day" (15:28).

The end of Saul's reign is also suggested by another image in v 8: the immediate circumstance of his attempt to force the answer is indicated on the temporal plane by a setting sun. The Hebrew word לילה carries the meaning not only of night but also of darkness, and

---

[20] Outside of the Deuteronomistic History, one might think of Rebekah who, in an effort to deceive Isaac, takes her eldest son Esau's clothes and places them on her younger son Jacob (Gen 27:15–16).

[21] Vv 13, 15 (3x), 20 (2x), 21 (2x), and 24 (2x). See Sternberg, *Poetics*, 482–515.

[22] Cf. 15:27–29. MT lacks the name "Saul" and reads "and he grabbed (ויחזק) the hem of his robe and it tore" (15:27). Samuel was the subject in the preceding clause, and Jakob H. Grønbaek (*Die Geschechte vom Aufstieg Davids [1 Sam. 15–2 Sam. 5]: Tradition und Komposition* [Copenhagen: Munksgaard, 1971], 695) argues that Samuel is the subject of the phrase in question (i.e., "and Samuel grabbed the hem of his robe"). Yet Fokkelman points out that a "difficult change of subject . . . is not uncommon in the OT" and is to be preferred here (*Narrative*, 2, 105 n. 30). Ralph Klein (*1 Samuel* [WBC 10; Waco: Word, 1983], 146 n. 27a) indicates that "4Q, LXX, Syr, Josephus" support the reading "and Saul grabbed."

The robe serves as a symbol of the monarchy. The transfer of royal power is also symbolized when Jonathan (from Saul's house) hands his robe to David (18:4). Subsequently, David cuts off a portion of Saul's robe in 24:4.

it will remain dark throughout this scene (v 25). The description provides yet another link to chapter 14, where Saul planned to attack the Philistines "by night" (v 36), but where his plans were foiled by his own people who ransomed Jonathan—thus causing Saul to withdraw (v 46). The king no doubt wishes to consult the medium at night because the darkness allows him to disguise his illegal actions and because his travels during the day might have made him an easy target for the Philistines, just as in chapter 14 the cover of night provided Saul an opportunity to rout the already enervated Philistine forces. But in both of these scenes night appears to serve a symbolic function as well. The absence of light accentuates Saul's inability to perceive God's volition.[23]

Initially, the narrator conveys the action in this chapter (vv 1a, 2ac, 3–6, 7ac), with characters speaking only on occasion (vv 1b, 2bd, 7bd). After Saul arrives at Endor, the dramatis personae address each other until v 19, with only occasional and brief interruptions from the narrator. The intrusions function almost exclusively as transitions from one character's speech to another's. Saul's attempt to find an answer will be highlighted by the spoken word that virtually dominates the story after he and his two men arrive in Endor (from vv 8b–19). As storyteller, the narrator may impress us as loquacious, reticent, or even silent when it comes to devising links in the plot chain. The narrator's silence,[24] like God's in 14:37 and 28:6, is self-imposed. Indeed, when characters address each other (or themselves through interior monologue), they speak with the narrator's approval. If any or all of the speech-events throughout chapters 14 or 28 could be summarized by the omniscient teller, why then does the narrator often prefer to render speech at crucial moments, making dialogue itself a narrative event? The distinction between dialogue and narration is important to recognize because the option the narrator often chooses[25] foregrounds the speech-event, making us aware of each of the characters as people addressing each other, defining relationships,

[23] Cf. 1 Sam 3 (esp. vv 2, 3, 8, 13) and the relationship between light, darkness, perceiving God's will, and the beginning of the end of another era (i.e., Eli's).

[24] Details about the trip to Endor, to mention just one example, are passed over altogether.

[25] Speech, as in 28:8b–19, for example. The narrator's preference for speech over narration is also apparent in chapter 14 after the report that Yhwh "did not answer [Saul] that day" in v 37. Cf. vv 38–46. No speech is quoted in the subsequent scenes of chapter 14 (vv 47–48, 49–51, 52).

and revealing through speech much (though certainly not all) of what we wish to know. Robert Alter has emphasized the importance of direct over indirect speech in Hebrew biblical narrative:

> Spoken language is the substratum of everything human and divine that transpires in the Bible, and the Hebrew tendency to transpose what is preverbal or nonverbal into speech is finally a technique for getting at the essence of things. . . . The biblical scene, in other words, is conceived almost entirely as verbal intercourse, with the assumption that what is significant about a character, at least for a particular narrative juncture, can be manifested almost entirely in the character's speech.[26]

Thus the report of the question answered with silence and Saul's attempt to force the answer this time stand out for at least two reasons: (a) the sequence of events establishes a link with chapter 14 where Saul's question to Yhwh was answered with silence,[27] and (b) the question-silence combination in chapter 28 also launches a full-blown series of questions by other characters. Subsequent interrogatives in the chapter are reported as direct speech.

The Woman's Questions (vv 9, 11, 12)

After the king's initial commands to the medium ("consult," "bring up"), the woman informs Saul of the danger he is putting her in. She duplicates a reference to the expulsion of "the mediums and the wizards from the land" (vv 3, 9), and from the reader's side, this informational redundancy underscores the duplicitous nature of Saul's effort to force the answer. She then addresses a series of questions to Saul (vv 9, 11, 12). Far from asking for information (as Saul had previously in v 6), two of her questions indict Saul. She accuses him of endangering her life: "Why then are you laying a snare for my life to bring about my death?" (v 9). She is not asking; she is chastising: This snare will kill me! מתנקש ("laying a snare") spoken by the woman here in v 9 is reminiscent of יתחפש ("disguised himself") reported by the narrator in the preceding verse. Once again, these words function at the phonological level as well as at the thematic level; the combination of sounds reinforces the serious consequences of deceit. The trap laid is for Saul—not for the woman.

[26] Robert Alter, *The Art of Biblical Narrative* (New York: Basic Books, 1981), 70.

[27] As mentioned above, 1 Sam 14:37 and 28:6 are the only two verses in the Deuteronomistic History where the formula לא ענה indicates God's silent response to an individual. See n. 13 above.

After learning Saul's true identity, the woman asks, "Why have you deceived me?" (v 12). Once again, the woman's indignant tone is understandable; this deceitful king is playing with her life. The phonetic connection of המיתני with רמיתני (death and deceit) in her two rhetorical questions is striking. She compresses למה . . . להמיתני of her first question (v 9) to למה רמיתני (v 12), and the issue of death (assigned hypothetically to the woman in v 9) will subsequently be reassigned to Saul (v 19). His fate will be sealed by the deceit he now practices.

Situated between these two rhetorical questions is an information-seeker. In v 11 the woman asks whom she should bring up, but contextually her question goes beyond plot exigencies. The issue of who is listening (i.e., obeying), so prevalent in this overarching story, comes to have new implications. The woman listens to her visitor even though, from her vantage point, the obedience she practices puts her life on the line. To underscore the point, the woman later returns to the scene just after Saul's conversation with Samuel, and says, "your servant has listened (שמע) to you; I have taken my life into my hand, and have listened (שמע) to what you have said to me" (v 21). The woman who is obedient to the king sounds an ironic note, and the repetition is certainly not accidental. The king, whose not listening to Yhwh had already been an issue at Gilgal (13:13) and reinforced subsequently in the Amalek incident (chapter 15), is now not even obeying his own edict (28:3)!

Saul's Questions Addressed to the Woman (vv 13, 14)

Saul immediately attempts to ease her mind ("have no fear")[28] before asking her what she sees (v 13). To this question the woman answers that she sees אלהים coming up from the earth. The word אלהים, typically translated as "God" or "gods," may here be a "divine being" (NRSV) or even "a ghostly form" (NEB). She suggests in her response that she will be able to assist Saul, but her words also produce suspense. The fact that someone or something is "coming up from the earth" may have encouraged her visitor, but the news also causes him to ask for more information: "What is his appearance?" (v 14). Both of Saul's questions addressed to the woman reinforce figuratively that he is in the dark. He sees nothing now, just as he heard nothing

[28] The reader knows that it is the client and not the woman who has reason to fear.

from God earlier. Saul is utterly dependent upon the woman to tell him what *she* sees, and even in the subsequent conversation with Samuel, the narrator mentions nothing about visual contact.

When Saul asks her the second question, the woman quickly supplies him with the information that he seeks. The reference to arising continues, but this time with a new subject: "an old man is coming up" (a description that would have delighted Saul). The next detail in v 14, drawn out to the last, does much to dispel Saul's (and our) suspense: "and he is wrapped in a robe." This reference to the garment calls attention to the different course that readers and characters travel along the path to enlightenment, because her answer to Saul's question about appearance rings differently in the ears of the king and the audience on the one hand and the woman on the other. That is, the reference to the robe has several implications to all but the unknowing woman because it is part of the prophet's characteristic garment. Even as a boy, Samuel received a new robe from his mother annually while at Shiloh (2:18–19). At the end of the Amalek incident, Saul[29] tore Samuel's robe, an action symbolizing the tearing away of the kingdom from Saul (15:27). Even in death, Samuel's robe is preserved, and after the garment is mentioned Saul knows (ידע) that the man he seeks has arrived even before the initial conversation. With this knowledge, the king responds by bowing his face to the ground in an act of obeisance (ויקד אפים ארצה וישתחו). The narrator refrains from any explicit explanations for what motivates the king to bow (קדד), but the context suggests at least two possibilities: Saul fears and respects this figure coming from the world of the dead, and/or he realizes that Samuel's ghost represents his last hope for gaining access to God. Ultimately, however, Saul demeans the rank of his office as he bows to the prophet, just as he had previously when he disguised himself with other clothes (v 8). These desperate actions are all precipitated by Saul's response to the question which was answered with silence (v 6).

Samuel's Initial Question (v 15)

Saul and Samuel finally meet, and the king's ill fate is suggested by at least two factors in their initial conversation. First, it is Samuel who starts the dialogue, even though Saul had initiated the meeting.

---

[29] See n. 22 above.

Second, the why-question that the prophet addresses to the king is highly charged. Like the woman before, Samuel opens with an accusing rhetorical question: "Why have you disturbed me by bringing me up?" (v 15). And the second-person verbal form הרגזתני that follows the interrogative למה accentuates Saul's responsibility for this unwanted disturbance. The language of the plot underscores that the efforts since Saul was rebuffed by silence have been heading to the central event of Samuel's resurrection; this image of bringing up (from the grave) has been repeated five times within this story,[30] and now that we have arrived, Samuel makes it abundantly clear that he does not appreciate being disturbed. The grave was, after all, understood to be a place where a person could rest in peace (cf. Job 3:13–19).

Saul Answers Samuel with a Question (v 15)

At the end of his extended speech in v 15, Saul does get around to posing a question ("so I have summoned you to tell me: what should I do?"),[31] but his query is prefaced by several revealing statements. While his speech duplicates much of what the audience already knows, it also conveys subtle, yet important differences in language. When the king answers Samuel's initial question, he explains that his misfortune stems from two factors: (a) the warring Philistines and (b) God who has turned away from him and who answers him no more. Contextually, the news is not surprising. The narrator had earlier reported that the spirit of Yhwh had departed from Saul (16:14) and that Yhwh was with David (18:12), and Saul had heard equally disturbing news from Samuel previously (13:13–14, 15:26). Readers might ask how the resurrected (and obviously annoyed) Samuel could possibly help this ailing king. When Saul complains that Yhwh answers him no more (ולא ענני עוד), he implies that this kind of silence is something new. Yet Saul and the audience know

---

[30] Previously, vv 8, 11 (2x), 13, 14. V 8: "bring up for me" (העלי לי); v 11: "Whom shall I bring up for you?" (את מי אעלה לך) and "Bring up Samuel for me" (את שמואל העלי לי); v 13: "I see a divine being coming up" (אלהים ראיתי עלים); v 14: "an old man is coming up" (איש זקן עלה).

[31] ואקראה לך להודיעני מה אעשה. A translation of מה as a relative (instead of as an interrogative) pronoun is also possible. The standard translations (JB, KJV, NAB, NEB, NRSV, NIV, REB, NJB) all understand מה as a relative, though cf. 10:8b where a similar phrase is found. In 10:8b the relative pronoun (cf. the modern translations) is conveyed with את אשר, not מה as in 18:15.

more and better. The first report of the question answered with silence was found in the initial portion of the narrative frame (14:37). In Samuel's presence, Saul says euphemistically, "I have summoned (אקראה) you," whereas earlier in vv 8 and 11 he had spoken more candidly by employing the verb עלה ("raise up")—as indeed the woman (vv 11, 13) and Samuel (v 15) had. Contextually, Saul's change from עלה to קרא underscores once again his duplicitous actions. Just as he must change clothes, he must also change words when he finds himself in Samuel's presence.

On what grounds might one argue that such changes in language reveal more than Saul's desire to show respect before Samuel? The answer brings another issue to the fore. The narrator does, of course, have the option to tell the story straight: what happens, why, what the characters think, how their actions square with the narrator's evaluative system, and so forth. The option that the narrator chooses—namely, to bring *speaking* characters onstage—produces an orchestration of voices, a systematic interplay of perspectives. This dimension of biblical narrative requires the narrator to relinquish certain privileges such as highlighting signification and passing judgment by way of commentary, but the choice to allow characters to address each other and us is not meant to imply that the narrator abandons such goals. The departure from straightforward communication requires the reader to pay attention to point of view—that is, to the system of perspectival relations that exists between narrator and characters, narrator and readers, and readers and characters. As we attempt to make sense of the Saul narrative we must perform reconstructive operations as best we can, and the process requires us to make inferences about such perspectives in relation to one another. One has ample opportunity to witness the narrator's skill of making the most of what, by modern standards, is scanty material. It is this process of reconstructing the story's perspectival parts into a coherent whole that makes the Bible such exciting reading and marks one of its artistic claims to notice. In chapter 28, the narrator (v 6) and Samuel (v 16) both refer to Saul as one who "asks" (שאל), but in conversation with Samuel (v 15), Saul uses other words. He explains that he has called (קרא) the prophet *to tell him* (להודיעני) what to do (עשה). The shift in point of view is accentuated by Samuel, who responds in the very next verse with words that remind us of the narrator's perspective: "Why do you ask me?" (למה תשאלני). Does the shift in language (from "ask" to "call to tell" back to "ask") have any implications? With respect to the overarching story, Saul's explanation in v 15 is reminiscent of Samuel's original instructions, all the way back at 10:8,[32] where the prophet anointed Saul in Ramah, saying, "I will tell you (הודעתיו) what you shall do (תעשה)." With the unlawful sacrifice at Gilgal, the Amalek fiasco, and his failed attempts in pursuing David behind him, it appears that with Samuel's ghost before him Saul is now eager to listen to the prophet.

Another aspect of Saul's answer to Samuel's question (v 15) is noteworthy. The king's description of the silence is similar to the narrator's report of the silence in v 6, but, of course, Saul omits a reference to the Urim in Samuel's presence: "God has turned away from me and answers me no more, either by prophets or by dreams" (v 15; cf. v 6). The narrator's explanatory comment in v 6, like Saul's in v 15, may appear to be unnecessary since the report that Yhwh/God did not answer is comprehensive. We may conjecture, however, that all of these words serve some rhetorical purpose. The narrator apparently wishes to stress that all doors are closed to Saul and that God's silence has an enduring quality about it at this point in the narrative. That is, Yhwh's silence is not just "for that day" (ביום ההוא) as it was in 14:37. What about Saul's omission of the Urim? Since the priestly oracle was embodied in the Urim, Saul may be intentionally avoiding an embarrassing reference to his botched efforts in the priestly role that he assumed in Gilgal, a scene where Samuel had reprimanded the king with harsh words: "You have done foolishly; you have not kept the commandment of Yhwh your God . . ." (13:13–14). Saul may also pass over the Urim in an effort to avoid alluding to the murdered priests of Nob who "wore the linen ephod" (22:18).[33] Saul does have good reason to forget the Urim in Samuel's presence because it was Saul who had commanded Doeg the Edomite to slay the priests of Yhwh at Nob. One priest, Abiathar, escaped from Doeg with the ephod (23:6) and brought it to David. Thus David the outlaw received the oracular device that he consulted with success on various occasions (23:8–12; 30:7–8). If Saul's amnesia in chapter 28 reminds us of this scene at Nob where the ephod plays an important role (23:6, 9), then one other detail stands out. In the midst of the description of Abiathar's escape from

---

[32] Fokkelman, *Narrative*, vol. 2, 611.

[33] Uriel Simon, "A Balanced Story: The Stern Prophet and the Kind Witch," *Prooftexts* 8 (1988), 161. See n. 17 above.

the slaughter and the report that he "came down [to David at Keilah] with an ephod in his hand" (v 6), we learn in 23:2 that David asks Yhwh if he should attack the Philistines. The narrator's report contrasts with the treatment Saul receives in the question-answer sequence of chapters 14 and 28: "Yhwh said to David, 'Go and attack the Philistines and save Keilah' " (23:2). David's troops then express their reservation, and when David inquires of Yhwh a second time, the narrator reports that "Yhwh answered [David], 'Yes, go down to Keilah; for I will give the Philistines into your hand' " (v 4). Immediately and on both occasions (vv 2, 4), after *David* inquires of Yhwh, the narrator reports that Yhwh instructs David to attack the Philistines at Keilah. The contrast suggested simply by the omission of the Urim as Saul speaks to Samuel in Endor is glaring: David twice gets direct answers from Yhwh and succeeds on the battlefield despite his army's protestations. In the subsequent scene of chapter 23 (vv 6–14), David again gets instructions on two separate occasions from Yhwh, and this time, he is apparently aided by the Urim. David says to Abiathar the priest, "Bring the ephod here" (v 9). The two answers that David gets from Yhwh are in this scene strikingly specific: "[Saul] will come down" (v 11) and "[the men of Keilah] will surrender you" (v 12). Biblical narrative, notorious for its sparsity of detail, is surprisingly rich in its creation of analogy.

All three of Saul's questions in chapter 28 that are recorded as direct speech are prefaced with מה ("what?"), and each interrogative sentence is short, consisting of only two words in the Hebrew: מה ראית ("What do you see?"); מה תארו ("What is his appearance?"); מה אעשה ("What shall I do?"). The cumulative effect of these terse questions underscores Saul's desperate attempts to get the facts, and they contrast with some of the more weighty, reflective questions raised in this context: ולמה אתה מתנקש בנפשי להמיתני[34], and ולמה תשאלני ויהוה סר מעליך ויהי ערך[35].

[34] "Why then are you laying a snare for my life to bring about my death?," spoken by the woman in v 9.

[35] "Why then do you ask me, since Yhwh has turned from you and become your enemy?," spoken by Samuel in v 16.

Samuel's Final Question (v 16)

The final question of the chapter, "Why then do you ask me, since Yhwh has turned from you and become your enemy?," launches a speech which, by biblical standards, is long. It is the second rhetorical question introduced with למה that Samuel puts to Saul, and the fourth unpleasant why-question addressed to the king in the chapter. Samuel is unyielding, and beginning with the question that launches his speech to Saul in v 16, the prophet expresses his regret with this anointed king who is unable or unwilling to comprehend the implications of God's silence. This final question leaves no doubt that Saul's asking is superfluous. The king knows everything that he should know; his fate has been decided long ago (13:14; 15:26), so why has he disturbed a dead man to ask more? While Saul's decline has long been forecast, Samuel now takes the opportunity to remove any ambiguity that remains. After a blatant reminder of Saul's disobedience in the Amalek episode, Samuel becomes arrestingly specific in v 18: "therefore (על כן) Yhwh has done this thing (הדבר הזה) to you today (היום הזה)." In the Hebrew, the author departs from the traditional word order (verb, subject, object), and ironically stresses God's silence by referring to it as *this thing*. Samuel continues this discouraging and specific message by indicating when ("tomorrow," מחר) Saul and his sons will join Samuel, and the prediction that Saul and his sons will be with Samuel in a descent to the realm of the dead (v 19) is ironically linked to Samuel's initial question (v 15) about the purpose of the forced visit up to the land of the living. "In this way," as Uriel Simon observes, "Samuel compounds Saul's sin with the personal injury done to the prophet of Yhwh, and thereby increases the catastrophe which will befall the king."[36]

In this speech (vv 16–19), language once again underscores a thematic point. Samuel portrays himself solely as an instrument of God. He refers to himself indirectly only in the suffixes in vv 16, 17, and 19. By contrast, Yhwh's proper name is invoked seven times and is the subject of verbal clauses on nine occasions, five times in vv 16 and 17 alone. As Saul seeks support and direction from Samuel, the prophet points back to Yhwh, whose authority is above them both.[37]

---

[36] Simon, "A Balanced Story," 161.

[37] Fokkelman makes this observation and supports it with the statistics in *Narrative*, vol. 2, 612.

Supporting Data

The argument that chapters 14 and 28 form an *inclusio* or narrative frame is supported by other images that the two chapters share. In both chapters, conflict with the Philistines serves an ancillary function, the theme of the famished character appears, and oaths and bans play an important role in the unfolding plot.

In the first episode, battle with the Philistines served as a backdrop to the actions of Saul, Jonathan, and the troops.[38] The scene opened with a description of Jonathan's successful initiative against the Philistine garrison. Jonathan—the narrator reminds us that he is "Saul's son" (v 1; cf. 13:16)—seeks and receives a prophetic sign just before launching an attack. In the second story of the narrative frame, four of the initial five verses focus on preparation for what appears to be yet another clash with the Philistines (28:1–2, 4–5). An imminent battle is suggested by the image of the Philistines who are assembled and encamped at Shunem. Yet the two scenes in these chapters are marked by contrasts. Saul's condition is now complicated by David's departure and collaboration with the Philistines (though cf. 29:1–11) who are preparing to fight against Israel. Verse 3a suspends the description to report that "Samuel had died, and all Israel had mourned for him and buried him in Ramah, his own city." These details appear to be out of place not only because they interrupt the story about the conflict, but also because the first portion of the verse duplicates information. Samuel's death, Israel's mourning, and Samuel's burial in his home town of Ramah had all been reported as recently as 25:1. Verse 28:3b, on the other hand, does provide some news: Saul has expelled the mediums and wizards from the land. Thus v 3 masquerades as repetition and rather innocuous details about a ban that Saul had previously instituted, one that is hardly surprising since it accords well with the biblical witness (Lev 19:31; 20:6; Deut 18:10–11). Its place in the narrative will become apparent as the action in vv 6–25 issues from two details conveyed in this verse: Samuel is dead, and Saul has expelled the mediums.

In contrast to Jonathan's earlier initiative, when Saul gathers the troops for battle at Gilboa, no sign is given. In chapter 14, Saul met the Philistine threat by gathering all Israel. He rallied his troops,

[38] 14:1–16, 19–23, 31–37, 45–48, 52.

went into battle against the Philistines (v 20), and was victorious because "Yhwh gave Israel the victory that day" (v 23). By the story's end, the people virtually reject Saul as they affirm Jonathan: "Shall Jonathan die? . . . Not one hair of his head shall fall to the ground; for he has worked with God today" (v 45). This kind of repetition with variation in the two chapters serves a rhetorical function. The author not only calls our attention to a similar sequence of events, but also suggests through analogy that the scenes in chapter 28 are more ominous. Now there is no report of victory as before, and Jonathan will not reenter the picture to be affirmed by the people. In fact, Samuel forecasts that Saul's sons will soon join the prophet in the land of the dead (v 19). As the second story of the narrative frame concludes, Samuel's resounding words drive one more nail in Saul's coffin: "Yhwh has turned from you and become your enemy" (28:16).[39]

[39] While the two chapters (14 and 28) share common features, they also exhibit major differences. One variation is the means of characterization. While a diverse repertoire of portrayal through speech and action is apparent in the Hebrew Bible, description inevitably centers on one of two alternatives: representation of the outer world where actions are described, or representation of the inner where feelings and thoughts are revealed. In contrast to chapter 14, Saul's decline is accentuated in chapter 28 by highlighting the inner life. The narrator provides a view of the inner life of the king in 28:5: "When Saul saw the army of the Philistines, he was afraid, and his heart trembled greatly." This description of Saul's mental state is hardly surprising, and the narrator's choice to convey such a view stands out only because the Hebrew Bible consistently prefers to describe action in the external world. Descriptions of the inner life, somewhat rare in the Hebrew Bible, have appeared before in 1 Samuel. When the Benjaminite arrives in Shiloh with the news that Hophni and Phinehas are dead, Eli is described as sitting by the road watching as his "heart trembles for the ark of God" (4:13). When the terrifying giant of the Philistine camp named Goliath orders the Israelites to produce a man so that they may fight together, Saul and all Israel are "dismayed and greatly afraid" (17:11). In chapter 28 attention is also given to a character's inner struggle. After the initial description that Saul is afraid in v 5, the king speaks to Samuel and tells him of "his great distress" (v 15) that is caused by the Philistines who are fighting against him, and of his recognition that God "answers [him] no more." After Samuel's extended and unfavorable response (vv 16–19), the narrator describes Saul's condition once again by informing us that he falls full length (מלא קומתו) to the ground because he is "filled with fear" (v 20). The fall is reminiscent of Saul's earlier action in Samuel's presence (v 14), but in v 20 we are told that Saul experiences great fear (ירא מאד). In chapter 28, much in both the internal and external worlds revolves around this word "fear." Early in the chapter, Saul is afraid because of the Philistine threat (v 5); subsequently his fear stems from the words that Samuel speaks (v 20); and finally, his fear is accentuated by means of analogy. His fearing contrasts with the woman's whose two rhetorical questions (vv 9, 12) reveal that she, too, is afraid. Yet Saul encourages her to "have no fear" (v 13), and in telling her this, he reminds us that he alone has reason to fear.

The twin image of the fast and resulting hunger, prominent in chapter 14, appears in a different form in chapter 28. In both places Saul is responsible for creating the conditions of hunger. In chapter 28, however, he chooses not to eat, a noteworthy counterpart to chapter 14, where the king ordered members of his army not to eat. The report in 28:20 that Saul had "eaten nothing all day and all night" subverts the true chronological sequence, and it may remind us of the earlier story where Jonathan (unknowingly) violated his father's order. Saul stood alone in condemning his son to death in chapter 14—despite Jonathan's protests in which he twice referred to the small nature of his offense ("I tasted a *little* honey," 14:29, 43), and despite the strong protest of the people (14:45). With Jonathan before, we knew why he was hungry; his success on the battlefield was well documented, and his appetite could be explained in part by his aggressive campaign against the Philistines. In 1 Samuel 28, we are not told why Saul has not eaten. The sequence of events seems to suggest that it is more likely that Saul's refusal to eat is to be understood as a psychological phenomenon aggravated by the hardship of the clandestine trip to Endor so close to enemy lines,[40] as opposed to a more narrow religious action.[41] Indeed, the word "fast" never appears in this chapter. It is ultimately the answer (28:16–19) to Saul's final question that precipitates physical collapse, but the fall is prompted by two factors according to v 20: Samuel's harsh words (ירא מאד מדברי שמואל) and enervation (גם כח לא היה בו). The woman, apparently unaware that Saul is destined for death on the following day, thinks that a hearty meal (v 24) will revive the king, but once again, more is at work here than an unfolding plot. She implores him to listen (שמע) to her now as she had listened (שמע) to him previously (vv 21–22); unknowingly, she underscores Samuel's accusation in v 18: "Because you did *not* listen (שמע) to Yhwh's voice . . . Yhwh has done this thing to you today."

A language of force, including a number of oaths spoken by Saul, was isolated in chapter 14. Saul has occasion to utter one oath in chapter 28. After the woman reminds her visitor of the potential

[40] Fokkelman (*Narrative*, vol. 2, 621) concludes that Saul's refusal to eat is an expression of depression or resignation and may even contain an element of self-destruction.

[41] Though see P. Kyle McCarter's argument (*I Samuel*, 421) that Saul's hunger is to be understood as his attempt to purify himself before the seance.

serious consequences that could result from practicing necromancy, Saul attempts to calm her fear. He, apparently, succeeds by invoking an oath. The narrator introduces the king's remark in v 10 with the words "and Saul swore to her by Yhwh" (וישבע לה שאול ביהוה לאמר). While variations on this formula are found elsewhere in the Hebrew Bible,[42] the emphasis on Yhwh, duplicated here by the narrator and a character—Saul repeats the proper name in the oath ("as Yhwh lives")—is rare.[43] Several observations accrue from the language of this oath. By invoking Yhwh's name, Saul accentuates the duplicitous nature of his invoking God, who has, after all, just answered him with silence. (Saul also invoked Yhwh's name in 14:39, despite the answer of silence that he received there.) While the phrase "as Yhwh lives" is part of Israel's stock vocabulary, it may serve an ironic function in this context, because it is spoken by one who is calling upon a dead prophet to answer him. The words call attention to Saul's tragic condition.

Conclusion

Chapters 14 and 28 of Samuel are organized around a single literary thread. The narrative frame of the two chapters contains explicit and unique statements from the narrator, who reports in 14:37 and 28:6 that Yhwh "does not answer" (ולא ענה) an individual (i.e., Saul). The multiple effects of the picture of a king unable to get answers combine to support the theme of decline, and the near duplication of images signals a distinct rhetorical strategy. The focus has been on questions—both chapters are loaded with them, and the king's name (שאול) is a constant reminder of asking—and on the answers they generate, but the interrogative form serves multiple functions beyond that of seeking information.

Subtle, important shifts in language have played an important role in characterization, and such changes have often underscored larger thematic points. Close attention to details has revealed that the biblical

[42] Josh 2:12, 9:18–19; Judg 21:7; 1 Sam 24:21; 2 Sam 19:8; 1 Kgs 1:17, 1:30, 2:8, 2:42.

[43] Cf. 1 Kgs 2:23. Uriel Simon makes this point and includes this reference (and those in the n. above) in "A Balanced Story," p. 170 n. 2. He also observes that this duplication can be found "to some extent" in 1 Sam 20:42 and Jer 12:16.

artist works with what by modern standards may appear to be rudimentary measures to accomplish various goals. Characterization has been achieved by means of analogy throughout: the language of oaths and bans, the images of characters who are famished, Jonathan's success on the battlefield, (preparation for) battle with the Philistines, even the clothes and the cover of night—all of these corresponding images and parallel situations in the two chapters advance the image of a king groping for information. At the phonological level, the narrator draws attention to the action through a play on words. Several events and thoughts are highlighted by words in close proximity that are remarkably similar in sound, such as שאול ("Saul") and ישאל ("inquired"); יתחפש ("disguised himself") and מתנקש ("laying a snare"); המיתני ("hasten my death") and רמיתני ("you deceived me"). Other words—בקש ("seek") and שמע ("listen"), for example—were also isolated because of the important role they play in underscoring thematic points. Finally, the reported questions in the two chapters play an important rhetorical function because they reveal the intentions of the speakers, and through them their positive and negative attributes.

CHAPTER FIVE

THE TRIUMPH OF IRONY BY MEANS OF A THREAD-AND-FRAME (1 SAMUEL 18:7, 21:12, AND 29:5)

In the previous chapter a narrative frame in 1 Sam 14:37 and 28:6 was isolated. This narrative frame serves a complex and rich rhetorical function in the characterization of the king as Saul's questions are answered with silence. In this chapter, we turn our attention to interrogatives that play an important role in a different type of narrative frame that functions in a myriad of ways. A celebrative song—"Saul has killed his thousands, and David his ten thousands"—appears in three different contexts, and in the hands of the narrator develops as something more than straightforward repetition.

What begins as a song of celebration becomes a portal that exposes Saul's fear and jealousy, and this couplet of a song serves another function as well. This refrain is in the first instance a narrative thread, but it is also used as a narrative frame that interlocks motifs and images around the Philistines/Achish and David. In time we come to discover no less than three different speakers and their points of view: the women who sing of Saul and David, the servants of Achish who recite the song to their king, and the Philistine commanders who also speak to Achish with persuasion on their mind. And when we consider the additional voice of the narrator, we discover different ironic points of view that have been woven together to show different levels of knowledge among characters and audience.

The triplicate appearance of the victory song is therefore both a thread that foreshadows the unfolding drama as the narrative moves inexorably away from Saul to David and also a frame that helps delineate the character zones of David and Achish. In the analysis that follows, attention is given both to the questions that surround and enhance the literary device of the thread-and-frame and to the multiple shades of irony that abound.

The Initial Narrative Thread

הכה שאול באלפו ודוד ברבבתו (1 Sam 18:7b)

The Subsequent Narrative Frame

הכה שאול באלפו ודוד ברבבתו (1 Sam 21:12b)

. . .

הכה שאול באלפו ודוד ברבבתו (1 Sam 29:5b)

The Song in Its Original Context

The celebrative song under discussion first appears in the Samuel narrative in a chapter that follows a description of David's triumph over the Philistine giant Goliath. The report that "David took the head of the Philistine and brought it to Jerusalem" has already foreshadowed David's rise to power in that city. The narrator stresses the festive mood now in this homecoming scene: "the women came out of all the cities of Israel, singing and dancing, to meet King Saul, with tambourines, joyful songs, and three-stringed instruments. And the women sang as they made merry" (18:6b–7a). The description of women celebrating with song and instruments looks back in narrative time to the Exodus, where the prophet Miriam was joined by all the women who went out with their tambourines and with dancing as the prophet sang her song of praise for deliverance. Jephthah's daughter also met him with timbrels and dancing (Jdg 11:34), just after her father's victory over the Ammonites. The narrator's introduction to the song is long by the Bible's standards, and it hints at upcoming complications in the plot. As the women come out to meet the commander Saul and warrior David, the narrator is explicit: they greet king (המלך) Saul; then subsequently Saul expresses his concern about what he assumes is David's desire for the kingdom (המלכה). The actual transfer of power will not occur until much later (2 Sam 5:1–5), but already the narrative is exploring the question of *who* is king. (The ironic implications of this question will be further exploited in the upcoming frame, where the song is repeated by the Philistines on both occasions.) At present, Saul finds himself unable to govern: he has little or no control over David, the people, even his own emotions. He is powerless, while David is on the rise. As chapter 18 opens, a number of important facts are established by the narrator before the song is reported: (a) Jonathan's deep and abiding love for David (v 1), (b) Saul's "adoption" of David (v 2), (c) Jonathan's political commitment to David (v 3), (d) Jonathan's extraordinary actions authorizing David for the throne (v 4), (e) Saul's elevation of David as commander over the army (v 5), and (f) David's unanimous support by all the people (v 5).

After this description of the support that David enjoys even within Saul's own family, the song is rendered:

> Saul has killed his thousands,
> And David his ten thousands.

In its context the victory song may not have been meant to disparage Saul. Since the numbers "thousands" and "ten thousands" are used synonymously in Ps 91:7 as well as in certain Ugaratic texts, the couplet may in fact not be suggesting a contrast between Saul and David at all. Intended to celebrate the success of Saul and David equally, the two words may both mean "many."[1] Yet from Saul's perspective an assertion even of equality is enough to cause him to interpret the song in the worst possible way. With a touch of irony the narrator is beginning to show that Saul is the key agent in his own demise: *He* transfers power to his neighbor, the one better than himself (1 Sam 15:28).

What is clear is that the political implications of the women's song of celebration are not lost on Saul, who, by means of interior monologue, recounts their words, "they have ascribed to David ten thousands, and to me they have ascribed thousands." Uttered through a prism of fear, Saul's reflection yields a rhetorical question: "What more can he have but the kingdom?" The counterpart to David's success is Saul's preoccupation with the thought that David may be destined for the throne. Yhwh, we know, is already with David (16:18), and Saul himself bestowed on David a divine blessing as recently as 17:37.

David has already been anointed king over Israel (16:1–13), but this ceremony took place in secret. Only Samuel, Jesse, his sons, and the audience know of it. We also know that the spirit of Yhwh recently departed from Saul (16:14) and that David is destined for the throne, and Saul appears, we might infer, to have more than a

[1] Ralph W. Klein, *1 Samuel*, WBC 10 (Waco, Tex.: Word, 1983), 188.

vague impression of what the future holds. In the preceding chapter, Saul, after lying repeatedly, has been verbally reprimanded by Samuel, and the meaning of the words is unambiguous:

> For rebellion is as much a sin as divination, and stubbornness is like iniquity and idolatry. Because you have rejected Yhwh's word, Yhwh has rejected you from being king (15:23).

> Samuel said to Saul, "I will not return with you because you have rejected Yhwh's word, and Yhwh has rejected you from being king over Israel" (15:26).

> And Samuel said to him, "Yhwh has torn the kingdom of Israel from you today, and has given it to your neighbor, who is better than you. And also the Eminence of Israel will not lie or have a change of mind for God is not a mortal, that God should have a change of mind" (15:28–29).

Thus an ironic tension is developing between what Saul is already fearing as a possibility and what the audience knows is inevitable. In brief narrative spaces we are told that Yhwh is with David (18:12, 14, 28), yet no longer with Saul (15:11, 23, 26–29, 35). And the narrator also makes clear that all Israel and Judah "love" David (18:16), as does Jonathan (18:1–5).

Saul's various stratagems are all destined for failure. He banishes David from his court, yet David ends up having "success in all his undertakings" on the battlefield so that Saul "stood in awe of him" (vv 12–16). The brief scene concludes with the narrator's report that Saul "eyed" David from that moment on (v 9). Saul correctly perceives David's rise, but in this trajectory he is blind to the damaging effects of his jealousy and self-serving anger.

The Song Recontextualized (Narrative Frame "A")

After David "rose and fled" from Saul, the celebratory song appears again, at the point in narrative time where David meets Achish, King of Gath (1 Sam 21:11–16). David in fact has been fleeing from Saul for some time already: in 19:18 he "fled and escaped" to find temporary refuge with Samuel; at 20:1 he "fled" from Naioth in Ramah, where he found Jonathan; and at 21:2 David met Ahimelech at the shrine of Nob. Subsequently, David continues to flee. He is next at the cave of Adullam (22:1–2) and in Moab (22:3–5), and Saul continues to pursue David until chapter 24, when David cuts off a corner of Saul's cloak. The song, the first part of a new frame, is thus embedded in an extended narrative that conveys David on the run as his relationship with the Philistines becomes increasingly complicated.

The verse that conveys David's flight contains oppositional links: David flees "from Saul" and goes "to Achish." It is worth noting that David does not flee to Gath, but to Achish, King of Gath. David has fled, escaped, or arrived in the presence of others previously—before Samuel in 19:18, Jonathan in 20:1, and the priest Ahimelech in 21:1—but now David appears to be going over to the enemy for the purpose of reaching a political agreement. If this is indeed David's goal, he does not succeed this time, but he will eventually (27:1–7, 12).

David's fame has spread. He is no longer an anonymous shepherd boy, and Achish's servants demonstrate that they recognize him when they invoke rhetorical questions as a prelude to the celebratory song, which the Israelite women sang earlier: (a) "Is this not (הלוא־זה) David king of the land?" (b) "Did they not (הלוא לזה) sing in dances . . .?" The duplication of the Hebrew interrogative words makes the point forcefully: David cannot hide, even in non-Israelite territory. His stature is expressed here not by the jubilant Israelite women, but by Philistines on the other side. They quote *their enemies*. The duplication of this song in the mouths of the Philistines, here and in the second part of the frame (29:5), shows just how far David's fame has spread. According to George Savran this song is introduced by a verbal form that suggests that the women are in fact still singing in order to stress that David remains a threat to the Philistines.[2] The double rhetorical questions presume an answer of "yes," and another equally forceful rhetorical device is found in their verbatim duplication of their opponents' victory song:

> Saul has killed his thousands,
> and David his ten thousands.

At its inception the victory song was contextualized to show David as a powerful warrior. In its new setting the song shows David not as warrior, but as "king of the land." Achish's servants' point of view is ironically linked to Saul's from the previous occasion: they, like Saul, wrongly infer David's "kingship" from the couplet song itself. That is, the song serves again as the basis for the conclusion that David must be king. David, of course, is not (yet) king, though he

[2] Savran, *Telling and Retelling*, 28, 125, n. 21.

finds himself fleeing from one and is now in the presence of another. How ironic that the Philistine servants perceive more than anyone in Israel concedes. They have no doubt heard the Israelite gossip, but their first rhetorical question makes a compelling case for the inevitability of David's accession to the throne. Their point of view coalesces with Saul's: both parties perceive David's "kingship" from the celebratory song itself. Additional irony is manifest in the concluding portion of the phrase. The man on the run is "king *of the land*." In time this monarch will indeed be more powerful than Saul and all the Philistine princes combined, and he will rule over an even larger territory.

Their use of this vague term, "king of the land" (מלך הארץ) makes both Achish and David uneasy. David takes their words to heart (בלבבו) and becomes much afraid (ירא מאד) of Achish, the king of Gath (מלך גת). The sitting monarch no doubt understands the danger that David would likely present to his own power as Philistine king, and David's immediate response to this "coronation" leaves no doubt that he has reason to worry, too.

Thus the report of the Philistines' perception of David as king highlights the danger in which David now finds himself, and this danger is stressed in the delayed revelation that Achish's servants have in fact detained David. At the end of the scene, Achish twice inquires about why they have "brought" (בוא, hiphil) David into his presence (vv 15–16). This delayed exposition shows in a dramatic and ironic way that although David is God's anointed one (chap. 16), destined for the throne—Samuel knows it; Jonathan and Michal know it; many in Israel, including Ahimelech, sense it, and now even the Philistines share in this perception—his life remains in grave danger both at home and in Philistine territory.

Trapped, this "king of the land" finds no recourse but to deny the control mechanisms that govern his daily life: he begins to play the part of a lunatic. By scratching marks on the doors of the gate and forcing spittle to run down his beard (v 14), David uses his instincts to impeach himself. It is not altogether clear in the Hebrew whether David made marks on the gate, whether he beat on them, or whether he spat on them.[3] What is unambiguous is that freedom lies beyond the gate and that he is now trapped. Feigned insanity

---

[3] Klein, *1 Samuel*, 217.

conveys both his despair and his desire to flee again. The next image—saliva dribbling down into his beard—is an unmistakable sign of madness: this lunatic is clearly inaccessible. Is there not an ironic contrast between the song that has been joyfully conveyed from mouth to mouth and this image of the "king" who appears to be beyond the universe of speech?

Even this action has ironic overtones, for what it demonstrates is that David is wise and shrewd. Indeed, he has little recourse but to feign madness in order to escape now from Achish and the Philistines. He has a problem on his hands. Just before meeting Achish, David received the sword of Goliath from Ahimelech (21:10). When the servants of Achish ask the question, "Is this not . . . ?" the narrator reports that David becomes afraid of "King Achish of Gath." The combination of their rhetorical question about David killing ten thousand and the narrator's report that David holds Goliath's sword may explain his fear and subsequent feigned madness before Achish, king in Goliath's hometown.

The ruse works. Achish turns to his men and tells them that David is mad (משתגע) and then invokes three rhetorical questions which point to his desire to have David removed from his presence: (a) "Why (למה) have you brought him to me?" (b) "Do I lack madmen that you have brought this to play the madman?" [no interrogative word]. (c) "Shall (הֲ)this come into my house?" This rhetorical excess leaves no doubt in the mind of the reader that Achish fails to perceive that *he* is the one who is being duped. From the audience's perspective Achish's questions are double-voiced—Who is the least perceptive?—with the second one fronting as an ironic jab at the Philistines themselves. The questions also contain delayed exposition that throws David's perilous fate into bold relief. We learn at this late stage that the soldiers had previously seized David: Achish twice asks why they "brought" him. The king's final question is also significant when the larger narrative is considered. This concluding question of the scene—"Shall this come into my house?"—can eventually be answered affirmatively. Though David does not join Achish now, he will in time (1 Sam 27:1–4).

In this scene we learn that the Philistines recognize David as a kind of king, and his resourcefulness on this occasion foreshadows his calculated and numerous escapes from Saul in the upcoming chapters. Other important events transpire as David moves from place to place within the contours of this large narrative block, framed by the Philistine speakers at 1 Sam 21:12b and 29:5b. While a thorough character analysis is beyond our scope, highlights include the following: David has an opportunity to kill Saul, but refuses to lift his sword against Yhwh's anointed. Indeed, David refuses to heed the prompting of his men to take Saul's life (24:1–6). This scene culminates in Saul's tender words to David: "You are more righteous than I. . . . I know that you shall certainly be king" (24:18–21). Subsequently, David spares Nabal (25:2–38), and also Saul once again (26:1–25). In each of these three chapters, David considers the deaths of Saul, Nabal, and Saul, but in each instance he does not perpetrate them. By refusing to kill—and the narrative shows that David has ample opportunity to take life—David avoids bloodguilt and earns the praise of several characters. For example:

> *Saul says to David*: "You are more righteous than I. . . . So may Yhwh reward you with good today for what you have done to me. And now behold, I know that you shall certainly be king, and that the kingdom of Israel shall be established in your hand" (24:18–21).
>
> *Abigail says to David*: ". . . for Yhwh will certainly make my lord a secure house because it is the battles of Yhwh that my lord is fighting, and evil shall not be found in you throughout all your days. If anyone should rise up to pursue you and to seek your life, the life of my lord shall be bound in the bundle of the living in the care of Yhwh your God. But the lives of your enemies he shall sling out from the hollow of the sling. And when Yhwh has done to my lord according to all the good he has spoken about you, and has appointed you prince over Israel, this shall not be for you a cause of grief or pangs of conscience to my lord for having shed blood without cause or for having saved himself, my lord. And when Yhwh has dealt well with my lord, then remember your servant" (25:28–31).
>
> *Saul says to David*: And Saul said, "I have sinned; return my son David for I will not harm you again, because my life was precious in your eyes today. Behold: I have been a fool, and have made a great mistake." And David answered, "Here is the spear, O king! Let one of the young men come over and take it. Yhwh rewards everyone for his righteousness and his faithfulness. For Yhwh gave you today into (my) hand, but I would not raise my hand against Yhwh's anointed. Behold: as your life was precious today in my eyes, so may my life be precious in the eyes of Yhwh, and may he rescue me from all tribulation." And Saul said to David, "Blessed be you, my son David. You will do many things and will succeed." And David went his way, and Saul returned to his place (26:21–25).

Verses 27:1–28:2 and 29:1–30:31 narrate David's sojourn among the Philistines, while 28:3–25, the intervening episode, describe Saul's rash attempt to hang on to power by means of a medium at Endor (see chapter 4). This middle episode functions to delay the action and to create a narrative pause as we contemplate the implications of the brief interchange between David and Achish which precedes it: "Achish said to David, 'You know, of course, that with me you are to go out in the army—you and your men.' David said to Achish, 'Very well, you shall know what your servant can do.' And Achish said to David, 'Very well, I will make you my bodyguard for life' " (28:1–2).

By removing David from the scene of Saul's death, these chapters serve a practical function at the level of plot. The action is launched by means of David's interior monologue: "I shall now perish one day by the hand of Saul. There is nothing better for me than to escape to the land of the Philistines; then Saul will become tired of seeking me any longer within the borders of Israel, and I shall escape out of his hands" (27:1).

David finds himself once again in the presence of Achish, who now accepts David and his men as mercenaries. Achish also gives him the city of Ziklag in exchange for his raids on southern tribes hostile to the Philistines.

> And David arose and went over, he and the six hundred men who were with him, to Achish, the son of Maoch, king of Gath. And David stayed with Achish at Gath, he and his troops, every man with his household. David with his two wives, Ahinoam of Jezreel, and Abigail, Nabal's widow of Carmel. When Saul was told that David had fled to Gath, he did not continue to seek him any more. And David said to Achish, "If I have found favor in your eyes, let them give me a place in one of the country towns, so that I may live there. For why should your servant live in the royal city with you?" So Achish gave him that day Ziklag. Therefore Ziklag has belonged to the kings of Judah to this day. The length of time that David lived in the country of the Philistines was a year and four months" (27:2–7).

King Achish of Gath now accepts David as a vassal, grants him control of Ziklag, and most significantly of all puts him in charge of his bodyguard (27:1–28:2). Achish no doubt reckons David's raids on Judah (27:8–12) have made him abhorrent in the eyes of all Israel, and if he is despised by the Israelites he must be a friend to the Philistines. Where else can he go?

The Song Recontextualized (Narrative Frame "B")

The song that hails Saul's killing of thousands and David's killing of ten thousands appears a third time, now in 1 Sam 29:5, as part of a larger unit that explains how David is extricated from the upcoming battle of the Philistines with the Israelites. (It is important that the future king not fight against his own people.) The Philistine officials (שר) question the presence of David and his company among their troops. Achish defends David's loyalty by means of yet another rhetorical question: "Is this not (הלוא־זה) David, the servant of Saul, king of Israel, who has been with me these days and these years? I have found nothing (wrong) with him since the time he defected (to me) until this day" (v 3). Achish's admission is yet another example of the predominance of irony within this narrative frame. The audience knows more than the characters who inhabit this narrative world, and as Achish seeks to exonerate David, his words call the reader's attention all the more intensely to David's ruse which began with the earlier "spittle" scene. David's frequent efforts to deceive Achish have succeeded.

As chapter 29 opens, the battle lines are drawn, with the Philistines and their forces at Aphek and the Israelites in Jezreel. David and his men have gathered with Achish, and the Philistine commanders express their concern by means of an interrogative: "What are these Hebrews (doing here)?" Achish attempts to assuage their concerns by means of yet another interrogative: "Is this not David, the servant of Saul, king of Israel, who has been with me now for days and years?" He responds to his own question in an effort to convince everyone: "I have found nothing wrong with him since he left me to this day." The Philistine commanders correctly perceive that David is indeed a faithful Israelite. David first deceived Achish by means of playing the lunatic in the scene where the narrative frame opens. It is also the case that Achish knows nothing of David's pro-Judean raids from Ziklag recounted in chapter 27 (see below). As Achish discloses what he perceives to be the truth, the audience's attention is drawn all the more directly to David's duplicity as well as to Achish's credulousness. It is ironic that Achish, the only one loyal to David in this context, is in fact also the only one deceived. In their effort to convince Achish, the commanders quote the well-known song.

> And the commanders of the Philistines were angry at him, and the commanders of the Philistines said to him, "Send the man back that he may return to the place which you have assigned him there. He shall not go down with us to battle, or else he will become to us an opponent in the battle. For how could this (man) reconcile himself to his lord? Would it not be with the heads of these men (here)? Is this not David, of whom they sing to him in dances,
>
> Saul has killed his thousands,
> and David his ten thousands? (29:4–5)

They correctly perceive that David poses a threat, yet even their perception falls short: they apparently do not connect David with the slaughter of hundreds of their own, including Goliath. (Does he still have Goliath's sword with him?) Saul and David have both been celebrated with song and dance. They are renowned fighters in Israel. Perhaps it is the popular song, once again spoken by non-Israelites, that implies in the present context that the two men might work again as a team. Achish must now convey the news to David.

> And Achish called David and said to him, "As Yhwh lives, you have been honest, and it seems good to me that you should march out and in with me in the campaign, for I have found nothing wrong in you from the day of your coming to me until today. Yet in the eyes of the lords, you are not viewed with favor. And now: turn and go back peaceably. Do nothing evil in the eyes of the lords of the Philistines." And David said to Achish, "But what have I done? And what have you found in your servant from the day I came before you until today that I may not go and fight against the enemies of my lord the king?" And Achish answered and said to David, "I know that you are as good in my eyes as an angel of God. Yet the commanders of the Philistines have said, 'He shall not go up with us to the battle.' And now: rise early in the morning—you and the servants of your lord who came with you. And start early in the morning, and as soon as you have light, leave." And David set out early, he and his men, to go in the morning, to return to the land of the Philistines. But the Philistines went up to Jezreel (29:6–11)

Narration gives way to dialogue in this scene as Achish's two speeches surround David's recorded words. In this interchange Achish concludes both of his speeches by imploring David to depart, and David's departure is, of course, the main concern of this pericope. It appears that David is trapped. What can he do? He cannot expose himself as the fraud that he is in the presence of Achish. He would certainly be branded a traitor and might even be killed. On the other hand, to fight against his own people is also perilous. In so doing, he would forfeit his own future kingdom as a traitor.

There is yet another reminder in Achish's speech of the presence of irony, and it revolves around the matter of David's ambiguous status. In commanding David to depart, Achish says "you and the servants of your lord" are to depart after rising early in the morning. But who is David's "lord"? Is it Achish, who is hereby asserting his claim to instruct David? Could it be Saul? Is it possible that even Achish recognizes David's true allegiance and has been profiting from a temporary alliance with this man on the run?

While the narrative's main concern is excusing David from the battle, this interchange has the effect of demonstrating just how far Achish's perceptions are from reality, while concurrently showing David in a much too positive light. With crescendo, Achish exonerates David: "I find no fault in him" (v 3); "I have found nothing wrong in you" (v 6); "You are as good in my eyes as an angel of God" (v 9).

After having already been vindicated by Achish in v 3, David is vindicated twice more by Achish in this scene (vv 6, 9), all on a false assumption. We know better, for David has been working in Ziklag to serve his self-interests (i.e., flight from Saul), and furthermore, he deceived Achish when he reported to Achish that he had made raids "against the Negeb of Judah," "against the Negeb of the Jerahmeelites," and "against the Negeb of the Kenites" in 27:10. David in fact had raided "the Geshurites, the Girzites, and the Amalekites" (v 8), and in a strategic move he took no prisoners and left no survivors who could report on his deception. The narrator confirms that this was David's regular practice all the time that he lived in Philistia, and also indicates that this subterfuge works: "Achish trusted David" (vv 11–12).

The Jerahmeelites and the Kenites were both southern people allied with Judah, and David deceives Achish into thinking that the raids have been against Israelite villages allied with the tribe of Judah. This grand deception is made for Philistine consumption. While on the run from Saul, David intends nonetheless to confuse and mislead the enemies of Israel. This relationship between David and Achish, so vital to the narrative at the points between the frame (21:12 and 29:5), is thus founded on an intentional deception on David's part.

"What have I done?" is one of David's favorite questions. He has asked it of Eliab (1 Sam 17:29), of Jonathan (1 Sam 20:1), and of Saul (1 Sam 26:18). What is David's purpose in asking this question now? We can assume from the question that follows—"And what have you found in your servant from the day I came before you until today, that I may not go and fight against the enemies of my lord the king?"—that the purpose is a rhetorical one since Achish has already responded to these questions. Indeed, David may intend it ironically. Perhaps he is relieved to know that he will not have to turn against Achish. His pleasant tone in the words "my lord the king" thus works in two directions simultaneously. Achish no doubt understands that he himself is being addressed, but is not David's loyalty ultimately with Saul and his people? The Philistine commanders are certainly correct in their assumption about where David's allegiance lies. Irony also abounds in David's declarative-interrogative to Achish: "may I not go and fight against the enemies?" Achish's support of David stems from his belief that while David is the servant of King Saul, he has in fact proven himself to be "loyal" to Achish, king of Gath. David is, of course, pressing the point, wanting to know why he has been judged "not good." He is playing with fire: if the facts were to be known there would be reason for Achish to agree with the verdict of the Philistine commanders. From David's side everything hinges on Achish's misperceptions. Indeed, so much in this narrative within the frame depends upon untruths. The commanders and Achish perceive David from different perspectives. Only "Achish trusted in David, thinking, 'He has made himself utterly abhorrent to his people Israel. Therefore, he shall always be my servant'" (27:12). The reality of David's exoneration is what ultimately matters in this narrative; it matters even more than the fact that he engages in deception to accomplish his goals. Achish does not know that the report of 27:10, which indicates that David raided the Judean tribes, contradicts the facts of 27:8–9, which show David raiding the Geshurites, Girzites, and Amalekites.

There is no explicit mention of God in this immediate context, and we are left to wonder if David's success here is a manifestation of luck or providence. (Yhwh is certainly "with" David elsewhere, 18:12, 14, 28). What is clear is that as the chapter opens David appears to be in dire straits, but by the end of the chapter David emerges not only unscathed but highly regarded by everyone as well.

And in conclusion, the rich irony and subtle ambiguity that propel the movement from narrative thread to narrative frame have been well described by George Savran:

> David is again placed in an awkward situation in 1 Sam. 29:5, as the Philistine officers repeat to Achish king of Gath the song first heard in 1 Sam. 18:7: "Saul has slain his thousands/David his tens of thousands." Earlier, in 21:12, Achish's own servants had quoted the same refrain to warn him of the potential danger of David. In a similar way the Philistine chiefs use the song to persuade Achish not to allow David to fight at Mt. Gilboa. Each time this song appears it clashes with its context in an ironic fashion. In 18:8–9 Saul "interprets" the song in a jealous manner, which leads to his attempt on David's life. In 21:12 the warrior praised in the song must degrade himself by acting deranged in order to escape the Philistines, even though he holds Goliath's sword. In 29:5 his very success in battle becomes an argument against his going to war. Even though David earned his reputation (and his song) fighting the Philistines, Achish wholeheartedly believes that David is loyal to him and not to Saul. Perhaps we are meant to understand this situation as similar to 27:1–12, where Achish is completely taken in by David's ploy, but the text leaves the truth of the matter embarrassingly unclear.[4]

[4] Savran, *Telling and Retelling*, 55–56.

CHAPTER SIX

SEQUENTIAL QUESTIONS I (1 SAMUEL 26:6–25)

The Deuteronomistic Historian sketches the reign of King Saul in both positive and negative terms. On the one hand, he prophesies after being overcome by God's spirit; he is proclaimed king in a jubilant celebration of "all the people" after being chosen by the sacred lots; he soundly defeats the Ammonites at Jabesh-Gilead; all Israel rejoices at a coronation celebration before Yhwh at Gilgal; and he and Jonathan rout the Philistines. But the tide turns. When Saul offers a burnt offering in haste as the people begin to turn away from him, he is rebuked by Samuel:

> You acted foolishly; you have not kept the commandment of Yhwh your God, which he commanded you. For now, Yhwh would have established your kingdom over Israel forever. But now your kingdom will not continue; Yhwh has indeed sought out a man after God's own heart. And Yhwh has appointed him to be ruler over Yhwh's people because you have not honored what Yhwh commanded you (1 Sam 13.13–14).

From this point forward, Saul opposes David, and the Historian portrays Yhwh championing David. Saul often stalks David as the question of who is fit to be king is resolved. Yet in scenes that parallel each other, Saul is twice at David's mercy, and David twice spares the life of Saul (chs. 24 and 26). A concentration of questions implies a distinct rhetorical tactic, one which we will soon explore. But first a few words about the similarities at the level of plot in these two chapters.[1]

In the first episode (ch. 24), Saul enlists three thousand men from Israel and seeks out David at Engedi. Both men arrive at the same cave. In the parallel episode (ch. 26), Saul once again takes three thousand chosen men of Israel to seek David. He travels to the

[1] Chapter 26 conveys the last meeting-exchange between the two heroes who have become rivals. Saul will appear again only in the disastrous night meeting of 28:3–25 and at his death scene (31:1–13).

wilderness of Ziph and encamps on the hill of Hachilah opposite Jeshimon. In contrast to the first scene, David takes the initiative and begins to stalk Saul. David sends spies and learns where Saul has encamped. Yet these two chapters display a remarkable degree of similarity. In both scenes,

(a) the two principal, rival characters find themselves together in close proximity.
(b) Saul initiates a chase with three thousand men.
(c) After David finds himself next to Saul, his own men prompt him to kill the king.
(d) While David has sleeping Saul in his power, David refuses to strike "the Lord's anointed." He defends his inaction with an oath: "Yhwh forbid that I should lift my hand against Yhwh's anointed."
(e) David forbids his men from injuring or killing Saul.
(f) David departs and then calls after Saul or his men.
(g) The occasion provides David an opportunity to argue that he intends no harm against the king.
(h) David stealthily confiscates Saul's personal belongings (the corner of his cloak, his spear, and his jug of water) and uses them subsequently to prove to Saul that he spared his life, even though he had the chance to kill him.
(i) Both men introduce the concept of sinning (חטא): David points out that he has not sinned; Saul, on the other hand, admits that he has sinned.
(j) Both narratives end with an exchange between Saul and David.
(k) David implores Saul not to hunt him.
(l) David compares himself to a mere flea.
(m) Saul responds to David with the question, "Is this your voice?"[2] The question calls attention to Saul's declining health, which in turn hints at his declining ability to govern. The plot moves steadily toward David's success and Saul's demise.
(n) We hear Saul say at the end of the scenes that David is the more righteous man: he did not kill Saul when he had the

[2] In both instances, Saul concludes the question with the endearing word בני ("my-son," 24:17 and 26:17). David addressed Saul as אבי ("my-father") in 24:12, but drops the family language in the second scene.

chance. We safely infer that Saul would not have hesitated if the tables had been turned.

(o) The sequence of events causes Saul to announce that David's future looks bright. In the first instance, Saul says, "You shall surely be king and the kingdom of Israel shall be established in your hand" (24:20). Subsequently, Saul predicts that David will accomplish many things and will be successful (26:25).

(p) In both scenes—and this last component is the most important for our present purpose—

David invokes a series a rhetorical questions to make his point. In chapter 24, he asks:

> After whom has the king of Israel come out? After whom do you pursue? After a dead dog? After a single flea? (v 15).

And in chapter 26, he asks:

> Are you not (הלוא) a man? And who (מי) is like you in Israel? And why (למה) have you not watched over your lord the king? . . . Why (למה) is it that my lord chases after his servant? For what (מה) have I done? And what (מה) guilt is on my hands? (vv 15, 18).

This linking of questions one after another represents a special literary phenomenon. After opening with an interrogative, the questioner does not allow the addressee to answer, but instead continues to make the rhetorical point through the question chain. The concentration is higher in chapter 26, to which we now turn.

The action may be divided into four scenes. In each scene David converses with another character, and in scenes ii and iii he invokes sequential questions:

scene i	David and Abishai (vv 6–12)
scene ii	David and Abner (sequential questions [vv 13–16])
scene iii	David and Saul (sequential questions [vv 17–20])
scene iv	David and Saul (vv 21–25)

Scene i. David and Abishai (vv 6–12)

> 6And David answered and said to Ahimelech the Hittite and to Joab's brother, Abishai the son of Zeruiah, saying, Who (מי) will go down with me to Saul into the camp? And Abishai said, I will go down

> with you. [7]And David went, and Abishai, to the army by night, and behold (והנה): Saul lay sleeping in the encampment, and his spear thrust in the ground at his head. And Abner and the army lay around him.
> [8]And Abishai said to David, God has given today your enemy into your hand. And now (ועתה), let me pin him, I pray, with the spear to the ground. One blow, and I will not strike him twice. [9]And David
> said to Abishai, Do not destroy him, for who (מי) can stretch out his hand against God's anointed one and remain innocent/unpunished?
> [10]And David said, As Yhwh lives, Yhwh will strike him down or his day will come and he will die, or in battle he will go down and be destroyed. [11]Far be it from Yhwh that I should stretch forth my hand against the anointed of Yhwh. And now (ועתה), take, I pray, the spear that is at his head and the jug of water, and let's go. [12]And David
> took the spear and the jug of water from the head of Saul, and they went away. No one saw it, or knew of it; nor did any one awake for they all were sleeping because a deep sleep from Yhwh had fallen over them.

This is not a chance meeting as it was in Engedi. Upon the prompting of the Ziphites, Saul and three thousand men of Israel sought David in the wilderness of Ziph. When David learns that Saul is pursuing him, David sends spies who discover the location of Saul's encampment. David arrives and sees from a distance that Saul is asleep within the encampment, surrounded by his army (26:1–5).

David initiates the action with a question addressed to two of his men, Ahimelech and Abishai: Who will go down with me to Saul into the camp? The narrator gives us more than the names of David's audience. The two men are Ahimelech the Hittite and Abishai, brother of Joab and son of Zeruiah. Zeruiah is David's sister, and her three sons, Joab, Abishai, and Asahel, are thus David's nephews. Abishai responds to David's question. While Ahimelech the Hittite is mentioned nowhere else in the Bible, the sons of Zeruiah are portrayed as David's loyal kinsmen on several occasions. Joab and Abishai urge and participate in the execution of a number of David's enemies: they avenge their brother's death by murdering Abner (2 Sam 3:30); and Abishai twice plots to kill Shimei (2 Sam 16:9, 19:22) before rescuing David by killing a Philistine champion (2 Sam 21:15–17). Why are these sons of Zeruiah and an obscure Hittite who is never mentioned elsewhere in the Bible singled out? The answer may lie in the unfolding plot.

It is Abishai who steps forward, and, though his response is laconic, the narrator shows his loyalty to David through words that mirror those just spoken. David asks, "Who will go down (מי־ירד) with me (אתי)?" Abishai answers, "I will go down (אני ארד) with you (עמך)." As the two men set out, the king is highlighted by the unusual singular verb which here denotes the actions of one man, then by ellipsis the actions of another: David went, and Abishai too. They travel by night. The nocturnal reference is not found among the many parallels in chapter 24 (see above). A sullen aura is sometimes conveyed by means of night travel. When Saul consults a medium at Endor, he disguises himself by changing clothes and travelling by night (28:8). But in chapter 26 the cover of night functions differently at the level of plot. The narrator's report of David's night travel is accompanied by a reference to Saul and his commanders who are asleep, lying on the ground. The full implications of the sleep are revealed, however, only subsequently: they all slept because a deep sleep from Yhwh had fallen over them (v 12).

The action is conveyed swiftly in v 7 through the Bible's free indirect discourse marker הנה "behold." While the description is rendered within the field of the narrator's voice, the scene is conveyed from David's point of view: he first perceives that Saul is not only lying down but is in fact asleep. (From a distance David saw that Saul lay with Abner nearby in v 5 [שכב־שם שאול ואבנר], but now, in close proximity, David first perceives Saul in isolation [שאול שכב ישן]). The second phrase conveys David's growing realization that it is the spear (and not Abner) which is near the king; indeed it is thrust in the ground next to his head. And finally, in the third phrase, the narrator conveys David's final perception: Abner in fact is with the army. He and they surround the king, and they too are lying. The threefold revelation is conveyed by a consistent syntactic sequence of subject, verbal form, place:

a) Saul, sleeping, encampment
b) spear, planted, ground/head
c) Abner/army, lying, around him

Between the twin images of lying that frame David's perception (signalled by הנה) is the spear. Its location, next to the king's head and thrust into the ground, is a provocative image from the larger story of the Saul-David confrontations. On more than one occasion Saul hurled his spear in an effort to pin David to the wall (18:11; 19:10), and he once hurled it at his son Jonathan (20:33). Allusions to this instrument will be made in each of the four scenes.[3] It is a symbol in this larger story of power and death, or, more to the point, the misuse of power which leads to death.

It was David's men who attempted to persuade him to kill Saul in chapter 24. Abishai assumes that role here. In contrast to the sleeping Saul, Abishai stands ready for action. Abishai, who now wishes to do with the spear what Jael once did with a tent peg (to Sisera in Judg 4:21) and who previously twice proposed killing Shimei, introduces the idea of executing Saul. A masterful rhetorician, Abishai makes the point that while this good fortune is divinely ordained (God has given), one must act today (now). He avoids Saul's name, and refers to him instead as David's "enemy." Abishai does not use the ordinary word for "give" נתן, but סגר, a word used in the Keilah scene to convey the intention of the Ziphites in 23:20. The words denote David as the victim, but here Abishai reverses the direction and places Saul as its object to the benefit of David.[4] Abishai knows that killing a king is no small matter. The son of Zeruiah proposes a plan whereby David's hands will remain blood-free: let me pin him—one blow, I will not strike twice. This shift from David (God has given your enemy into *your* hand) to Abishai (let *me* pin him) is signaled by the narrator's use of עתה. The plan would appear to have odds in David's favor. In contrast to David's position on a previous occasion, Saul, asleep on the ground, would have little chance of dodging the spear. The spear, Saul's head, and the ground were all mentioned previously by the narrator. Abishai does not now mention Saul's head, however, and the reason is obvious should the efficient plan of murder be carried out: If the spear is to travel "to the earth" in only one blow, we know what it will strike as it travels.

David's response is presented in two parts, both introduced by the speech formula "and David said." Since the duplication is unnecessary we may infer that the repetition serves to split the second part of the speech from the first. The initial speech, addressed to Abishai, is short. The second one is longer and since no addressee is named, David's words have a more encompassing quality. Abishai had promised swift action; David answers promptly at the verbal level:

[3] Scene i: vv 7, 8, 11, 12; scene ii: v 16; scene iv: v 22. In scene iii, the reference is implicit in the hunting reference.

[4] Fokkelman *Narrative*, vol. 2, 534.

Do not destroy him. David once again shows that he knows the value of restraint (cf. 24:6–7). He makes his point through a rhetorical question, the first in what develops as a cluster of questions in scenes ii and iii. The answer should be obvious to the addressee: no one can strike God's anointed and remain innocent/unpunished. David will later act upon this conviction. When an Amalekite conveys news that he killed the languishing Saul on Mount Gilboa, David instructs one of his men to kill the Amalekite for destroying Yhwh's anointed (2 Sam 1:1–16).[5] With the benefit of hindsight, we begin to understand Abishai's role in the unfolding drama. In contrast to Ahimelech the Hittite, Abishai would have been familiar with the taboo of killing Yhwh's anointed. But Abishai is an impetuous man, driven by a desire to remove Saul from the throne. He serves as a foil to the prudent, patient David whose words bear witness to a conviction beyond the sight of this ambitious soldier. Saul must not die in a way that implicates David. In the previous, long chapter David has explained why he avoids bloodguilt against Nabal. How much more he will avoid it with Saul!

David begins the second part of his speech with an oath, "as Yhwh lives," and suggests possibilities whereby Abishai's wish for a dead king might be realized. It is not that David shrinks from the welcome prospect of Saul's death. He quickly mentions three options of how Saul might die.[6] The depictions of the deaths of Nabal, Uzzah, and the firstborn child of David and Bathsheba all testify to the possibility of the first option—Yhwh may strike him down. Death by natural causes or death on a battlefield are the second and third possibilities. (The Historian will later reveal that the third option is realized: Saul and three of his sons die at the hands of the Philistines on Mount Gilboa.)

David then frames the options with a concluding oath, "Far be it from Yhwh that I should stretch forth my hand against the anointed of Yhwh" (cf. v 10a). He is more farsighted than the bloodthirsty Abishai, and this soon-to-be king's words testify to his theological conviction which is also beyond the vision of the eager soldier. These

[5] Abishai later asks David to put Shimei to death for cursing Yhwh's anointed. David refuses and self-confidently retorts, Shall anyone be put to death in Israel this day? For do I not know that I am this day king over Israel? (2 Sam 19:22).

[6] For the same options later offered to David, see 2 Sam 24:12–13.

words are reminiscent of 24:7. There David's oath is followed by the narrator's report of the rebuke and prohibition against an attack on Saul. At the end of the extended speech in this scene from chapter 26, David offers an alternate plan: they will rob Saul of his valued spear and water jug, and then quickly depart. The effects of the robbery will become apparent in time. At present, David avoids bloodguilt as he had in the previous two chapters (against Saul, ch. 24, and Nabal, ch. 25). The spear has already been mentioned. A multifaceted symbol of authority, anger, defense, and death, it seems to be everywhere Saul is. Now it is in David's hands. The jug of water is a new element in the drama, and should not be dismissed as the work of a copyist.[7] If death is symbolized by a spear, a jug of water in an arid region is certainly a sign of life.[8] The two elements are thus counterposed in this story of a man whose time as king is waning, just as the day of David's anointing is approaching. In addition, by means of a counterproposal, David demonstrates his ability to exercise restraint, a feat which reveals his ability to act judiciously. He prefers the symbols of power over the king's life even as he reveals his view that Yhwh shapes history.

The narrator's conclusion to the scene jars with David's speech on two counts. First, it is David—not Abishai—who seizes the spear and jug (cf. v 11). The initiative shows him to be a man in charge. Once the plan is drawn, he will act upon it. David once received the sword of Goliath from Ahimlelech, an event which precipitated Saul's murder of the priests of Nob (1 Sam 22:6–23). The robbery here has the opposite effect: Saul's life is spared. The man who has shown remarkable restraint in chapter 26 is now a man of calculated action. Second, the contrasting symbols of life and death (water and spear) are foregrounded by the narrator. The spear has twice been described as close to the head of Saul, once as recently as the conclusion to David's speech in v 11. But in the narrator's report the two symbols appear together beside the head of Saul for the first time. This latest revelation leads to another surprise in v 12. If both spear and jug are by the head of Saul, their capture represents

---

[7] Alfons Schulz makes this case in "Narrative Art in the Books of Samuel," in *Narrative and Novella in Samuel: Studies by Hugo Gressmann and Other Scholars (1906–1923)*, ed. David M. Gunn (JSOTSup 116/HTIBS 9; Sheffield: Almond, 1991), 131.

[8] According to J. P. Fokkelman (*Narrative*, vol. 2, 537), one would have to drink five liters of water per day in this region to avoid dehydration.

a distinct risk to David and Abishai. Will Saul stir? Will he or any of the three thousand men who lie around him see or hear the robbers? The narrator is quick to quell the reader's suspense: no one sees, no one knows. But the narrator's third qualifying clause is portentous: no one stirs; they are all asleep because Yhwh had caused a deep sleep (תרדמת) to fall over them. This divinely induced "deep sleep" makes David safe and Saul vulnerable, and the motif advances this chapter beyond the parallel chapter 24, where no such allusion is found. This shift hints at the way in which Yhwh now works for David (and against Saul). While in chapter 24 Saul's "escape" may have been fortuitous, chapter 26 highlights Yhwh's presence and commitment to David. From the narrator's vantage point, more is at work than the actions of mortals.

This account of divinely orchestrated slumber is chronologically misplaced. We have suspected all along that Saul and his men sleep merely for the obvious reasons that night has fallen (v 7) and they are weary from chasing David to the wilderness of Ziph and from setting up camp on the hill of Hachilah (vv 1–3). The reader travels with David through most of the scene without the knowledge that Saul and the men will not rouse. (Indeed, Adam sleeps so soundly—the same root, רדם, is used in Gen 2:21 and here in 1 Sam 26:12—that surgery is performed.)[9] The third mention of sleep in scene i shows divine involvement in the events that are transpiring: Yhwh is aligned with David, against Saul. The work is thus carried out at two levels: first, the human efforts of the Ziphites who aid Saul (v 1) and his three thousand men (v 2), the description of Abner as commander of Saul's forces who surround and try to protect the king, and second, Yhwh's involvement in this affair. And the reader who has followed the Historian's twists and turns knows who will prevail.

In scene ii, we arrive at the first sequence of questions that drew us to this passage. Six questions are invoked in this brief scene. Three appear in v 15 in a sequential pattern. The narrator's propensity for the interrogative form is also apparent in the next scene, where three of the four questions invoked are part of another sequential pattern.

[9] Peter D. Miscall (*1 Samuel*, 159) states that, but does not explain why, Saul's "deep sleep" is not in the same class as that of Adam (Gen 2:21) or Abraham (15:12).

Scene ii. David and Abner (vv 13–16)

> [13]And David went over to the region beyond and stood on the top of the mountain at a distance with a great space between them. [14]And David called out to the army and to Abner son of Ner saying, Will you not (הלוא) answer Abner? And Abner answered, and he said, Who (מי) are you that calls out to the king? [15]And David said to Abner, Are you not (הלוא) a man? And who (מי) is like you in Israel? And why (למה) have you not watched over your lord the king? For one in the army came to destroy the king your lord. [16]This thing is not good that you (sg.) have done. As Yhwh lives, you (pl.) are dead men because you (pl.) have not watched over your (pl.) lord, the anointed one of Yhwh. And now (ועתה), look around. Where (אי) is the king's spear and the jug of water that was at his head?

David's retreat from Saul's camp is accentuated by the phonologically related sounds. First, he goes over to the other side (ויעבר דוד העבר). But this new scene is also linked to the previous one by the important word ראש. David now stands on top (ראש) of the mountain. (Previously, he went down, ירד, into Saul's camp.) In scene i, with Saul and all of his troops asleep on the ground, the narrator three times mentions that the spear is close to the king's head (ראש). A loyalist is ready to act and spare David the bloodguilt. David, by contrast, is a man who shows remarkable restraint. A contrast is also drawn early in scene ii by the three verbal forms. David "went," "stood," "called." At the conclusion of scene i, none of Saul's troops "saw," "knew," "awoke."

While David is now separated from Saul and the troops by a great space, the two groups are able to communicate by shouting. The narrator focuses the meeting by means of a direct conversational exchange.[10] David calls out to the army and to Abner, but, the narrator hints, not to Saul! What are we to make of the narrator's quotation formula, "David called out to the army and to Abner son of Ner," which contrasts with Abner's response, "Who are you that calls out *to the king*?"[11] Scene i sheds some light. Throughout

---

[10] For a different view, see F. H. Cryer, who argues that vv 14–16 are "secondary in their present context" in "David's Rise to Power and the Death of Abner: An Analysis of 1 Samuel xxvi 14–16 and Its Redactional-Critical Implications," *VT* 35 (1985), 388.

[11] The LXX (Τίς εἶ σὺ ὁ καλῶν με.) lacks the reference to the king in Abner's question.

much of the first scene, the narrator separates Saul at the spatial level from Abner and the army. David originally schemes to go down and meet Saul, but he and Abishai travel to meet the army. Through free indirect discourse, signalled by הנה in v 7, we witness David's perception first of Saul in the camp, then of Abner and the army. Abishai encourages David to kill Saul, but David refuses to lift a hand against Yhwh's anointed. But by the scene's end, the three subjects (Saul-Abner-army) are no longer differentiated: no one saw, knew, or awoke; Yhwh caused a deep sleep to fall over them all. This congruence is preserved at the opening of scene ii: David is separated from all of them. But as David calls out from the top of the mountain, he addresses only the army and Abner, fearless field commander and cousin of Saul (1 Sam 14:50). As David speaks, the plot moves away from the subject of David's restraint and to the matter of Abner's neglect. This dichotomy of Abner-army vs. Saul had been highlighted before. In the previous scene, "Saul lay sleeping" while "Abner and the army lay around him" (v 7). The return to separation hints at the problem of command. David does not address the king. David speaks instead to the king's loyal and trusted servant. But Abner asks who is it that calls out to the *king*. Who has power within Saul's camp? The Abner-Saul split will also allow David's character and Saul's character to be further delimited.

David responds to Abner, but without providing information to the who-are-you question. David instead turns attention back to Abner through a series of annoying questions. The impact of this interrogative string is significant. Abner is not allowed to respond to the individual questions that David shouts out, and in the process Abner's character is delineated in terms of the rhetorical flow of the pattern itself. Their full rhetorical significance can be gauged by their combined weight.

"Are you not a man?" The question is, of course, rhetorical. Abner's campaign record leaves little doubt that he is a stalwart leader. A blood relative to David, he has been placed in a position of trust. His important position has been indicated by the seat he occupied next to the king at the New Moon festival (1 Sam 20:25). He now sleeps next to Saul in the role of the king's personal bodyguard. Abner's status can also be seen in the Chronicler's report that Abner dedicated war spoils for the maintenance of the temple (1 Chr 26:26–28) alongside Samuel and Saul. (Since the temple did not exist at the time of these individuals, it seems likely that Abner has been elevated in the Chronicler's account.) It is because of the important position he holds that David chides him for not having kept a close enough watch over Saul.

"Who is like you in Israel?" The second rhetorical question is like the first, but David's point is carried further. The question refers to the warriors of the land, especially those who are lying close to Saul. Posed in a manner than elevates Abner, the question compares him with others even as it praises Abner. But this rhetorical flourish serves an explicit purpose. With his guard down, Abner is overwhelmed by the next question.

"Why have you not watched over your lord the king?" After laying the groundwork by means of the first two questions, David now moves to highlight Abner's negligence. Such an exceptional general should watch over his lord the king! David exposes the fundamental problem. Saul, the divinely anointed, has been neglected. He has been left unguarded. By means of this interrogative string, David exalts Saul at Abner's expense. Abner had previously referenced Saul as "the king." In his speech, David now reiterates the words three times. Indeed, he advances the previous speech when he also refers to "the Lord's anointed." But these rhetorical questions also indict Abner. The one who had the important responsibility of guarding the king has been negligent. He did what a soldier on watch should never do. He slept. But of course this line of questioning and the caustic statements that follow are all ironically charged: David, Abner, and all the men of the army are unaware of what the narrator shares: Yhwh is responsible for their slumber. The powers that be are allied with David. Saul will surely fall.

From atop the mountain David concludes his speech to Abner with a series of statements. Their negligence (notice the shift from singular to plural "you") almost cost Saul his life; one came to destroy (שחת) the king. The Hebrew verb looks back to the action of vv 9–10. Abishai had asked permission to pin (נכה) and strike (שנה) Saul, but David would not allow the king to be destroyed (שחת). The duplication of שחת now in scene ii is an example of what Mikhail Bakhtin calls the double-voiced nature of language and speech: David recounts the scene in Abner's hearing while tacitly indicting Abner again.[12]

---

[12] See esp. Mikhail Bakhtin, *Problems of Dostoevsky's Poetics* (Theory and History of Literature 8) ed. and trans. Caryl Emerson (Minneapolis: University of Minnesota

The verb duplication allows the reader to perceive with the aid of hindsight that David's initial prompting—Who will go down with me to Saul into the camp?—left much unsaid. What is David's purpose as he set out? If he does not wish to destroy (שחת), what does he intend? The text never hints that David knew of the deep sleep sent from Yhwh, certainly not prior to arriving in Saul's camp. And, of course, the notion that David travels to pay Saul back *lex talionis* is ruled out by the action and dialogue in scene i. David's initial, open-ended, provocative question, therefore, allows the writer to draw a rather flattering portrait of the man who will be king, a view that is reinforced as he now speaks to Abner. Indeed, he three times refers to Saul as "the king," three times as "your lord," and once as "the anointed one of Yhwh" in Abner's hearing.

With negligence recounted, David turns to moral evaluation: this thing is not good that you (sg.) have done. This value judgment leads to a prediction: you (pl.) are dead men because you (pl.) have not watched over your (pl.) lord. David's original address to Abner in this scene becomes, at the end, an indictment for all in Saul's army. When the questioning began, David moved from Abner (sg.) to all Israel (pl.): Will you not answer? Are you not a man? Who is like you *in Israel*?[13]

David concludes his speech in this scene, just as he did with Abishai in the previous scene, by referring to spear and water. The ועתה once more signals a new direction in speech, and, as with Abishai, David highlights these two objects which once lay close to Saul's head. The spear which hastens death and the valuable water which preserves life are now missing from beside Saul's head. It is this talk that stirs Saul to speak.

Press, 1984), 185–205. David's charge here to Abner for neglecting to watch (שמר) over Saul is another example of the twofold directions of discourse. In the larger story of Saul, Samuel previously excoriated the king: "You have done foolishly; you have not kept (שמר) the commandment of Yhwh your God, which Yhwh commanded you. Now, indeed, Yhwh would have established your kingdom over Israel forever. But now, indeed, your kingdom will not develop. Yhwh has sought out a man after God's own heart, and Yhwh has commanded him to be ruler over the people because you have not kept (שמר) what Yhwh commanded you" (1 Sam 13:13–14).

[13] Ralph W. Klein, overlooking this artistic pattern, refers to the shift from sg. to pl. in v 16 as the author's "negligence" (*1 Samuel*, 258).

Scene iii. David and Saul (vv 17–20)

> [17]And Saul recognized David's voice, and he said, Is (ה) this your voice, my son David? And David said, My voice, my lord the king. [18]And he said, Why (למה) is it that my lord chases after his servant? For what (מה) have I done? And what (מה) guilt is on my hands? [19]And now (ועתה), hear, I pray, my lord the king, the words of his servant: If Yhwh incited you against me, may Yhwh smell an offering, but if it was mortals, may they be cursed before Yhwh for they have expelled me today from joining myself in the inheritance of Yhwh saying, Go, serve other gods. [20]And now (ועתה), do not let my blood fall to the ground away from the presence of Yhwh because the king of Israel has come out to seek a single flea, like one who hunts the partridge [lit. the one calling on the mountains].

The stage is now cleared of all supporting characters—Ahimelech, Abishai, Abner, and the army. Saul and David speak to each other for the first time. Indeed, they are the only speakers in scenes iii and iv, and in both scenes the narrator interrupts only with quotation formulae. While Abner did not recognize David's voice, Saul does. The king's question of David is identical to the one he asked in 24:17[24:16],[14] but there the narrator informed us that David first spoke *to* Saul (אל־שאול). In chapter 26 the narrative portrays the king, roused from a stupor, overhearing David's conversation *with Abner*. While David did not identify himself after Abner's who-are-you question, he does reveal his identity to Saul in a short three-word response, my-voice my-lord the-king. This brief answer contrasts with his long-winded speech to Abner.[15] It is, therefore, highlighted by the contrast in words. The lord-king combination picks up from the three appearances of "your lord the king" from scene ii, in David's conversation with Abner. Here in scene iii the level of intimacy increases with "my lord the king" (twice).

On each of the three occasions that Saul addresses David in scenes iii and iv, he calls him "my son David." David eschews such familial language here (though he used it in 24:12[24:11]. He speaks respectfully, though impersonally, to Saul: "my lord the king" (2x),

---

[14] Where Hebrew and English versification differ, the English is given in brackets.

[15] While David's speech continues through v 20, it is broken once again (cf. vv 18a and 9–11).

"my lord," "the king" (2x), and Saul's "servant" (2x). Such epithets are, of course, ironically charged. While Saul holds power, it is David who has exercised power through restraint (contra Abishai).

After the question that launches this third scene, and after the initial three-word answer, David continues with three more sequential questions. In this fast-paced brilliant rhetorical move, David supplies answers to his own questions, all in an effort to underscore his innocence: You must know that I am doing nothing wrong! he tells Saul with many words. David moves quickly to the issue with his first question, and the key word רדף ("hunt," "chase") will later by used (v 20) to frame the speech: Why is-it-that my-lord chases after his-servant? (6 words). The follow-ups are also brief and to the point: For what have-I-done? (3 words); And-what-on-my-hands guilt? (2 words).

The question series highlights for us the precarious situation of David on the battlefield against Saul. Indeed, Saul appears to be triumphant: "And David said in his heart, 'I will now perish one day by the hand of Saul. There is nothing for me better than that I should escape to Philistine land'" (1 Sam 27:1). But the narrator is more concerned with the theological undercurrent that moves in a different direction from the current military situation. That is, the narrative is ultimately concerned with the inexplicable work of Yhwh.

To his own laconic questions, David answers loquaciously. The shift in grammatical mood is signalled by the word ועתה, and the initial pairing of opposites is followed by a long hypothetical consisting of two parts, both introduced by אם: (a) if Yhwh is against me, may Yhwh . . .; (b) if mortals are against me, may they. . . . In an attempt at comprehensiveness, David allows for the possibility that his present misfortune may be the result either of divine or human action. In this first option, David offers a type of recompense. But David (like us) certainly does not believe that Saul's pursuit is instigated by Yhwh. If the second option should be true—if Saul has received poor advice—David sees no need of reconciliation. He curses his opponents for expelling him from Yhwh's inheritance and quotes them as enticing him to serve other gods. (David will in fact find himself with the Philistines in chapters 27 and 29.) Since David uses more words to discuss the second possibility (human action), Fokkelman concludes that David thinks it more likely, a distinct possibility supported also from the events of the larger story context.[16] The allusion to sacrifice would certainly have been understood as pleasing to God.[17] Either way, such relentless pursuit of David will cause him to leave Israel.

David concludes his speech as he had at the end of the two prior scenes: ועתה ("and now") serves as a signal for his summation point. He asks that his blood not fall to the ground away from Yhwh. Though the word "blood" has not appeared before, the story is filled with allusions to it—pin him, strike him, destroy him, stretching out the hand against Saul. While the tetragrammaton has appeared ten times before v 20, the phrase, "away from the presence of Yhwh," is new. The narrator here presents David as one more fearful of being cast away from Yhwh than of being hunted by the plotting, spear-throwing Saul himself. David concludes his appeal to the king of Israel by comparing himself to insignificant prey. The notion of a king pursuing a flea—an image utilized in the question-answer interchange of 24:15[24:14]—is, of course, farcical, but David does not stop here. In the conclusion to the scene, Saul's actions are compared to one hunting "the one calling on the mountains," the Hebrew idiom for the partridge. David is the hunted caller from the mountain (vv 13–14).

Chapter 24 ended with the king's summation speech. Saul admitted that David is the more righteous and expressed the wish that Yhwh reward David for his kindness. Saul admits that he perceives that David will next sit on the throne, just before the two men part company. The conclusion to chapter 26 is strikingly similar.

Scene iv. David and Saul (vv 21–25)

> [21]And Saul said, I have sinned. Return my son David for I will never do anything evil to you again because my life was precious in your eyes today. Behold (הנה): I have played the fool and have made a mistake in a great way. [22]And David answered and said, Behold (הנה): the spear, O king. Let one of the young men come over and get it. [23]And Yhwh restores to everyone his righteousness and his faithfulness for Yhwh gave you today into a hand, and I would not stretch out my

[16] J. P. Fokkelman, *Narrative*, vol. 2, 546.
[17] Cf. Noah and Utnapishtim after the flood.

> hand against the anointed of Yhwh. [24]And behold (והנה): As your life was great this day in my eyes so my life may be great in the eyes of Yhwh and may Yhwh deliver me from all distress. [25]And Saul said to David, Blessed are you my son David. Moreover, you will do many things and you will be successful. And David went his way, and Saul returned to his place.

Saul begins his petition with the bold, unqualified admission that he has sinned. Such precise language contrasts with his deceit, hesitation, justification, and explanation of his "sinning" in the Amalek incident: "I have sinned because I feared the people" (15:24 and cf. 15:8–9). "I have sinned yet honor me now" (15:30). His latest admission of sinning looks back both to the parallel chapter 24 and to David's statement that he had not sinned against Saul (v 12[11]). By contrast, Saul neglects to say against whom he has sinned in this opening to scene iv—Yhwh, David, both?[18] Instead, he quickly implores David to return (שוב) before promising to never do evil against David again. Saul's confession of wrongdoing is much more explicit than any of his statements in chapter 24. His words—and we have heard similar ones before in the History—have the ring of desperation. One can almost discern the petition of a scolded, punished child who promises to "never do it again."

If superlatives are a sign of desperation, further proof of Saul's decline is found in his words that follow the הנה statement. In a departure from his summation speech in chapter 24, Saul now admits to playing the fool and making a grand mistake, but does not mention Yhwh's name and says nothing of David becoming king. His memory of Samuel's indictment after the Gilgal fiasco appears not to have faded from 1 Sam 13:13: "You have acted foolishly. You have not kept the commandment of Yhwh your God, which he commanded you." And, from David's angle, Saul's words have a distinct déjà vu quality to them. Abigail recently told David, "Do not take, my lord, this ill-natured fellow, Nabal, seriously. For as his name is, so is he. Nabal [fool] is his name, and folly is with him" (25:25).

David responds to Saul's supplication in a magisterial tone, "O king," and uses הנה twice for the first time in a single speech event. The address of "O king" serves in this context as a modification of the previous "lord-servant" language that appeared throughout scenes

[18] Cf. n. 10 in chapter 4 and the discussion there on "sinning."

ii and iii. Saul retains his title, but David sets the terms of the return! David begins by highlighting the spear, but omits the water. Is this the narrator's hint that Saul's life will end soon? While Saul may have previously overheard David's conversation with Abner, David chooses to make clear to the king in this speech that he stole his very own spear, the story's symbol of power and death. In scene ii David responded to Abner without directly answering the who-are-you question. Now in scene iv his negative response to Saul's request for David to "return" can also only be determined by indirect means. David transforms the idea of returning into a stratagem, substituting an object for his person. If the spear is to be returned, one of Saul's men will have to retrieve it.

David concludes his first הנה speech with a statement that borders on self-congratulation. Saul, who knows that his spear has been seized, now hears David explicitly declare that he did not stretch out his hand against Yhwh's anointed (משיח). The final mention of "anointed one" rounds out the picture. David twice referred to God's משיח in Abishai's presence (scene i) and once in dialogue with Abner (scene ii). Now Saul, David's third dialogue partner, hears the word again, and from the reader's side this fourfold repetition serves to underscore the view that David perceives the workings of Yhwh. Even after Saul hears from David about what Yhwh has done, the king speaks of David as "blessed" and bound for future "success," but without reference to any divine initiative.

The key words "righteousness" and "faithfulness," which David attributes tacitly to himself, oppose Saul's explicit self-characterizing descriptors: I sinned, played the fool, made a great mistake. David's actions are characterized by righteousness (צדק) and faithfulness (אמונה): he spared Saul when he might have killed him. In David's first הנה statement of scene iv, Yhwh's name appears no less than three times. Saul had used the title "my son" when addressing David in his three speeches. David never addresses Saul as "father," and Saul never speaks of Yhwh (though David does multiple times). In his second הנה statement, David continues to use language with religious overtones. In his last words spoken to Saul, David suggests an analogy, and the incongruity in the parallel lines moves the issue in David's favor:

> As your life [Saul's] was great in my eyes [David's]
> May my life [David's] be great in the eyes of Yhwh, and may Yhwh deliver me from all distress.

The "parallel" lines are unbalanced. David concludes with a wish that Yhwh will deliver him from all distress, a thought not expressed in the first line. The frequent mention of Saul's spear and David's offer to return it to one of Saul's men necessitates his expressed wish, and the offer to return the weapon from which he has twice narrowly escaped leaves no doubt now that his trust is in Yhwh. David's offer and the asymmetry in parallel lines converge to portray David as a man of good character—for the moment at least.

David does not explicitly reply to Saul's request that David "return." Instead, he implies that their world is based upon moral symmetry, wherein God treats them according to their conduct. By sparing Yhwh's anointed David has shown his moral character. His "righteousness" and "faithfulness" set him apart from Saul. David not only vindicates himself. His words anticipate the throne he will receive as a just reward for his faithfulness.

The final quoted speech of the scene is Saul's. From his mouth, David is legitimized, and the sweeping blessing is a virtual relinquishing of power. Coming from Saul, the blessing and overture to success sound promising, but the king does not mention Yhwh—David did four times in his two brief statements—and one might recall that this king now bestows blessings indiscriminately. Saul had blessed the Ziphites as recently as 23:21 for disclosing David's hiding place!

The king's גם—גם construction matches David's הנה—הנה in frequency, but when compared to the previous speeches, this one is short. Saul calls David "son" for the last time, and his acknowledgement that David will be successful iterates the narrator's point from 18:14–15, the report that David twice eluded Saul who hurled his spear: "David was successful in all his ways for Yhwh was with him. And when Saul saw that he was very successful, he stood in awe of him." Saul's declaration contains two infinitive absolutes: the verdict is thus strong and intense, and confirms what the reader has for some time known. All that remains is the narrator's terse conclusion. David does not return to Saul (v 21). As in the conclusion to the parallel scene in chapter 24, David goes his way and Saul returns home. But the rhetorical statements and descriptions of action escalate beyond their counterparts in chapter 24. The two men never see each other again. Saul has spoken a powerful benediction over David, a man the king has more than once tried to kill. David will now leave Israel and enlist with the Philistines, and will return only after Saul is dead.

CHAPTER SEVEN

SEQUENTIAL QUESTIONS II (2 SAMUEL 19:32–44)[1]

No fewer than twenty-three questions appear in 2 Sam 19:9b–44. Indeed, the concentration in the Deuteronomistic History is nowhere else as high as here.[2] Within this narrative block, one finds other examples of the sequential question type. 2 Sam 19:32–44, which features Barzillai and David in conversation at the beginning (vv 32–41), and the Judahites and Israelites in collective dialogue at the end (vv 42–44), exhibits sequential interrogatives. We will consider the sequential questions in both scenes after reviewing the larger narrative block of which they are a part.

The Narrative Context

The Bible's story of David interweaves sordid family affairs with military struggles and political maneuverings. In the span of only three chapters (2 Sam 11–13), one reads of David's adulterous affair with Bathsheba, his murder of Uriah, the court prophet's condemnation of the king, the death of David and Bathsheba's first child and the birth of another (who in time will become the next king of Israel), Amnon's rape of his half-sister Tamar, and Absalom's plot and murder of Amnon. It is because of fear after the execution of Amnon that Absalom flees from his father, King David. Absalom finds refuge with one Talmai, king of Geshur. After three years David's heart begins to turn and the narrator reports on the effect: "And David the king longed to go to Absalom, for he was consoled over the death of Amnon" (13:39). After father and son are reunited—Absalom

[1] I follow the Hebrew verse enumeration throughout this chapter. The passage is numbered with a single verse differential in most English translations, 19:31–43.

[2] Robert Polzin, *David and the Deuteronomist: A Literary Study of the Deuteronomic History (Part Three): 2 Samuel* (Bloomington and Indianapolis: Indiana University Press, 1993), 192 and 231 n. 21. Cf. 2 Sam 19:11, 12, 13, 14, 22, 23 (3x), 26, 29, 30, 35, 36 (4x), 37, 42, 43 (3x), 44 (2x).

lives in Jerusalem two years before seeing his father (14:28)—the plot takes a decisive turn.

While in Jerusalem Absalom becomes popular: he "stole the hearts of the Israelites" (15:6b). And his thoughts turn to politics: "If only I were judging in the land. Then anyone with a suit or cause might come to me, and I would render them justice" (15:4). Under pretext of paying a vow to Yhwh in Hebron, Absalom conspires there against his father with the help of Ahithophel. Absalom's popularity among the people continues to grow. His support becomes so strong that David decides to flee from Jerusalem. The passage with sequential questions, 2 Sam 19:32–44, to which we will soon turn, serves as the second part of a frame of David's departure and return from Jerusalem.

Narrative Frame

> And David said to all his servants who were with him in Jerusalem, "Get up! And let us flee, or there will be no escape for us from Absalom" (15:14a).
>
> And all the people crossed over the Jordan, and the king crossed over . . . and he returned to his own home [in Jerusalem] (19:40).

Within the frame of 15:14 and 19:40, the plot unfolds in important ways. Verbal forms call attention to the action: fleeing, returning, and, most prominently, crossing over (עבר) the Jordan. The following outline highlights this design and points to some of the motifs that are developed in 19:32–44.

15:13–18	David and "all his household" (but not his ten concubines) flee from Jerusalem. They pass on (עבר) before the king.
15:23	David crosses (עבר) the wadi Kidron.
15:24–25	David sends the priests Abiathar and Zadok back to Jerusalem with the ark. They set the ark down while the people pass out (עבר) of the city. David expresses hope that he may one day return to Jerusalem.
15:32–37	David discourages Hushai the Archite from going on (עבר) with him. David then sends him back to Jerusalem with instructions to conspire against Absalom. Hushai is to communicate with Zadok, Abiathar, and their sons on the subject of conveying news to David of events transpiring among Absalom and his friends.

17:16 Hushai, after proposing a plan (17:7–13) that differs from the one Ahithophel had proposed (17:1b–3), clandestinely sends word to David to cross over (עבר) the Jordan lest the king and army be swallowed up.

17:21–22 Ahimaaz and Jonathan advise David to "arise and cross (עבר) the water quickly." The narrator confirms that David and all the people "crossed (עבר) the Jordan." Indeed, "no one was left who had not crossed (עבר) the Jordan."

17:27–29 Shobi, Machir, and Barzillai give provisions to David and the army in Mahanaim.

18:9 Though David orders Joab, Abishai, and Ittai to "deal gently . . . with the young man Absalom" (18:5), the king's son dies after his mule continues to walk on while Absalom's head is caught in an oak tree.[3]

With Absalom's rebellion quashed, the plot turns to David's return from Transjordan to Jerusalem. Everything turns on two matters: (a) What is to be done now that Absalom's revolt has failed? (b) What is to be done about King David, who fled from Jerusalem and has been living across the Jordan? The strain is expressed in the collective speech of "all the people of Israel":

> And all the people were at strife throughout all the tribes of Israel, saying, The king delivered us from the hand of our enemies, and saved us from the hand of the Philistines; [but yet] he has fled from the land from Absalom. But Absalom, whom we anointed over us, is dead in battle. So behold: why do you say nothing about bringing the king back? (2 Sam 19:10–11).

Thus this larger story is concerned with getting the king from Transjordan back to Jerusalem, with activity aimed at joining him in procession. As David approaches the Jordan, the Judahites arrive to meet him and to bring him back. With the Judahites poised at Gilgal, eager "to go to meet the king to bring the king (over) the Jordan" (19:16), narrative attention turns to three personal meetings between David and individuals whom the king had previously encountered on his way out of Jerusalem. The meetings that transpired as David left Jerusalem all dealt with the matter of questions and conflicts. Now in chapter 19, the parallel meetings offer resolution

[3] The death is recorded as a two-stage event: Absalom's head is caught in an oak, then Joab thrusts three spears into the heart of Absalom who hangs from the tree.

and reassurance. But the conclusion to the scene (vv 42–44) will show that the issue is by no means resolved. The king's return precipitates an outbreak of sectional hostility that will be settled in time, thus ensuring that the kingdom is secure at last. The parallel meetings that occur as the people of Judah arrive at Gilgal and as David arrives at the Jordan are between David and the following individuals:

(a) Shimei 19:17–24 || 16:5–14
(b) Mephibosheth 19:25–31 || 16:1–4
(c) Barzillai 19:32–41 || 17:27–29

In (a), Shimei the Benjaminite acknowledges that he was previously antagonistic toward David (16:5–14). He now offers the king a gesture of support that may in fact secure his survival. Abishai, as before, calls for Shimei to be executed for cursing Yhwh's anointed. David, again, rejects the advice (cf. 16:9–10 and 19:22–23). The initial meeting took place after David crossed the summit of the Mount of Olives and reached Bahurim, the village of Shimei's house. At that time, Shimei cursed David, but now he graciously welcomes the king home, as he admits to doing wrong. As David grants Shimei a full pardon, the narrator portrays David in magnanimous terms, generous toward Saul's former followers.

In (b), Mephibosheth, a lame man, son of Jonathan, comes down to meet with David at the Jordan. Ziba had previously reported that Mephibosheth viewed Absalom's coup as an opportunity for him to reclaim Saul's throne (16:1–4). Mephibosheth now comes forward to suggest that he did not defect from David on his own volition. It was Ziba who deceived him. With an unkempt look, he has been mourning for David all along. The description of appearance goes far beyond traditional mourning rituals: "he had not dressed his feet, or trimmed his beard, or washed his clothes, from the day the king left until the day he came back safely" (19.25). He now refers to David five times as "my lord the king," speech obviously intended to demonstrate his loyalty, obedience, and subservience. Mephibosheth succeeds. In an instant, David understands that Ziba was deceitful, and the king again makes a magnanimous offer—this time to Mephibosheth—one which no doubt shows David's goodwill toward Saul's supporters.

Shimei and Mephibosheth, the men around whom the action moves in these first two reunion scenes, are Israelites. They accompany David. The final conversation scene (c) is between David and

Barzillai, a wealthy landowner from Gilead. The tone of the third meeting sequence is more amicable than the first two. Barzillai had earlier provided provisions to maintain and sustain David's men (17:27–29). In contrast to Shimei and Mephibosheth, Barzillai's support for David is unwavering. It is worth noting that the stability of David's political power depends upon a carefully managed series of alliances. This one is crucial. After quelling Absalom's rebellion, David proposes a reward for faithful Barzillai: residence in the palace in Jerusalem. When David invites Barzillai to join him in Jerusalem, the Gileadite demurs, then offers his son Kimham in his place.[4] From David's point of view, the substitute plan is as good as the original one; either man embodies a strong political force allied with David. It is in this third conversation that we find a string of sequential questions.

> [32]And Barzillai the Gileadite came down from Rogelim, and he passed over with the king to the Jordan to escort him to the Jordan. [33]And Barzillai was very old, eighty years old in fact. And he had supplied food for the king during his travels at Mahanaim for he was a very wealthy man. [34]And the king said to Barzillai, Pass over with me, and I will supply food for you by my side in Jerusalem. [35]And Barzillai said to the king, How many (כמה) years do I have left to live that I should go up with the king to Jerusalem? [36]Eighty years old I am today. Can (ה) I discern between good and evil? Can (אם) your servant taste what I eat or what I drink? Can (אם) I still hear the voice of singing men and singing women? And why (למה) should your servant be an extra burden to my lord the king? [37]A little distance your servant will pass over the Jordan with the king. And why (למה) should the king reward me with such a reward? [38]Pray, let your servant return that I may die in my city close to the grave of my father and my mother. And behold (הנה): your servant Kimham. Allow him to pass over with my lord the king, and do to him whatever seems good in your eyes. [39]And the king said, Kimham shall pass over with me, and I will do for him whatever is good in your eyes. And all that you

[4] The identification of Kimham as Barzillai's son is based on inference rather than textual evidence. Stephen Dempster's conclusion merits quoting: "Although it is not stated that Chimham was the son of Barzillai, this can be reasonably inferred. Some Greek versions and the Syriac add 'my son' to Chimham's name in 2 Samuel 19, and Josephus (*Ant* 7.11.4) believed that Chimham was the son of Barzillai. As one of his last requests, the dying David asked Solomon to continue to show favor to Barzillai's 'sons' who lived at the royal residence (1 Kgs 2:7). It can be assumed that others had joined their kinsmen (lit. brother) Chimham there" (*ABD*, i:909).

desire of me I will do for you. [40]And all the people passed over the Jordan, and the king passed over and the king kissed Barzillai and blessed him. And he returned to his home. [41]And the king passed over to Gilgal, and Kimham passed over with him; all the people of Judah brought the king over, as did half the people of Israel.

The voices within the scene are arranged chiastically:

Narrator
  David
    Barzillai
  David
Narrator

David's quoted speech is rendered within the first level of the narrator's frame. His speech frames Barzillai's speech, which lies at the center. In volume terms, Barzillai's speech is the most substantial element in the five-part arrangement. Its length surpasses the combined speeches of David which frame it.

In the opening verse of the scene, the key word עבר appears. It functions as a narrative thread throughout this and the next scene. It also links the plot dynamics discussed above (i.e., beginning with David's hasty departure from Jerusalem in 15:13–18). The verb appears ten times in this scene and can mean both "to go over" and "to go on." This double valence makes it difficult to determine at what point David actually crosses the river.

Despite his old age, Barzillai travels from Rogelim for the purpose of escorting David to the Jordan. Along with Shobi and Machir, Barzillai had previously provided beds, basins, earthen vessels, sheep, and an array of food to maintain David's fighting forces (17:28–29). David asks Barzillai to continue accompanying him past the Jordan and offers to repay Barzillai's kindness with food. David's royal recompense offer has the added benefit of a position for Barzillai at court (עמדי, "at my side.)" The proposed parallel (Barzillai gave David food, etc./David will give Barzillai food, etc.) is displaced at the syntactic and phonological levels in vv 33–34:

verb and subject (king's voice) וכלכלתי : והוא־כלכל (narrator's voice)
object (king's voice) אתך : את־המלך (narrator's voice)
general location (king's voice) עמדי : בשיבתו (narrator's voice)
specific location (king's voice) בירושלם : במחנים (narrator's voice)

To David's simple request (seven words) Barzillai responds with rhetorical overkill (sixty words). His stirring response consists of no less than six rhetorical questions which serve the singular purpose of declining David's offer. The six interrogatives are introduced with the following words: כמה, ה, אם, אם, למה, למה. The choice to represent characters in dialogue is always an option the narrator might reject in conveying the plot. As the speech of David and Barzillai is quoted, the reader gains insight into a creative tension that exists in the narrator-character alliance of the unfolding drama. What is the nature of this character-narrator alliance? Barzillai's first question picks up the narrator's report of Barzillai's advanced age: how much longer will an old man live? (He also asks about going up to Jerusalem, a felicitous contrast to the narrator's report of Barzillai coming down from Rogelim. In view of his old age, it is no small matter that he has "come down from Rogelim." The man "very old" does not wish "to go up to Jerusalem.") Barzillai asks this question, then answers it, and in the response foregrounds his age by means of an unexpected word order (construct precedes subject): "Eighty years old I am today." According to the narrator's prior report, Barzillai is "very old, eighty years old in fact." The purpose of this repetition will become evident in time, for Barzillai has a plan in mind.

Building on the point about his many years, Barzillai's next three questions adumbrate the effects of old age: discernment, taste, and hearing all dull with the passing of time. His question about discerning between good and evil probably denotes what he likes from what he dislikes and may indeed be a euphemism for sexual (im)potency.[5] Duplicating the narrator's report of eighty years, his question about tasting what he eats looks back in contrast to the time when he had supplied food to David. What is the purpose, Barzillai intones, of a man with a diminishing capacity to enjoy life's pleasures, establishing residence in a new, moneyed home? But he focuses not only on himself. The cost to David, couched in defer-

---

[5] Cf. P. Kyle McCarter, Jr., *II Samuel: A New Translation with Introduction, Notes, and Commentary*, AB 9 (Garden City, N.Y.: Doubleday, 1984), 422, and Peter R. Ackroyd, *The Second Book of Samuel*, CBC (Cambridge: Cambridge University Press, 1977), 182. Cf. also Gen 3:7, Isa 7:15, and Gilgamesh 1:4, 29, 34 (*ANET*, p. 75), where wisdom and understanding come with sexual experience.

ence and homage language, would be considerable: why should your servant be an extra burden to the king? His five references to "the king" surpass the four references of the narrator, and the narrator's unadorned references to "the king" are embellished: though he is from the narrator's vantage point "a very wealthy man," he presents himself in the hearing of David as the king's "servant" four times and calls the king "my lord" twice. The narrator's description of Barzillai passing over with the king to the Jordan is also enhanced in Barzillai's speech:

> Should I go up *with* the king to Jerusalem?
> Your servant will pass over the Jordan *with* the king.
> Allow [Kimham] to pass over *with* my lord the king.

The rhetorical flourish has its effect on David: "Kimham shall pass over *with* me."

In the midst of the interrogative sequence is woven a simple statement consisting of only five words: a little-distance your-servant will-pass-over the-Jordan with-the-king. Let me not leave the wrong impression, Barzillai now implies with this statement that interrupts the interrogative flow. I am willing to comply, if only for "a little distance." He twice declares his intention of escorting David over the river (vv 32, 37), and, after he completes this task, he recrosses the river to go home. The final question (and second "why" למה interrogative) closes the questioning sequence: why should David reward a man who is too old to enjoy such a reward? In an effort to underscore the age point—if only he were younger—Barzillai brings up the issue of his pending death and his desire to be laid to rest beside his closest of kin. His initial question featured the word life (חי). He now closes the interrogative sequence with the words death (מות) and grave (קבר). His homeland and grave mean more to him than anything else (cf. 2:32a; 17:23b). The meaning of Barzillai's six questions is clear, but does anything lie behind them? What motivates Barzillai to demur with such rhetorical flourish? Should we take him *au pied de la lettre*, or are his words to be understood as part of a clever bargaining scene on a scale of the powerful chieftains such as Jephthah and the elders of Gilead (Judges 11:5–11)? Answers to these questions will be found in time.

A change in Barzillai's direction of thought is signalled by the appearance of הנה, "behold." Attention is focused at the grammatical level through הנה and the unexpected subject "your servant

Kimham," which precedes the verb "pass over." The nine words that follow this key word sharpen the reader's sense of superfluity. Barzillai had previously spoken a form of four of the words (your-servant, pass-over, with, the-king) in a manner that highlighted the novel idea of something good being done for Kimham.[6] Barzillai's charged rhetoric on old age, we now discover, has laid the groundwork for a novel counterproposal: who better than his youthful son Kimham to enjoy the benefits of David's goodwill.[7] All of the questions of Barzillai assumed negative answers, either directly or indirectly. After a long series of negatives, Barzillai is offering a positive alternative: Kimham can go.

Barzillai thus conveys his intentions only at the end of a sophisticated, highly charged rhetorical speech. In self-deprecatory language, Barzillai represents David's repayment offer as quite generous. Barzillai is a man, in the hearing of David, who values his family grave more than a sumptuous life at court. Yet, the one who would have his audience think he has difficulty in reasoning (האדע) offers a counterproposal that shows him wise enough to commend his son to the king. To Barzillai's extended speech, David offers a comparatively brief response which suggests that Barzillai has twice succeeded. The statement, Barzillai shall pass over with me (issuing from David's point of view in v 34), becomes Kimham shall pass over with me (from David's point of view in v 39). And Barzillai's proposal, Do to him whatever seems good in your [David's] eyes (v 38), becomes I will do for him whatever is good in your [Barzillai's] eyes (v 39).

Old and frail, Barzillai is determining what is good, and the king's concluding carte blanche statement—"all that you desire of me I will do"—is icing on the cake. From David's side, the Kimham

---

[6] Your-servant Kimham. Allow-him-to-pass-over with-my-lord, and-do-to-him whatever seems-good in-your-eyes.

[7] While MT does not identify Kimham as Barzillai's "son" בן, the inference is reasonable. In addition to the support for this view cited in n. 4 above, cf. also Hans Wilhelm Hertzberg's point that Kimham is "almost certainly a younger son," (*I & II Samuel: A Commentary*, OTL [4th ed.; Philadelphia: Westminster, 1976], 367. A similar view is expressed by A. A. Anderson, *2 Samuel*, WBC, 11 (Dallas: Word Books, 1989), 239: "Chimham must have been Barzillai's son (so G[L] Josephus, *Ant.* 7.274). According to 1 Kgs 2:7 David's consideration must have been extended, at least eventually, to several sons of Barzillai." Cf. also Ackroyd, *Second Book of Samuel*, 182.

substitution is certainly propitious. He is as valuable (maybe more valuable) to the king as Barzillai because he will embody powerful, youthful allied support for David on the return to Jerusalem.

The first part of the conclusion to the narrator's frame (v 40) accentuates movement: (a) the people, the king, and Barzillai cross over the Jordan; (b) the king bestows a parting kiss and blessing upon Barzillai; (c) Barzillai returns home.

Given Barzillai's insistence upon not crossing over, the opening sequence seems unusual. At least two solutions to the matter are possible. If one translates the phrase with pluperfect forms, "the king had kissed Barzillai and had blessed him," Barzillai does not cross the Jordan. Or, in the light of the narrator's introductory note in v 32 that Barzillai passed over with the king to the Jordan, one might view Barzillai crossing the Jordan only to turn quickly back because he does not wish "to go up to Jerusalem with the king." J. P. Fokkelman's prudently observes that the text does not consider this issue to be so important that it fully answers the question.[8]

The image of David's departure from and possible return to Jerusalem was introduced beginning in 15:12. By 15:23 a form of the verb עבר had appeared three times. The narrator, who introduced the scene in 19:32, concludes it by again featuring the key word עבר (five times).[9] In the concluding verse of this scene, the passing over עבר theme (mentioned three times) continues even as the place name Gilgal is brought back into the picture. (The Judahites had come to Gilgal to meet David and bring him back across the Jordan [19:16] just before David met with Shimei, Mephibosheth, and Barzillai.) Robert Polzin has called attention to the important role that Gilgal plays as a crossing-place for the king who is returning to Jerusalem:

> from the inception of kingship onwards. . . . Gilgal is where the kingdom was first renewed, and where the people made Saul king (1 Sam 11:14–15). . . . We now find that Gilgal is the place to go when Israel's anointed, Absalom, has died, and the matter of returning with the

[8] Fokkelman proposes the two options discussed above in *Narrative*, vol. 1, 310. Cf. also H. W. Hertzberg's statement: This verse "need not be understood to mean that the parting took place *after* the king had crossed the Jordan" (*I & II Samuel*, 367, original emphasis).

[9] Four times in the qal stem, "pass over" (vv 40–41), and once in the hiphil, "brought over" (v 41).

> king is once more raised. Gilgal, then, is the place where kingship is born, broken, and renewed, a royal crossing where one makes or breaks kings, and where kingship itself is renewed.[10]

The final verse splits the passing over (עבר) sequence into a threefold drama, and, as in the preceding verse, the narration leaves the unity-disunity issue unresolved: (a) the king passes over (עבר); (b) Kimham passes over (עבר) with him; (c) all the people of Judah and half the people of Israel pass (עבר) the king over. The processional accompaniment is paramount in getting the king across the Jordan and back to his house in Jerusalem. The important preposition puts Kimham "with" David in (b), and while "all" the people of Judah escort David, only half of Israel makes the trip in (c). The conclusion to the scene links the two ideas of "crossing over with the king" and "bringing the king across," that had previously been articulated. The king "returns" (19:15, 16) and "gets brought back" (19:11, 12, 13, 44). So, too, he also "crosses over" (19:19, 32, 34, 37, 38, 39, 40, 41) and "gets brought across" (19:16, 19, 41, 42).[11] If the conclusion hints that the northerners may resent the southern initiative of vv 14–15, the scene that follows makes it clear that old, deep tribal differences linger.

> 42And behold (הנה): all the people of Israel came to the king and said to the king, Why (מדוע) have our kindred, the people of Judah, stolen you and brought the king and his household over the Jordan, whereas all David's men are with him? 43And all the people of Judah answered the people of Israel, [We did so] because the king is near of kin to us.*[12]* And why (למה) does this thing make you angry? Have (ה) we eaten anything at the king's expense? Or (אם) have gifts*[13]* been given to us? 44And the people of Israel answered the people of Judah, and said, We have ten shares in the king, and also in David we are more than you. And why then (מדוע) do you treat us with contempt? Were

---

[10] Polzin, *David*, 195.

[11] עבר has appeared as a concern throughout: vv 32, 34, 37, 38, 39, 40, 40, 41, 41 = qal (9x), but 41, 42 = hifil (2x); also hifil in 19:16, 19. Polzin (*David*, 195) comments that "the concern is not over simply bringing back the king, for as we have seen, the procession is also one of *crossing over* with the king, of bringing him *across* from the place where he has been, for a time, in exile."

[12] Lit. "to me." The Hebrew reads collective "I," "me," "my" in vv 43–44.

[13] Reading משאת for the MT's problematic נשאת (a possible ni. or piel inf. abs. of נשא, "to take away"). LXX reads ἢ δόμα ἔδωκεν, "or has he given us a gift," which McCarter (*II Samuel*, 419), prefers over MT.

> we (לא היה) not the first to speak of bringing our king back? But the words of the people of Judah were fiercer than the words of the people of Israel.

After David converses with Shimei, Mephibosheth, and Barzillai (vv 17–41), the plot returns to the matter of civil strife in the form of a quarrel scene between the armies of Israel and Judah. In a tripartite structure initiated and concluded by the speaking armies of Israel, six questions are invoked: one by Israel, three by Judah, and two by Israel. The Israelites and Judahites now compete for the premier place in a hierarchy of honor as David and his entourage cross the Jordan. This scene and the one that precedes it are a study in contrasts. The first one flaunts etiquette and decorum: (a) What David had regarded as a reward to a friend, Barzillai regarded as a burden to a friend; (b) in the midst of a long rhetorical question series, Barzillai interrupts the flow to say that he will cross over a little distance—it may be the case that this is the only distance Barzillai can go ("eighty years old I am today"), but it is certainly the case that he wishes to go; (c) Barzillai's request of the king—Take Kimham and do with him whatever seems good in your eyes—is eclipsed by the king himself, who says, "I will do for him what is good in *your* eyes." In contrast, this second scene highlights the rift that has developed between the two armies. It shows that the previous accounts are in no way to be interpreted as "happy endings." This scene poses the question of who can claim a place of honor with the king, while looking back in narrative time to the north-south division that had surfaced in this chapter prior to the Shimei-David (vv 17–24), Mephibosheth-David (vv 25–31), and Barzillai-David (vv 32–41) scenes discussed above. David had invited the Judahites to assume the premier place in this hierarchy of loyalty. His message to the elders of Judah was:

> Why should you be the last to bring the king back to his house? . . . You are my kin, my bone and my flesh you are. So why should you be the last to bring the king back? And to Amasa say: Are you not my bone and my flesh? Therefore may God do to me, and more, if you are not commander of my army in my presence from now on, in place of Joab (2 Sam 19:12b–14).

David's appeal to the Judahites, which may have been motivated in part by the Israelites' dispersion to their homes and rancor among the tribes, is met with success:

> And he swayed the hearts of everyone in Judah as one, and they sent (word) to the king: Return, you and all your servants. And the king returned and came back to the Jordan, and Judah came to Gilgal to go to meet the king and to bring the king over the Jordan (vv 15–16).

The conclusion to David's conversation with Barzillai serves as a link between the two scenes: all the people (i.e., army) of Judah and also half the people (i.e., army) of Israel brought him over (v 41b). This link-verse hints at an issue of loyalty to the king, and the quarrel scene brings this issue to the fore. Robert Polzin has aptly shown that physical presence with the king hints at a larger issue. The matter is more than allowing or inviting the king to return. One must be physically present with him when he returns. Loyalty is measured in part by one's physical proximity with the king. David had encouraged Ittai, the leader of a mercenary troop from Philistine Gath, to return home. Why should Ittai, a foreigner in exile, take upon himself David's burden (15:19–20)? Ittai, however, refused and swore to remain physically present with David: "As Yhwh lives, and as my lord the king lives, wherever shall be my lord the king, whether for death or for life, there also your servant will be" (v 21). David rewards Ittai's devotion by appointing him to command one-third of the troops in the war against Absalom. Joab and Abishai command the other two-thirds of the army (2 Sam 18:2). In contrast, David condemns Mephibosheth for his absence: "Why did you not go with me, Mephibosheth?" (19:26b). Polzin concludes,

> [Ittai] personifies a central aspect of the story: *being with the king* in a physical sense pictures forth for us larger themes of siding with him in terms of loyalty, devotion, and allegiance. The best way "to return the king" is "to return with him." And like the History's use of blood brothers, bloodied heads, and material houses as graphic representatives of their less tangible counterparts, this emphasis on *physically* accompanying the king in and out of the land stands for larger ideological and historiographic issues involving allegiance to David, his house, and even kingship itself.[14]

The narrator's introduction to the Israelite's emotionally charged question is significant on two fronts. First, it is introduced by הנה, which calls the reader's attention to the shift in tone, the conflict at hand. Second, the Israelites come "to the king." A shift in perspective

[14] Polzin, *David*, 193, original emphasis.

is underscored by the narrator's speech formula introductions: the people of Israel come to the king and speak to the king, but they are answered by the people of Judah. Excepting the narrator's speech formula introductions, the following voices emerge: narrator; Israelites; Judahites; Israelites; narrator.

The people of Israel speak to the king qua king—in contrast to the people of Judah, who speak of David as their kin, of the same bone and flesh (cf. 19:13–14). (These perspectives will continue to diverge as Israel claims more of an interest in the king because of their ten tribes and their claim to be "more than" Judah, v 44).[15] This Israelite perspective, reinforced by the narrator, emerges in their collective speech. Speaking to David, the Israelites ask why the Judahites stole and brought the king and his household over the Jordan. Their "why" question works in two directions simultaneously. They seek information and also make a spirited rhetorical point. They hope to learn why Judah has been favored (information), but their choice of the word "steal" moves in the direction of judgment (rhetoric).[16] From the reader's vantage point, the answer can be found easily. When the Israelites hesitated (19:9b–10), David turned to the Judahites (vv 12–14). Israel now condemns the Judahites ("stole"), though it was David who initiated the overture. Perhaps they are unaware of David's conversation with the Judahites, or perhaps their rhetoric is moderated through diplomacy: no need to offend the suzerain now. Indeed, their reference to the people of Judah as "our kindred" gives the initial impression of tranquility.

David disappears from view as they respond. The question, twice referenced by the narrator as "to the king," is answered by the people of Judah. The shift is anticipated in the Israelite's question: Why have they stolen *you* and brought *the king* over the Jordan? The people of Judah respond that David is a beloved relative; they enjoy a special relationship of privilege with him. He is their favorite son. Reference to kinship will no doubt further alienate the Israelites. And, as if to squelch their interrogators, the Judahites demur that they have received no special favors. They have received neither food nor gifts from the king.[17]

---

[15] LXX reads: "We [Israel] are firstborn in respect of you [Judah]."

[16] Their moral indignation also looks back in narrative time to Absalom who "stole" (גנב) the hearts of Israel (15:6).

[17] Cf. n. 13 above.

This central collective speech of the Judahites, framed by the Israelite speakers, consists of an explanation followed by three questions. The Israelites had asked for information, and they get it. This defensive move can only threaten an already tense situation. Their first question asks about what right the Israelites have to express anger. The two follow-up questions both touch on the subject of money: We have cost you nothing, and we received no special gifts from the king. The single effect of this approach is conveyed with a condescending tone. The three implied answers to these rhetorical questions all have a negative cast, and one hears a crescendo in the sequence. The increasingly pointed questions provoke further protest from the people of Israel.

In the last round (and in contrast to their opening), Israel no longer addresses David, but the people of Judah. The Judahites appealed at a psychological level to blood relationship. Israel now counters with the politically charged argument that they are larger in size (ten shares).[18] Their part in the building up of the kingdom is dramatically greater than Judah's role. They return to their ploy of offering a single-word value judgment, as they did in their first rhetorical question in v 42. Previously, they accused the Judahites of stealing (גנב) David. They now accuse them of acting with contempt (קלל). In their follow-up question the Israelites bring up an issue that has appeared before in the chapter: they were the first to speak of bringing the king back (cf. v 12). Though Israel is the first *to speak of* returning the king, Judah's more prominent role in actually returning him is evident both in the reaction of Israel (vv 41a, 44b) and in the narrator's frame that surrounds the speeches:

> *all* the people of Judah and also half the people of Israel brought him over (v 41b).
>
> But the words of the people of Judah were fiercer than the words of the people of Israel (v 44b).

Robert Polzin has observed that this issue of privilege is indeed a central concern of the narrative:

> Not only is it important to be part of the procession that returns with the king, that returns the king, that crosses over with the king, or that brings him across, it is especially important to be "the first" and not

[18] Cf. 1 Kgs 11:31.

"the last" to do so. David twice asks Judah, "Why should you be the last to bring the king back?" (19:12, 13), Shimei says to David, "I have come this day, the first of all the house of Joseph to come down to meet my lord the king" (19:21), and Israel asks David, "Were we not the first to speak of bringing back our king?" (19:44). Some precede while others follow. This is the rule for processions as well as for evaluative positions choreographed in the narrative.[19]

It is now the Judahites' turn to speak, but the narrator silences them to tell us that they have prevailed: their words are fiercer (or: harsher, קשה) than those of the Israelites. In the face of David's earlier successful political maneuverings ("the king kissed Barzillai and blessed him," v 40), deep tribal differences now linger as David consolidates power over Israel and Judah. The sight of Judah leading David to Jerusalem has provoked Israel, belatedly, to think of its own stand in relation to the king. David's united kingdom is tenuous; earthly powers vie for control. (Yhwh is never mentioned in these scenes.) The flow of the narrative plainly places David on his way back to Jerusalem, but it ends amid old tensions that are as ancient as the tribes themselves (cf. Judg 8:1; 12:1). The result of the conflict that has surfaced in this quarrel scene between the armies of Israel and Judah will become the focus in the chapters that follow. Sheba, a dissident from the Ephraimite hills (20:21), will soon lead a revolt as the old strife (Absalom's revolt) gains new momentum.

[19] Polzin, *David*, 194.

CHAPTER EIGHT

SEQUENTIAL QUESTIONS III (1 SAMUEL 20)

The Bible contains a number of scenes that tell the story of characters who put God to the test. For example, Gideon twice tests God before routing the Midianites:

> Behold: I am laying a fleece of wool on the threshing floor; if there is dew on the fleece alone and on all the ground it is dry, then I shall know that you will (really) deliver by my hand Israel, as you have said. . . . Let me speak once more; let me, please, make trial with the fleece only once more (Judg 6:37–39).

On another occasion, Jephthah, having received the spirit of Yhwh (Judg 11:29), makes a foolish vow, which also puts God to the test:

> If you will really give the Ammonites into my hand, then whoever comes out of the doors of my house to meet me when I return victorious from the Ammonites, shall be Yhwh's, and I will offer him up as a burnt offering (vv 30–31).

In other instances, tests or trials are devised as characters scheme by means of projected coded language. In the simplest of terms, A talks to B who in turn transfers A's message to C; A communicates with C through B, even as B is kept from understanding the implications or full meaning of the original words. For example, after Uriah is killed in battle, Joab sends word to David by a messenger. The news that David's plan to murder Uriah has succeeded reaches David's ears by the messenger; yet the messenger does not realize that he has shared it (cf. 2 Sam 11:18–25).

Another instance of three-way duplicitous communication occurs in the story of the struggle for succession at the beginning of 1 Kings. Nathan, having learned of Adonijah's aspirations for the throne, conspires with Bathsheba:

> And now, come, let me advise you so that you may save your life and the life of your son Solomon. Go quickly to King David and say to him, Did you not, my lord the king, swear to your maidservant saying: Indeed, Solomon your son shall reign after me, and he shall sit upon my throne? So why is Adonijah reigning? All of a sudden, while

> you are still speaking with the king, I will come in after you and confirm your words (1 Kgs 1:12–14).

Their plan, which depends upon the right words spoken at the right moment, succeeds. Oblivious to the machinations of Nathan and Bathsheba, David, duped, tells Bathsheba what she had hoped to hear: "As Yhwh lives who has redeemed my life from every adversity, as I swore to you by Yhwh the God of Israel saying, 'Solomon your son shall reign after me, and he shall sit upon my throne in my place'" (1 Kgs 1:29–30).

Tactics such as these are not lost on the Deuteronomistic Historian in 1 Samuel. By means of a sham archery session in chapter 20, David and Jonathan agree upon a plan whereby arrows will be shot and a boy will be sent to retrieve them. Using coded language, Jonathan and David will communicate through the lad, even as they keep him unaware of the implications of their words. The charade is a sequel to the scene in which David and Jonathan conspire against Saul in their devised plan to excuse David from the New Moon festival. Chapter 20, which is but one of many that exploits the theme of duplicity at the royal court, is launched with sequential questions.

The two lengthiest narratives in which Jonathan appears are here in 1 Sam 20 and in 1 Sam 14. (In the episode of chapter 14, Jonathan proves himself a brave warrior who defeats a Philistine garrison accompanied only by his armor-bearer.) The action in chapter 20 opens with an extended conversation between two friends. One of them, David, knows that the stakes are quite high and the threat to his own life is real. Jonathan, his conversation partner, is not convinced that David's life is threatened ("Far from it! You shall not die," v 2), but will become enlightened by the scene's end. Saul, who had hurled his spear at David as recently as 19:10, will hurl it again—this time at his own son (20:33).

Chapter 20 may be divided into seven scenes. Narration gives way to dialogue in each of them, except in scene iv, which is carried entirely by the narrator. Characters speak in the following scenes:

(a) vv 1–11	David and Jonathan
(b) vv 12–17	Jonathan
(c) vv 18–23	Jonathan
(d) vv 24–25	—
(e) vv 26–29	Saul and Jonathan
(f) vv 30–34	Saul and Jonathan
(g) vv 35–21:1	Jonathan

Jonathan is the principal speaker in this chapter. He speaks in each scene where characters are quoted. He is the only speaker in three scenes. The speeches reflected in these scenes also lead us to an observation, the most important one for our purposes: the initial scene (i) and concluding scenes (v–vii) contain numerous interrogative forms.[1]

The first words, "and David fled (ברח) . . . and came (בוא)," link the opening scene with the previous meeting between David and Samuel. In 19:18, David also "flees" and "comes" to Samuel, but their meeting is conveyed in considerably less narrative space, and, in contrast to his meeting with Jonathan, the words of conversation in the initial meeting are not recorded.[2] They are summarized by the narrator as David tells Samuel "all that Saul had done to him."

> 1 And David fled from Naioth in Ramah and came and said before Jonathan, What (מה) have I done? What (מה) is my guilt? And what (מה) is my sin before your father that he seeks my life? 2 And he said to him, Far from it! You shall not die. Behold (הנה): my father does not do[3] anything great or small without revealing it to me. And why (מדוע) should my father conceal this matter from me? Such would never happen! 3 And David swore again and said, Your father knows well that I have found favor in your eyes and he thinks, Do not let Jonathan know this lest he be grieved. But indeed as Yhwh lives and as your soul lives only a step exists between me and death. 4 And Jonathan said to David, What do you yourself say? I will do it for you. 5 And David said to Jonathan, Behold (הנה): the New Moon is tomorrow and I would definitely sit with the king at the table. But let me flee and hide myself in the field (until) the third evening. 6 If your father misses me at all, then you say, David begged leave of me to run to Bethlehem his city for there is a yearly sacrifice there for all the family. 7 If he says Good, it will be well with your servant. But if he shows great anger, know that evil is determined by him. 8 And show *ḥesed* to your servant for into a covenant of Yhwh you have brought your servant with you, but if there is in me guilt kill me yourself. And

---

[1] It is possible that a question ("Will I not send and disclose it to you?") is also invoked in v 12 without an interrogative word. Cf. GKC §150a: "A question need not necessarily be introduced by a special interrogative pronoun or adverb. Frequently the natural emphasis upon the words is of itself sufficient to indicate an interrogative sentence as such." The NASB, NRSV, and RSV translate the phrase as a question. AB, JB, KJV, NAB, OTL, and WBC all translate the expression as a statement.

[2] The verbal sequence in 19:18 is fled (ברח), escaped (מלט), came (בוא). In 20:1, it is fled (ברח), came (בוא). The word "escaped" (מלט) appears in 20:29.

[3] Reading MT qere (לא יעשה) and LXX (οὐ μὴ ποιήσῃ) for MT ketib (לו עשה).

to your father why (למה) should you bring me? [9]And Jonathan said, Far be it from you, if I knew for certain that evil was determined by my father to come upon you, would I not tell you (ולא אתה)?[4] [10]And David said to Jonathan, Who (מי) will tell me if your father answers you harshly? [11]And Jonathan said to David, Come let us go out into the field. And they went out both of them into the field.

The plot in the first scene unfolds almost entirely by words spoken. The narrator's spatial descriptions in vv 1 and 11—"David fled from Naioth in Ramah and came" and "they went out both of them into the field"—are exceptional statements. At all other times, the narrator interrupts the speaking characters with speech introductory formulae for the sole purpose of shifting attention from one dialogist to the other in their four rounds of conversation:

David complains (v 1) and Jonathan is astonished (v 2)
David complains again (v 3) and Jonathan grants David carte blanche (v 4)
David plans (vv 5–8) and Jonathan reassures David (v 9)
David inquires (v 10) and Jonathan responds (v 11)

The Historian often introduces scenes with simple speech introductory formulae. In 15:1, for example, "Samuel said to Saul" is used. In 27:1, the narrator signals interior monologue with the formula, "David said in his heart." But in 20:1, the dialogue scene is preceded by the narrator's introduction, which portrays David "fleeing" (ברח) from Naioth and "coming" (בוא) and "saying" (אמר) before Jonathan. The triple verb sequence calls attention, of course, to action; the words anticipate David's anxious state of mind. He has been fleeing (ברח) from Saul (19:12–17; 19:18–24), and he will continue (21:11–16; 22:17–23; 27:1–4). David speaks "before" (לפני) Jonathan, not "to" him as we would expect. The unexpected word will soon be matched by David, who inquires about himself *before* Jonathan's father. Psychological shading is apparent: David, in speech, places Jonathan alongside his father, while distancing Jonathan from himself. A confident warrior loyal to his father, Jonathan is also David's close and loyal friend. Jonathan may here be weighing these two loyalties, to father and friend.

[4] Cf. n. 1 above.

Sequential and Nonsequential Questions in Scene i

David's rhetorical flourish consists of three questions that reveal his state of mind. They are characterized by staccato and crescendo. All three begin with the word "what" (מה), which is followed by forms with first-person singular suffixes. One- and two-word questions (What have-I-done, What-is-my-guilt) are followed by a six-word interrogative (and-what-is-my-sin before your-father that he-seeks my-life). The third question looks back to earlier events, when Saul tried to pin David to the wall with his spear. At this point in the narrative, the king has three times attempted to kill David with the spear (18:10–11, 19:9–10). The spear is, of course, Saul's weapon of choice, but it is also his scepter, a symbol of power and authority. Close to the end of his life, the narrator reports that Saul keeps his spear within reach as he sleeps (26:7). While Saul had both a sword and a spear at Michmash (13:22), he offered David only his armor, helmet, and sword when he fought against Goliath. Indeed, Saul's spear-scepter passes out of his hands only when he hurls it at David (18:11, 19:10) or his own son (20:33), or when he has it taken from him while he sleeps (26:12).

The weight of these sequential questions should probably be taken rhetorically—I have done nothing!—but David may also be asking Jonathan to reveal his father's motives. David clearly intends a severe attack on the character of Saul. His agitation is accentuated by the rhyme: have-I-done (עשיתי), my-guilt (עוני), my-sin (חטאתי), my-life (נפשי). His first question has been asked before, of Eliab in 17:29, and will be invoked again, of Achish in 29:8. David also asks about his "guilt" and "sin."[5] He does not ask what his sin was before Saul, but before "your" (i.e., Jonathan's) father. Both nouns are labels for negative conditions and conduct, used often in religious contexts. The predominance of offenses is directed against Yhwh—it is a sin against Yhwh to transgress the Lord's commandment (1 Sam 15:24–25)—but one may also "sin" against another person: one can make an offense against a brother (Gen 42:22), or rebel against one's

[5] The two words are used in a variety of ways in the Samuel narratives, yet deliberation on their semantic fields is beyond our scope here. Shades of meaning can be traced in the following passages. On sin, see 1 Sam 2:17, 12:23, 14:34 and 38, 15:23 and 25, 19:4 and 5; 2 Sam 12:13, 19:21. On guilt, see 1 Sam 14:41, 25:24, 28:10; 2 Sam 14:9 and 32, 19:20, 22:24, 24:10.

king (1 Sam 24:12). It is also the case that masters can sin against servants (Gen 31:36), and kings can mistreat subjects (1 Sam 19:1–7). It was in this passage (19:4–5) that Jonathan had just talked of "sin" in the context of Saul's attempt to kill David.

Jonathan responds to David's highly charged rhetorical questions with a disclaimer, weighted equally in terms of its rhetorical force. The narrator's introduction of two words (and-he-said to-him) is short when compared to its eight-word counterpart in v 1. The narrator's narrow attention now on speaker-addressee exposes Jonathan's rhetorical rejoinder. By highlighting a few of Jonathan's words, we see the force of his opposing response to David's sequential questions:

חלילה	(Far from it!)
הנה	(Behold)
דבר גדול או דבר קטן	(Anything great or small)
מדוע	(Why?)
אין זאת	(Such would never happen!)

Jonathan dismisses David's questions outright. His first word חלילה ("Far-from-it!") is strong in its rhetorical weight. It turns the line of argument, and such redirecting continues in Jonathan's follow-up. David presented his case that Saul sought his life. Jonathan denies the thought outright—"You shall not die"—in an attempt to convince David that Saul poses no real threat. We might infer that Jonathan is either attempting to convince himself of this point or that he is taking his father's recent change-of-heart comment as a statement of fact. As recently as 19:1 Saul had encouraged Jonathan and the servants to kill David, and the threat was real enough there to cause Jonathan to warn David to hide because of his father's murderous intentions. Jonathan is able to convince Saul, if only momentarily, to spare David, and in 19:6 Saul, persuaded by his son, swears (שבע): "As Yhwh lives, he [David] shall not be put to death." By chapter 20, Jonathan appears to have taken his father's oath to heart.

Previously directed by Saul to kill David, Jonathan is now arguing on behalf of Saul. What are we to make of Jonathan? Is he, as H. W. Hertzberg suggests, the Bible's "real nobleman of high sensibility?"[6] His loyalty to David is certainly well attested (18:1, 19:1–7).

[6] Hertzberg, *I & II Samuel*, 172.

He is also son of Saul, a real companion on the battlefield (13:16) and advisor to his father (19:4–5). We may infer that he is torn by conflicting loyalties to his father and friend. But how can he now be resolved in the thought that his father will not kill David? Part of the answer is certainly found in what Jonathan does *not* know. While Jonathan is aware of his father's desire to kill David (19:1–2) and his father's change of heart (19:6–7), it is also the case that Jonathan has not learned of his father's most recent attempt to kill David with the spear (19:9–10). But is he a man of "high sensibility"? Jonathan appears to be a rather innocent, simple-minded person. He will soon devise a plan involving coded language and arrows. The plan is not especially dangerous, though it is not without risks. And—it will be shown in time—this duplicitous scheme proves unnecessary. Robert Polzin has made a convincing case that Jonathan's lack of knowledge here and elsewhere stems from his "uncomplicated directness," his "uncomplicated view of people and events."[7]

Jonathan responds to David's questions by denying them outright. The notions that David has "guilt" or "sin," or that he has reason to fear for his life, are countered by Jonathan's provocative response, one which suggests he does indeed have an uncomplicated view of life: Since my father has not spoken to me about the matter you raise, David, what you say must be false. We should note that Jonathan's assumption that his father keeps no secrets from him has a counterpart: Jonathan did not discuss his plan of attack on a Philistine garrison with his father in 14:1–15, nor did he talk with his father of his friendship with David in 18:1–5. Indeed, the plan that Jonathan and David will soon agree upon is contrived against Saul, and Jonathan's explanation to his father concerning David's whereabouts in v 29 is an outright lie: "for this reason he has not come to the king's table" (cf. vv 12–24a).

Jonathan's use of the word "conceal" (סתר) serves to remind the audience of a plot that has been developing along the lines of deceit begetting deceit, deeds begetting misdeeds all along: (a) Saul offers a burnt offering at Gilgal, then explains to Samuel that he forced (אפך) himself to do it; the action and explanation rouse the anger of Samuel: "You have acted foolishly; you have not kept the

[7] Robert Polzin, *Samuel and the Deuteronomist: A Literary Study of the Deuteronomic History, Part Two (1 Samuel)* (San Francisco: Harper and Row, 1989), 189.

commandment of Yhwh" (13:13a). (b) When Jonathan routes the Philistines he is assisted by his young armor-bearer. Saul, unaware of his son's action, makes an oath that curses anyone who eats before he is avenged of his enemies. Jonathan, unaware of the regulations, eats a little honey, and is then condemned to death by his father (14:44). (c) In the incident at Amalek, Saul is commanded to utterly destroy "man and woman, child and infant, ox and sheep, camel and donkey" (15:3). He disobeys the command (v 8; cf. v 9), and in a reunion scene with Samuel, Saul's initial lie "I have carried out the word/command of Yhwh" (v 13) is followed by a dozen more lies and half-truths (vv 15–31). (d) In 19:11–17 Michal, David's wife (and Saul's daughter), helps David escape through a window, and then, with teraphim, goats' hair, and ingenuity thrown in, makes it appear that David is in bed. When Saul's messengers arrive, Michal informs them that David is sick in bed. Saul, in anger, subsequently turns to Michal, and says, "Why in this way did you trick me?" (v 17).

Jonathan concludes his response to David with the kind of rhetorical force that he used in his opening. He frames his speech in the following manner:

חלילה "Far from it!"
אין זאת "Such would never happen!"

Jonathan has responded to David's questions, but he has not answered them. The momentum of Jonathan's speech continues even as the narrator shifts attention back to David.

The narrator introduces David's speech and again departs from using the common introductory speech formula ויאמר ("and he said"). David is "swearing again" (שבע עוד) as he addresses Jonathan. The attention to family continues. For the fourth time, Jonathan's "father" is referenced. With forceful language, David now attempts to prove Jonathan wrong. In his effort to persuade, David assumes to know the mind of Saul. Saul knows (ידע ידע) and thinks (ויאמר אל־ידע זאת), David says, that this matter would grieve (עצב) his son. David responds forthrightly to Jonathan's why-would-my-father-conceal-the-matter question. The answer, it appears, is easily found: your father conceals the matter to spare you grief. For this reason, David avers, Saul shields his son by concealing his desires or plans to kill David. The sentiment which David is projecting, Saul's concern for Jonathan, is not without problems. If Saul were indeed concerned about sparing his son from grief, he would not be seeking the life of his son's best friend. The issue is presented as a fact. Indeed, David relates that Saul "knows well" (ידע ידע). This repetition in the Hebrew (qal infinitive absolute and qal perfect) emphasizes the point that Saul is keenly aware of the bond of friendship between Jonathan and David. It also looks back to Jonathan's statement that his father would not conceal anything from him, and the "knowing" anticipates, by way of opposition, David's point that Saul intends for his son not to know (אל־ידע). Indeed, the issues of knowledge and lack of knowledge appear throughout the chapter. David, in the know, is now revealing what has been "concealed" from Jonathan.

David, who is "swearing again," concludes his thought with an oath formula which twice calls attention to life (חי): "But indeed as Yhwh lives and as your soul lives." Yet it is death which David fears is imminent. He had alluded to it in his first speech to Jonathan (v 1), and now, immediately after the oath, David accentuates his perilous situation: only one step separates him from death.

The entire scene is characterized by urgency in language. David opens with three rhetorical questions, and then adds an oath. Jonathan responds initially with an exclamation, and moves the plot forward with a question and a promise. He proposes a solution to the problem at hand: whatever David shall ask, Jonathan will do. Does Jonathan hear David's opening questions as an invitation for help? Does David intend for Jonathan to hear him in this manner? The quick turn in the plot beginning at v 5 may indeed indicate that David opens with questions that are intended to move the principals to action. The single Hebrew word ואעשה־לך ("I-will-do-it-for-you") sets in motion a duplicitous plan of action. No one can doubt Jonathan's devotion to David. An extraordinary bond of friendship exists between the two men. Jonathan is, as Polzin remarks, "loyalty personified."[8]

David's plan, which proceeds from the thought that Saul indeed plans to kill him and that David's presence in Bethlehem confounds Saul's plans, is presented through quoted speech, the longest in the opening scene. Fifty-six words in the Hebrew, David's speech is loaded with: hypotheticals ("if", "if", "if"), a projection of Jonathan's

---

[8] Polzin, *Samuel*, 193.

speech ("David begged leave of me to run to Bethlehem his city for there is a yearly sacrifice there for all the family"), a projection of Saul's speech ("Good"), a projection of Saul's demeanor ("shows great anger"), a highly charged rhetorical plea ("show *ḥesed* to your servant")—all framed by the deictic הנה ("behold") and a rhetorical question.

David's plan to prove a point to Jonathan by confounding Saul rests on the notion that David has been detained by his family at their annual sacrifice festival, scheduled to begin the next day. It is clear from the words and action that follow this conversation—though not from any other biblical sources—that David is expected to sit with the king. This honor might derive from his kinship (son-in-law) with the royal house (18:27), his prestige (18:6–8), his work as Saul's armor-bearer (16:21), or some combination of the three. His opening statement reveals his dilemma. Though he fears for his life (vv 1, 3), he still feels loyal to his father-in-law: he "would definitely sit with the king at table" (v 5). Incongruity dissolves, however, through verbal forms: he *would* sit, but he *will* hide and flee as he has previously (19:2). For the first and only time in the chapter, David makes reference to "the king." By contrast, the word "father" has often been spoken (vv 1, 2 [2x], 3) and will be uttered again (vv 6, 8, 9, 10). By means of this unique reference, David distinguishes high responsibility at court from family matters. When explaining that the issue will be undertaken away from the court (in the field), David quickly draws Jonathan's father back into the picture. The idea of escaping to the field had previously been proposed by Jonathan in 19:3: David is to hide while father and son are nearby in the field. But now, under David's plan, Saul will not be with them. The subtle change signals that David's complete break with the royal court is imminent.

Jonathan has volunteered to do what David *says* (v 4). In v 6, David informs Jonathan what he is to *say*. The plan is, of course, a charade: David will not go to Bethlehem, and the yearly sacrifice for all the family is either a pretext (David's family may hold the annual sacrifice) or an outright lie (no event is scheduled). As the plot moves from the saying by Jonathan in v 4 to the saying that David projects in v 6, we discover that David's plan will make Jonathan more than a collaborator; he will be a conspirator, a point not lost on his father in v 30: "son of a perverse, rebellious woman.

Do I not know that you have chosen the son of Jesse to your own shame, and to the shame of your mother's nakedness?"

The plan is carefully contrived. David counts on the power of persuasion: He projects himself not only asking, but begging (נשאל נשאל) to be excused from the royal table. The matter is presented with an utmost sense of urgency, for David is running to Bethlehem. The annual sacrifice is an event for all the family. He would be missed there, too. And to ensure the least resistance, Jonathan is not to approach the king with all this news, but must instead wait for the king to miss David and initiate conversation himself.

David projects that if Saul inquires about his absence, the king's response will be expressed either in positive or negative terms. The first possibility, positive, is projected through speech: if he says "Good." The consequences are narrated concisely by means of two words: it-will-be-well with-your-servant. The conciseness can be explained by the fact that if Saul responds positively, the would-be crisis is averted. There is, of course, another reason that David invests few words in the first possibility. He "knows" (ידע) what the outcome will be. Saul has already sought to kill him twice, and David has himself admitted that he is but a step from death. He intends to provoke Saul to anger and thus prove to Jonathan his father's murderous intentions. Using the imperative "know," David would now have Jonathan recognize what he had previously refused to accept, namely that Saul seeks David's life. "Your father knows and knows well (ידע ידע) that I have found favor in your eyes" has become "know (דע) that evil is determined by him." The test is to cause Jonathan to know all that David knows. The second possible royal response, the negative, is projected in terms of Saul's demeanor: if he shows great anger. If the interpretation is correct that the object of David's plan is to force Jonathan to discover what David is already convinced of, namely that Saul seeks David's life, then we may assume that David is also interested in knowing when Jonathan gains knowledge. David shows respect for Jonathan, but not for Saul, by invoking the language of court decorum. Three times David refers to himself as Jonathan's "servant." Unequal to, subject to Jonathan, David is projecting a scene whereby he is asking permission not from the king, but from the king's son.

In v 8 David turns attention away from Saul's possible response to Jonathan himself. The imperative clause "know that evil is determined by him [Saul]" is followed by another imperative clause, which has Jonathan as its implied subject: "show *ḥesed* to your servant for into a covenant of Yhwh you have brought your servant with you"—a request that puts Jonathan opposite Saul, who may display "great anger." While the word "covenant" is new to this scene, in 18:3 Jonathan made a covenant with David "because he loved him as his own soul." Made just after David slays Goliath, this covenant is the first of three between the two men. Its nature is left unspecified. Terms and conditions would bind the two parties, but in this instance nothing is spelled out. It is clear, however, that Jonathan is captivated by David: "Jonathan stripped himself of the robe that was upon him, and gave it to David, and his armor—even his sword and his bow and his belt" (18:4). Jonathan, whose soul is "knit" to the soul of David, has transferred royal garments and trappings, thereby elevating David to princely status. The second covenant, in 20:8, is sealed as a solemn oath made in a religious context. This agreement is "a covenant of Yhwh." Jonathan's obligation to inform David of what transpires within the royal household is developed as a sacred agreement: "And if I am still alive, show me the *ḥesed* of Yhwh so that I may not die. And do not cut off your *ḥesed* from my house forever, even when/if Yhwh cuts off each of David's enemies from the face of the earth" (vv 14–15).

Under this agreement the two parties have equal status. Neither will destroy the other, or the other person's family, in a rivalry for power.[9]

The talk of covenant is not the only way that David demonstrates loyalty through language. He three times refers to himself as Jonathan's "servant" in a brief narrative space, and their joint effort is emphasized not only by the covenant itself but also through repetition of second-person pronominal forms: show *ḥesed* to *your* servant; *you* have brought *your* servant with *you*.

Near the conclusion of his speech, David introduces yet another hypothetical clause, which turns the plot in a new direction. "If there

[9] The third and final covenant of David and Jonathan is narrated in 23:17–18. David in exile hides in the wilderness of Ziph when Jonathan reaches him and strengthens his hand: "And he said to him, 'Do not be afraid, for the hand of Saul my father shall not find you. And you shall be king over Israel, and I shall be to you second. And also Saul my father knows this.' And the two of them made a covenant before Yhwh, and David remained at Horesh, and Jonathan went home."

is guilt in me," David appeals to Jonathan, "kill me yourself."[10] The thought expressed is, of course, a rhetorical device, which looks back to David's opening question. This initial question ("what is my guilt?") has its own answer lurking beneath the surface, which is still operative here: "I am not guilty!"

David's question—Why should you bring me to your father?—should, as Fokkelman has pointed out, be read against the backdrop of 19:7c: "Jonathan took David to Saul."[11] It appears that David now in 20:8 is rejecting any attempt on Jonathan's part at reconciling David with Saul. The issue is once again presented in life-and-death terms. If I am guilty, David says, kill me. In v 3 the oath, "as Yhwh lives and as your [Jonathan's] soul lives," precedes David's claim that he lives only a step from death. These statements and the initial question ("why does your father seek my life?") all hint that there is no room for compromise, no place for reconciliation.

Jonathan begins his response to David's lengthy, self-absorbed speech with the forceful word חלילה ("far from it"), just as he did previously in v 2. In both instances Jonathan is responding to David's introduction of the possibility of his own "guilt" (עון). Jonathan twice characterizes David as an innocent man by means of outright denial: Far from it (v 2) and Far be it from you (v 9).

Jonathan's loyalty to David is emphasized by yet another conditional clause: if he learns for certain that his father seeks to harm David, Jonathan will reveal the news to his friend. The narrator has in the past assured us of Jonathan's devotion and love for David (18:1–4; 19:1–3) and will again (20:17; 23:15–18). The two חלילה statements commingle with these other love and covenant references to reveal Jonathan's perspective: the bonds of friendship and covenant supersede family ties. Jonathan expresses loyalty to David through language. David had said: know that evil is determined by him (דע כי־כלתה הרעה מעמו), and Jonathan now says: if I knew for certain that evil was determined by my father to come upon you, would I not tell you? (כי אם־ידע אדע כי־כלתה הרעה מעם אבי לבוא עליך ולא אתה אגיד לך).

[10] Absalom's plea to Joab is strikingly similar in 2 Sam 14:32: "Behold, I sent to you, saying, 'Come here, that I may send you to the king to say "Why have I come from Geshur? It would be better for me still to be there." And now therefore let me see the king's face. If there is in me guilt, let him kill me!'"

[11] Fokkelman *Narrative*, vol. 2, 305.

The scene has developed around the central idea of the acquisition of knowledge, and it is brought to the foreground again in these parallel speeches of David and Jonathan: know that evil; if I knew that evil. David and Jonathan are counterposed by the narrator: David knows that Saul seeks his life; Jonathan thinks, naively, that his father has no murderous intentions. If Saul were to plot against David, Jonathan thinks that his father would share his intentions with him first. The sham archery session that will soon be devised will serve the singular purpose of making Jonathan as knowledgeable as David.

In the final round of the initial scene of chapter 20, the dialogists are laconic. The highly charged rhetoric of the previous three rounds of speech gives way to concise, practical matters. David speaks seven words: Who will-tell me if your-father answers-you harshly? Jonathan speaks three words: Come let-us-go-out-into the-field. David's question calls attention again to the matter of acquiring knowledge: who will tell him if Saul answers harshly? Any theoretical positive response of Saul is now dropped in David's speech (cf. v 7). As Fokkelman has observed, it is only a small step from this if-question to its import: "who will inform me *that* your father answers harshly?"[12]

The issue of how questions are answered in this scene (and, indeed, in the Bible) is worth considering. In this instance, Jonathan instantly turns attention away from the informant (who will tell?) to a covert plan (let us go). His request is, we may safely assume, for the purpose of devising a plan beyond the hearing of others.[13] This detail of going "into the field" looks back first to v 5, for David proposed

[12] Fokkelman, *Narrative*, vol. 2, 308.

[13] The Bible's frequent mention of the "field" suggests that it is an important place. Its literary significance is too complex to trace here, but a cursory survey of two books is instructive. It is a place in Genesis associated with the creation of plants and animals (Gen 2:19–20, 3:18), but it is also a place associated with intrigue, duplicity, violence, and murder. It is where Cain kills his brother (4:8); where Sarah, Abraham, and Jacob are buried (23:9, 11, 13, 17; 25:9–10; 49:29–32; 50:13); the location where Esau hunts (25:27); a place associated with Jacob's deception of Esau and Isaac (25:29, 27:3); and also a place associated with the rape of Dinah (34:5, 7, 28). In the book of Samuel the field is where battles are waged (1 Sam 4:2; 2 Sam 18:6), but it is also a place owned by Joab which Absalom's servants set on fire (2 Sam 14:30), where the woman advised by Joab to deceive David says that her two sons fought until one killed the other (2 Sam 14:6), where Amasa, covered with blood, is dragged after Joab murders him (2 Sam 20:10–12); and a place that figures prominently in the story of David's affair with Bathsheba (2 Sam 11:11, 23).

that he would flee and hide there, but it also looks back to the time and place where Jonathan spoke to his father and told him of David's good deeds (19:2–7). Now Jonathan proposes that they go together. The subsequent scenes will reveal that the field is the place where Jonathan and David agree on a plan of duplicity. Indeed, the archery session itself will take place in the field (v 35). Jonathan's request that they go into the field also serves a distinct purpose for it generates curiosity in the mind of the reader. Why the field? Jonathan gives no explanation. We may surmise the following: no witnesses will be present. Away from the court the field provides a more intimate setting for the private conversation of conspiratorial friends. It is also a place large enough for David to hide (v 24), and large enough, too, for Jonathan to shoot his arrows beyond his attendant and thereby communicate with David (v 36).

The next two scenes (scene ii, vv 12–17, and scene iii, vv 18–23) take place in the field. In both of them David listens as Jonathan speaks in two long monologues. In scene ii Jonathan agrees to ascertain from his father's reaction if David's fear is justified. Jonathan promises David with oaths and a covenant that he will reveal Saul's reaction. The scene concludes with the narrator's report of Jonathan's love for David: "and Jonathan again made David swear by his love for him for as he loved his own soul he loved him." After the narrator introduces the speaker, scene iii is filled entirely by Jonathan's speech to David. Jonathan develops David's plan to absent himself from the king's table with specific details: he instructs David to go to the place by the stone where he hid before. He will shoot arrows and send a boy to retrieve them. Short shots indicate that David is safe in Saul's presence; long shots reveal the opposite. The plan is sealed with Jonathan's account of divine approval: Yhwh is between me and you forever. Scene iv is brief (vv 24–25). With characters silenced, the narrator describes their locations: David hides in the field; the king sits down before bread (the allusion to "the house of bread" [Bethlehem] is not accidental); Jonathan stands; Abner sits by Saul's side; David's seat is vacant.

The Remaining Questions of Chapter 20

In the three concluding scenes of chapter 20 (vv 26–29, 30–34, and 35–21:1), five questions are invoked (vv 27, 30, 32 [2x], 37). At least one appears in each of the scenes. As the first of these three scenes opens, Jonathan finds himself in the unenviable role of mediator between father and friend.

> [26]And Saul did not say anything on that day for he thought (אמר) he has been in an accident. He is not clean; surely he is not clean. [27]And it was on the next day, the second day of the new moon and David's place was vacant. And Saul said to Jonathan his son, Why (מדוע) has the son of Jesse not come either yesterday or today to the meal? [28]And Jonathan answered Saul, David begged (שאול נשאל נשאל) leave of me to go to Bethlehem. [29]And he said, Let me go I pray for our family holds a sacrifice in the city, and my brother commanded me (to be there). And now (עתה) if I have found favor in your eyes, let me slip away I pray, and I will see my brothers. For this reason he has not come to the king's table.

The scene opens with the narrator's report of Saul's inner life, which is conveyed through the work of two Hebrew words. Saul does not say (לא־דבר) anything; he thinks (אמר) instead. The blurring of speech and thought can be reflected in the singular Hebrew word אמר, as one can speak to others, or one can speak to oneself (i.e., think). Saul first assumes that David does not come to the table for the New Moon festival because of ritual disqualification (Lev 15:16–18), and the thought is represented by the writer as a scant perception, which evolves into crystallized thought:

he has been in an accident	מקרה הוא
he is not clean	בלתי טהור הוא
surely he is not clean	כי־לא טהור

But the king fails to convince himself. Can Saul be oblivious to what might motivate David to be away? Can he or anyone at court forget that he previously directed his son and servants to kill David? When on the next day David's seat remains vacant, interior speech gives way to dialogue. Saul now speaks (אמר) to Jonathan his son. The kinship reference is, of course, unnecessary, but by playing on family perspectives the author accomplishes several literary goals. In the quoted speech that follows, the word "son" is duplicated, as Saul inquires after the "son-of-Jesse." The close proximity of this duplicated word gives rise to highly charged rhetoric:

ויאמר שאול אל־יהונתן בנו	and Saul said to Jonathan his son (narrator's voice)
מדוע לא־בא בן־ישי	why has the son of Jesse not come? (Saul's voice)

Saul is implying that his son knows David's whereabouts. The question is obviously abrasive in tone—a "where is David?" interrogative would have been harmless enough—and we might assume that Jonathan is not expecting a neutral response from his father on the matter of David's absence. Saul will later say, "No one discloses to me when my son deals with the son of Jesse" (22:8a). The king repeatedly speaks despairingly of the "son-of-Jesse,"[14] a bloodline fact he first learned from David himself (1 Sam 17:58). In contrast to both Jonathan and the narrator, who use David's name throughout chapter 20, Saul never utters the name. The fact that he cannot speak David's name is also represented by the narrator as the king thinks (in interior monologue) about the man: he has been in an accident; he is not clean; surely he is not clean. Saul's inability to name David is highlighted in two other ways: (a) by way of contrast in the narrator's duplicated statement which frames the report of Saul's thoughts—*David's* place is vacant (vv 25, 27) and (b) just after Saul asks, Why has the son of Jesse not come to the meal? to which Jonathan answers, *David* begged leave of me to go to Bethlehem. With his question, Saul points out that "the son of Jesse" has been twice absent. This question highlights Saul's anguish (yesterday and today), and the coupling technique is also a part of the narrator's strategy: both before and after Saul's thoughts are conveyed in v 26, the narrator reports that David's place was vacant.

While it is Jonathan who deceives his father, it is at David's bidding. Having been coached by David on what to say, Jonathan gives an answer to the "why" question that consists of a frame around his quotation of David's speech, projected in scene i. Transforming speech, Jonathan says,

> [frame:] David begged leave of me to go to Bethlehem. And he said,
> [inset:] Let me go I pray for our family holds a sacrifice in the city, and my brother commanded me (to be there). And now if I have found favor in your eyes, let me slip away I pray, and I will see my brothers.
> [frame:] For this reason he has not come to the king's table.

In v 6, David told Jonathan what to say: If your father misses me at all, then you say, "David begged leave of me to run to Bethlehem his city for there is a yearly sacrifice there for all the family."

[14] See 1 Sam 22:7, 8, 13.

The projected speech undergoes considerable transformation in the telling of Jonathan. In Jonathan's telling, the drama of David's begging (נשאל נשאל) becomes a *description* of David's speech, rather than words which David had projected as actual speech. The two new frame components allude, indirectly and directly, to a central item: food. David is now, Saul is led to believe, in Bethlehem, and it is because of David's need to be there that he is absent from the king's table. The anguished Saul is left to wonder if the food served at the "house of bread" is better than that served at the royal table!

The inset is a fine example of deception through language. In v 28 three key words appear consecutively: שאול נשאל נשאל. A duplication occurred within the speech that David had originally projected in v 6 (נשאל נשאל, "begged"), but in the new context the narrator reports that Jonathan is speaking to Saul (שאול) immediately before quoting the words alike in sound. The close connection between the voices of the narrator and Jonathan is thus seen in the phonologically similar שאול ("Saul") and נשאל נשאל ("begged"). This triplicate emphasis on the root שאל ("ask") highlights Saul's dilemma: Jonathan indicates that David—the name contrasts with the appellation son-of-Jesse, which Saul had just uttered—asked leave of him. While David has asked permission to be away from the king's table, he has asked it of the prince! The incongruity calls to mind a chief concern of the Historian: Who has authority in this court?

In v 6, Jonathan is directed to say: "David begged leave of me." In many English translations of Jonathan's speech the words appear to be duplicated verbatim, but he changes the original preposition ממני ("of me") to מעמדי ("of me"). The term עמדי also signifies "with me," but concurrently conveys a sense of separation after having been together.[15] By means of word substitution, Jonathan positions himself closer to his father in this delicate loyalty balancing act.

Another modification of speech can be traced to the business of travelling to Bethlehem. David had suggested "running" or "hurrying" (רוץ). This verbal form never appears in Jonathan's retelling, but the idea appears no less than three times. Movement is conveyed in the first instance by the simple preposition עד in the frame: David begged leave of me (to go) to (עד) Bethlehem. This sense of motion is followed by two verbal forms in the quoted speech, both

[15] Shimon Bakon, "Jonathan," *JBQ* 23 (1995), 147–48.

underscored by the particle of entreaty נא: שלחני "let me go" and אמלטה "let me slip away." This transformation from "running" to "going"/"slipping away" is rhetorically loaded. On a prior occasion Michal "let David go," only to be scolded by Saul.[16] Jonathan retains the idea of running since מלט conveys an image of haste, but the original thought is now amplified. Jonathan, wittingly or unwittingly, introduces the novel—though hardly surprising—idea to his father that David is not only "going away" (שלח), but "slipping away," "fleeing" (מלט), a view not far in meaning from "let me escape."

Jonathan retains the nominal forms—sacrifice, family, city—but modifies the original syntax by shifting the possessive pronouns. He changes the original "his [David's] city" to "the city," the sacrifice that is for "all the family" becomes an event for "our [David's] family," and his attendance in the retelling becomes a command (צוה) from David's brother. In his formulation, David had personalized the city and made the sacrifice out to be a rather objective event (for "the family"). As Fokkelman has observed, "[the original statement] has an air of being self-evident, which makes it difficult to oppose; anyone who would dare to do so places himself outside the social order, for he will appear not to know how things are or what are the requirements of the rite."[17] We should also note that in David's telling, this sacrifice is an "annual" event. In context, the point would not be lost on Saul that the event in Bethlehem happens less frequently—thus his presence is more important—than the regularly occurring New Moon festival. But in Jonathan's voice the contrast in frequency is lost altogether. He omits the "annual" reference, and replaces the religious element with a new focus on personal dynamics. Three times Jonathan turns the issue in the direction of family concerns:

> *our family* holds a sacrifice;
> *my brother* commanded me;
> I will see *my brothers*.

We might expect this new emphasis on David's family to have little calming effect on Saul, and, indeed, the narrator will soon report

---

[16] Cf. 19:17, for example, where the verbal form שלח appears twice and מלט once.

[17] Fokkelman, *Narrative*, vol. 2, 331.

that Saul's anger rises (v 30). The whole issue of loyalty to Bethlehem instead of at "the king's table" affects Saul dramatically. It is David's brother's command (צוה) that pulls David away from the king himself. This issue of Saul's lack of authority is also highlighted in Jonathan's introduction of the new idea that David hopes that he has found favor in Jonathan's eyes!

Jonathan concludes the scene with a four-word explanation: for-this-reason he-has-not-come to-the-table-of the-king. His final words have rhetorical implications at two levels. First, son Jonathan refers not to "his father's" table or even to "your" table, but instead to "the king's" table. This choice of words contrasts with the new references to David and his family, of which Jonathan has just spoken, and this disjunction highlights a matter that will increasingly become one of the central concerns of the narrative: the relationship among Saul, his son, and others at court is fractured beyond repair. Second, the reference to table also highlights a central concern of the larger story. Because of Saul's actions and David's response to them—"What is my sin before your father that he seeks my life?" David had asked when the chapter opened—table fellowship is becoming increasingly problematic.

This scene has masqueraded as effortless dinner conversation about a missing member of the court who left to attend a family feast. Efforts at decorum cease in the next round, framed by the narrator, who portrays both a father and a son rising in anger (ויחר־אף שאול, ויקם יהונתן בחרי־אף):

> [30]And Saul's anger rose against Jonathan, and he said to him, Son of a perverse, rebellious woman. Do I not (הלוא) know that you have chosen the son of Jesse to your shame and to the shame of your mother's nakedness? [31]For as long as the son of Jesse lives upon the earth neither shall you be established nor your kingdom. And now (ועתה) send and bring him to me for he shall surely die. [32]And Jonathan answered Saul his father and said to him, Why (למה) should he be put to death? What (מה) has he done? [33]And Saul hurled his spear at him to strike him, and Jonathan knew that it was set by his father to put David to death. [34]And Jonathan rose from the table in fierce anger and did not eat on the second day of the month bread because he was grieving for David because his father humiliated him.

In addition to the symmetry of the narrator's frame in this scene (father then son angered), the episode is also fashioned by the speeches of father and son. Both Saul and Jonathan invoke interrogatives in this scene, and all three of their questions—Saul asks one question and Jonathan asks two—are rhetorical. Saul turns the narrative with electrifying rhetorical force. His speech consists of four parts: name calling (son of a perverse, rebellious woman); rhetorical question (Do I not know that you have chosen the son of Jesse to your shame and to the shame of your mother's nakedness?); ominous prediction (for as long as the son of Jesse lives upon the earth neither shall you be established nor your kingdom); and a command introduced with עתה (and now send and bring him to me for he shall surely die).

Saul's rage is not against David, but "against Jonathan," the closer target. The sudden verbal lash of the whip at the opening of this scene contrasts with the royal silence at the beginning of the previous one. Perhaps Saul is not surprised by the subterfuge of David, but the thought of his son-heir joining in the conspiracy causes him to rail. He curses his own son in terms charged with sexual torment. Initially, Saul attempts to make Jonathan a degenerate rebel by shaming him. Saul calls him a "son of a perverse, rebellious woman" and concludes his speech by calling "the son of Jesse" (בן־ישׁי) a "son of death" (בן־מות). In the first instance, "son of" (בן) functions as a metonym for a class of people who are unfaithful to the ones they owe loyalty, and, in context, is a reminder of family discord, plots and subplots that pit son and father against each other. As recently as v 27, the narrator reminded us that Saul speaks to his son about the son of Jesse. He now calls Jonathan a son of a perverse, rebellious woman and accuses him of shaming himself by showing favor to the son of Jesse. And furthermore, it is the son of Jesse who is portrayed as a threat to Jonathan's kingdom. Family language abounds. Jonathan himself has referred in this chapter to his father often.[18] Jonathan will soon rise from the table because, the narrator reports, his father humiliates him. This family language calls attention to an important matter, because much turns on the subject of family (dis)loyalty. In his speech, Saul sets Jonathan's love for David against his disloyalty toward family. Jonathan has, Saul contends, disgraced the one who gave him birth. By "choosing" David, Saul would have Jonathan believe that he shames himself and his mother's nakedness.

[18] In vv 2 [2x], 9, 12, 13 [2x]. Both David (vv 3, 6, 8, 10) and the narrator (vv 32, 33, 34) also refer to Jonathan's father.

Jonathan, like Yhwh, has chosen David. Saul has unknowingly verified David's claim back in v 3: Saul knows that David has found favor in Jonathan's eyes. Though mad, Saul sees with clarity: David and Jonathan have conspired against him.

With heavy psychological shading, Saul attempts to convince Jonathan that David is a threat to his own future. David is no longer Saul's rival; David threatens Jonathan, Saul would have his son believe. Saul appeals to his son's self-interest so that David might be lured back to the court, but Jonathan has already served his own interests by making a covenant with David and by concealing David's fears and plans from the king. In a brilliant stroke, the author links Saul's warning to his son to the renewal covenant between the two young men. In v 14 Jonathan had asked David to show him the *ḥesed* of Yhwh if he is still alive (חי); Saul now speaks of the son of Jesse's life (חי). Jonathan had spoken of David's enemies cut off from the face of the earth (האדמה, v 15); now Saul warns Jonathan that his kingdom will not be established while the son of Jesse is upon the earth (האדמה).

Saul concludes his speech with a double-barreled command, "send" (שלח) and "bring" (לקח) David to the court. His threat on David's life is unambiguous: he shall surely die. The directive is followed by the narrator's introductory speech formula, which, in this instance, consists of two verbal forms, "answered" (ענה) and "said" (אמר). Jonathan's quoted speech is also double voiced. His two questions are an altered form of the questions David voiced in the opening scene. Saul had just revealed his knowledge that Jonathan had chosen (בחר) the son of Jesse, and the extent of the friendship is now seen in Jonathan's two rhetorical questions, each consisting of only two words: Why-should-he be-put-to-death? and What-has he-done?

Jonathan's attempt to reason with his father has failed. Saul understands the two staccato-like questions as forceful, indignant negative responses to the command to go and bring David. He responds by hurling his spear at his son, a response not unlike what he has shown David before (18:10–11; 19:9–10). We may assume that Saul never puts his spear away. He has it close at hand, even at the royal banquet table, just as he earlier kept it within reach even as he slept. In a figurative sense, the enraged monarch is blind. He makes no distinction between David and his son. The two friends, aligned, suffer the same life-threatening effect of Saul's wrath. The singular image of the spear thrown serves to unite Jonathan and David as allies. The monarch had lamented that neither Jonathan nor his kingdom would be established. Now it is Saul who threatens both with the thrust of his spear.

The scene concludes with the narrator's description of Jonathan and his response to the hurled spear. The launched spear enlightens Jonathan, who now knows that his father does indeed intend to put David to death, a startling conclusion since Jonathan was the target! He now knows (ידע) what he refused to accept as David's knowledge in v 3. When the narrator informs us that Jonathan rises from the table in anger and does not eat bread because he is grieving for David, we have the opportunity to make literary connections between Jonathan and Saul on the one hand, and Jonathan and David on the other. Saul has just risen against Jonathan in anger; his son now rises in anger, unable to eat. The reference to Jonathan not eating bread links him to David, who is also not eating, at least not "from the table" at "his seat as was his custom" (vv 25, 34). Indeed, he would have the king believe that he has travelled to Bethlehem, the "city of bread." The reference to Jonathan grieving for David also looks back to an earlier time in the chapter when David had informed Jonathan that his father did not want his son to grieve. It is a sign of Jonathan's noble character that he grieves for David just after his father has attempted to murder his son. The divine rejection of Saul has now come home: Jonathan's "grieving for David" is tantamount to a rejection of his father.

Jonathan knows what David has known for some time: Saul can no longer be reasoned with, and David's concern for his life at the king's hand is legitimate. The high drama ends as two friends are reunited in the field. At the end, they kiss and weep. The scene has only one interrogative.

> [35]And in the morning Jonathan went out to the field to the appointed place with David and a young boy with him. [36]And he said to his boy, Run, find, I pray, the arrows which I am shooting. The boy ran and he shot an arrow past him. [37]And the boy came to the place of the arrow which Jonathan had shot, and Jonathan called after the boy and said, Is not (הלוא) the arrow beyond you further down? [38]And Jonathan called after the boy, Make haste; hurry; do not stand still. And Jonathan's boy picked up the arrows[19] and came to his master.

[19] Reading with qere חצים "arrows" for MT חצי "my arrow."

> [39]And the boy knew nothing. Only Jonathan and David knew the matter. [40]And Jonathan gave his possessions to his boy, and he said to him, Go, take (them) to the city. [41]The boy went, and David rose from beside the mound[20] and fell with his face to the ground and bowed three times. And they kissed each other and wept with each other—David wept the more.

The final scene is different from the preceding ones in several respects: (a) Saul is neither mentioned nor present, and his absence explains in large measure the scene's change in tone; (b) the action moves from the intense, life-threatening atmosphere of the previous scenes to a sham archery session where nothing is said about the possibility of death, a prominent motif earlier; (c) David appears at the close of the scene, in a tender reunion with Jonathan; (d) only Jonathan's speech is recorded in the scene.[21] He gives directions to the lad in brief command statements:

> Run, find, I-pray the-arrows which I am-shooting. (7 words)
> Is-not the-arrow beyond-you further-down? (4 words)
> Make-haste; hurry; do-not-stand-still. (3 words)
> Go; take-(them) to-the-city. (3 words)

Ensconsed in this series of commands is the scene's only question, and it is Jonathan who asks it: "Is not the arrow beyond you further down?"

What was projected as a statement of fact (v 22) becomes an interrogative in the enactment scene. The question functions as a sign by which Saul's negative reaction is communicated. By following through on the sign, Jonathan gains an opportunity to discharge the youth, and thus avoids arousing his suspicions. The conventional verb used to introduce speech (אמר) is not used here. Jonathan's triple command, "make haste; hurry; do not stand still" is called out (קרא) to the boy. The subtle variation in verb choice points to the fact that Jonathan is not speaking to the boy but calling out and hoping that David hears. The tripartite command has its desired effect: the boy picks up the arrows, returns to his master, and then returns to the city upon Jonathan's command. Using the key word

---

[20] Reading "mound" or "stone heap" (הארגב) with LXX εργαβ, instead of MT הנגב ("the south").

[21] Jonathan's solo speech was also recorded earlier in scenes ii and iii.

"know" (ידע) twice, the narrator reports that the boy knew nothing; only Jonathan and David knew the matter.

David's ceremonious rising and falling with his face to the ground, bowing three times, is reinforced with the report of their show of emotion (kissing and weeping). Jonathan utters the final speech in the scene as the narrator reports explicitly that he speaks to David. This speech is Jonathan's third and final invocation of an oath, one that creates a bond between friends, and binds them in a covenant that extends to their descendants.

> 42 And Jonathan said to David, Go in peace for we have sworn both
> of us ourselves in the name of Yhwh, saying, Yhwh shall be between
> me and you and between my descendants and your descendants for-
> ever. 21:1 And he got up and left; and Jonathan went into the city.

The rules of the archery session had been spelled out: "If I say to the youth, 'Behold: the arrows are beyond you,' Go because Yhwh has sent you away." The drama of the arrows was played out in the resolution. But the arrow episode proves less critical than we had been led to expect. When David learns the news, he does not flee. Indeed, he and Jonathan converse face to face as soon as the boy departs from the field. In this ironic twist, the ensuing action of the friends violates the terms of their agreement. David was to come back if it is peaceful, but if Jonathan determines that Saul intends harm, David was to flee.

It would appear that the prearranged face-to-face conversation between friends renders the prearranged signal with the arrows superfluous, but a few observations are in order. Considerable narrative space is devoted to planning and executing the archery session, but since David and Jonathan talk face to face, why all the subterfuge? When planning, Jonathan may have legitimately assumed that the archery would be performed in the presence of Saul himself. Having set the plan in motion, Jonathan carries through on it and then discharges the boy without arousing his suspicion. On the other hand, the prearranged plan may have been a ruse all along. Perhaps Jonathan has a penchant for display or covert operations? We are on much firmer ground when we isolate the archery session's function from a literary standpoint.

(a) The covert nature of the scene calls attention (again) to the danger and risks in and around Saul's court.

(b) The projected scene dramatizes the actual face-to-face reunion scene of Jonathan and David, for the reader expects the two men to part without having had the opportunity to speak. The kissing and weeping scene is unanticipated. By means of the narrator's indirection and misdirection, the friendship alliance is rendered in dramatic terms.

(c) The projection and fulfillment of the archery scene gives rise to the making of oaths and covenants. David concludes his initial proposal in scene i regarding his contrived absence at the king's court using covenantal language: "show *ḥesed* to your servant for into a covenant of Yhwh you have brought your servant with you." Jonathan reveals in scene ii that he will disclose his father's disposition toward David. Then Jonathan makes a covenant with David's house and makes David swear by his love for him. While scene iii lacks covenantal language, it is replete with references to divine blessings: Yhwh lives; Yhwh has sent you away; Yhwh is between you and me forever. In the next and final scene in which Jonathan and David are present (scene vii), Jonathan's final words blend his previous oaths and covenants while underscoring the presence of Yhwh as provider and guarantor.

(d) The similarity between Saul's spear and Jonathan's arrows invites comparison. Jonathan, who directs David throughout this chapter, skillfully shoots the arrows. Saul has by this stage of the narrative four times launched his spear and missed his mark each time. Saul's decline can be seen in the light of Jonathan, who directs David with words and deeds.

(e) The arrow scene also highlights Jonathan's role as prince in charge. He devises the plan, and also modifies it in the fulfillment stage. He directs the entire incident. Even at the end, it is Jonathan who commands David: "Go." David bows to Jonathan three times, a grandiose show found nowhere else in the Bible.[22] Jonathan is the only speaker in the scene. In fact, his speech is recorded in each scene where characters are quoted (scenes i–iii and v–vii). In contrast, David's speech is recorded in scene i, but never again in scenes ii–vii.

(f) Jonathan's transfer of his possessions (or: weapons) to the boy is unanticipated (cf. vv 20–22). Why does the laconic narrator convey

[22] Characters elsewhere do, of course, bow. Abraham consistently bows before addressing the Hittites in Gen 23, but in action interspersed with dialogue. David's three sequential bows are unique.

this detail? We know that when Jonathan calls out to the boy his words are ultimately addressed to David. The transfer of possessions to the boy (and ultimately to David) parallels 18:4, where Jonathan tears off his robe and gives it—along with his armor, sword, bow, and belt—to David. These actions of transference are fraught with symbolic meaning, for we know that Yhwh has torn (קרע) the kingdom from Saul and given it to his neighbor who is better than (הטוב מן) Saul (15:28).

(g) The unexpected conversation scene allows Jonathan to send David away. He sends him "in peace," a contrast to the life-draining thrust of Saul's sword, which has been hurled at David and Jonathan.

(h) A key word appears twice in the archery session: the boy knew nothing (לא־ידע); only Jonathan and David knew (ידע) the matter. This alignment in awareness between friends is important because the chapter has been about the education of Jonathan, or, more to the point, about bringing Jonathan to the same level of knowledge as David. The opening sequential questions had made it clear that David knew for certain that Saul sought his life.

But the final scene ultimately leaves important matters unresolved: What does David think about these oaths and covenants he is swearing to? David does not speak about them, and the narrator does not report his thoughts. And what is driving Jonathan to contrive this archery session? Political ambition? Friendship and loyalty? Subsequent chapters will resolve some of this ambiguity, but in tragic terms for Jonathan and his father. We meet Jonathan on only two more occasions. In 23:15–18 he comes to encourage David, who is fleeing again from Saul. Here at Horesh Jonathan and David make a "covenant before Yhwh" again. David never again returns to Jonathan for encouragement or advice. When we meet David's friend again it is on Mount Gilboa in 31:1–7—slain along with his brothers, Abinadab and Malchishua, by the Philistines.

CHAPTER NINE

QUESTIONS AND THE CHARACTERIZATION OF GOD (2 SAMUEL 7:1–17)

> "The [Bible's] protagonists are characterized not only by direct means, but also, and in fact primarily, by what they say and do."
>
> —Shimon Bar Efrat

Introduction

In 2 Sam 7 David is suffering from a guilty conscience because he is settled in his palace in Jerusalem while the ark of God resides in a tent. Just after David implies that now is the time to build a temple for Yhwh, he receives the commendation of the prophet. Immediately thereafter, however, Nathan receives word from Yhwh that David's thoughts are incompatible with God's. Generations-old discussions about this chapter focused on what has been perceived to be its complex literary history, and the author (or editor, if the argument about an elaborate literary tradition is accepted) has not fared well. According to Robert Pfeiffer, for example, the author is responsible for "the muddle" and the "dreary prose of II Sam 7." The author "sinks into a mire of unintelligible verbiage," and "his style is consistently wretched."[1] Now that the days of undervaluing the Bible's art have passed, a new perspective based on the integrity of the text of 2 Sam 7 is possible.

---

[1] Robert Pfeiffer, *Introduction to the Old Testament* (New York: Harper & Brothers, 1941), 372. Cf. also Henri Bussche, "Le texte de la prophétie de Nathan sur la dynastie davidique," *ETL* 24 (1948), 354–94; Heinz Kruse, "David's Covenant," *VT* 35 (1985), 139–64; Martin Noth, "David and Israel in II Samuel VII," *The Laws in the Pentateuch and Other Studies* (ed. Martin Noth; London: SCM, 1966), 250–259; Marcel Simon, "La prophétie de Nathan et le Temple: Remarques sur II Sam 7," *RHPR* 32 (1952), 41–58; Matitiahu Tsevat, "The House of David in Nathan's Prophecy" *Bib* 46 (1965), 353–56; Matitiahu Tsevat, "What was David Promised in II Sam 7:11b–16?" *HUCA* 34 (1963), 71–82.

From a thematic standpoint, the chapter stands out for at least two reasons: generally, it belongs to the category of divine revelations concerning temple building that was common in the ancient Near East,[2] and, more specifically, it highlights the Davidic dynasty. From a rhetorical standpoint, the chapter has another claim to notice: the narrator, in self-imposed silence throughout most of the chapter (vv 2b, 3b, 5–16, 18b–29), departs from the biblical norm. After a brief description of action and conversation (vv 1–4) and a short transitional passage (vv 17–18a), all of the remaining verses are given over to the speeches of Yhwh (vv 5–16) and David (vv 18b–29).

The Bible does, of course, allow its characters to speak, but more often the narrator of biblical prose provides commentary to help the reader find his or her way through the stories. But in this chapter we hear from the narrator only in six verses, and at times only in portions of these (vv 1–4, 17–18). The surrounding chapters, 6 and 8, are instructive because they are made up almost entirely of the narrator's words. By the time David is allowed to speak in 6:9, we have already learned of his military initiative, the size of his army, the setting, details about the ark, David's dance before Yhwh, instruments used for accompaniment, the consequences of Uzzah's contact with the ark, and David's emotional response (vv 1–8). Most of the events that follow in this chapter are also described by the narrator (the characters speak subsequently only in vv 12, 20–22). In the chapter that follows 2 Sam 7, the narrator highlights David's ability as a fighter. After striking down King Hadadezer, David takes "one thousand seven hundred horsemen and twenty thousand foot soldiers" (8:4). When the Arameans from Damascus arrive, David "kills twenty-two thousand men of the Arameans" (v 5). He also seizes a great amount of bronze as he travels around the towns of Hadadezer (vv 7–8), and the narrator makes it clear that Yhwh is responsible for David's success (v 6). Indeed, we do not hear directly from any of the characters during the entire episode; all of David's exploits in 2 Sam 8 are reported by the narrator. The narrator, who is responsible for such direct expressions of characterization in 2 Sam

[2] Readers interested in temple building in the ancient Near East may wish to consult Victor Hurowitz's fine comparative and phenomenological study *I Have Built You an Exalted House: Temple Building in the Bible in Light of Mesopotamian and Northwest Semitic Writings*, JSOTSup 115; JSOT/ASOR Monograph Series 5 (Sheffield: Sheffield Academic Press, 1992).

6 and 8 (and elsewhere), wields a kind of supreme authority. Only the narrator has access to the inner thoughts of characters, God's included, and as one who fashions and tells the tale, even the narrator's choice to *allow* characters to speak indicates a dimension of authority.

In an effort to show that 2 Sam 7 is not "unintelligible verbiage" and that the author's style is something other than "consistently wretched," we may pose one question: How is God portrayed? In chapter 7, where virtually every phrase sheds light on God's character, the question arises: If the preponderance of dialogue represents a departure from the norm in the deuteronomistic history, why is it used for the characterization of God? One should bear in mind that the characterization of God represents a special case because most aspects typically associated with character—appearance, social status, place of residence, and so forth—have no bearing on God at all.[3] Certain information-seeking questions that human characters sometimes ask one another (Judg 12:5, 18:3, 19:17; 1 Sam 28:14, 30:13; 2 Sam 1:13) are not addressed to God.

When assuming a less pronounced role in telling the story, the narrator allows characters to advance the plot by means of their spoken words, and this shift in point of view requires us to attend to the contours of speech. But even when withdrawn, the narrator is never completely absent. The narrator frames the characters' speech by introducing the speakers and often nuancing their words: "the *king* said to *the prophet* Nathan" (v 2); "*in accordance with all these words and with all this vision*, Nathan spoke to David" (v 17); "then *King* David *went in and sat before Yhwh*, and said" (v 18a).

Shlomith Rimmon-Kenan's analysis of character provides us a starting point. She asserts that the biblical narrator provides two basic types of character identification. Borrowing from Joseph Ewen, she labels these as "direct definition" and "indirect presentation." The first type names the character trait by an adjective ("she was good-hearted") or an abstract noun ("his goodness knew no bounds"). The second type, on the other hand, allows the reader to infer the quality of certain traits without mentioning them explicitly. She concludes, "such naming of a character's qualities counts as direct

[3] Meir Sternberg, *The Poetics of Biblical Narrative: Ideological Literature and the Drama of Reading* (Bloomington: Indiana University Press, 1985), 323.

characterization only if it proceeds from the most authoritative voice in the text [i.e., from the narrator]."[4] The implications of this analysis extend beyond the narrator. In a chapter such as 2 Sam 7 where the dramatis personae assume much of the responsibility for characterization, we see that such direct and indirect methods of portrayal also extend to the characters themselves. For example, David supplies "direct definitions" of God's character when he prays and says, "You have wrought all this greatness . . . Therefore you are great" (vv 21–22). And after repeating God's (or Yhwh's) name twenty-five times in the span of only twelve verses, David says toward the end of the prayer, "O Yhwh God you are God" (v 28). This frequent reference in the narrative to Yhwh's name and position affects the reader's understanding of both the speaker and the addressee.

Certain portions of the chapter may also be described in terms of "indirect presentation." Yhwh's first words to Nathan, "Go and tell my servant David" (v 4), suggest a particular type of relationship between God and David before God delivers the oracle. This type of portrayal may also be observed in the very first verse of the chapter, where we learn that the rest that David now enjoys is the result of Yhwh's actions against the king's enemies. And finally, God's uniqueness is also suggested on both the temporal and spatial planes by God's own words in v 6: "I have not lived in a house since the day I brought up the people of Israel from Egypt to this day, but I have been moving about in a tent and a tabernacle."[5] Obviously this distinction of direct and indirect portrayal helps to show how characterization is achieved, yet more is at work here. Because of the preponderance of dialogue, we might focus on the characters' speeches themselves. After all, a narrator reluctant to offer direct and explicit comments about characters may still put words in their mouths that shed light on the speaker or addressee (or both). As Shimon Bar-Efrat notes:

> Traits of both the speaker and the interlocutor are expressed through speech, or to be more precise, all speech reflects and exposes the speaker, while it sometimes also brings to light qualities of the person

[4] Shlomith Rimmon-Kenan, *Narrative Fiction: Contemporary Poetics* (London and New York: Methuen, 1983), 59–60. Cf. Joseph Ewen, "The Theory of Character in Narrative Fiction" (Hebrew), *Hasifrut* 3 (1971), 1–30; Joseph Ewen, *Character in Narrative* (Hebrew) (Tel Aviv: Sifriyat Po'alim, 1980), 47–48.

[5] Other examples can be found, such as in v 8b.

> being addressed (or reveals the speaker's opinion of that person). What people say witnesses not only to their thoughts, feelings, etc., but is often slanted to accord with the character, mood, interests and status of their interlocutor.[6]

An analysis of the portrayal of God is bound to yield complexities and nuances far beyond what can be explored here, but a more careful look at the dialogue may reveal how God's character is drawn, while concurrently suggesting how earlier commentators missed the mark.

Nathan's Role: The Tables Turned

The characterization of God begins in the opening verse as the narrator conveys two pieces of information: (a) the king is settled in his house; (b) Yhwh had given David rest from all his enemies. While the two images are linked by a simple conjunction (ו) that is typically translated as "and" (the king is settled *and* Yhwh had given him rest), the issue is more involved because both author and audience share in a game of reading between the lines. By linking these particular two ideas the author invites the following interpretation of the *vav* conjunction: the king is settled in his house *but only because* Yhwh had given him rest from all his enemies around him.

This reference to David's security and rest reverses the true chronological sequence: Yhwh gives David rest; then the king is able to settle in his house. Such manipulation of temporal ordering is one of the hallmarks of biblical narrative,[7] and by reversing the sequence the author calls attention to the cause-effect relationship. With respect to the overarching story of David's rise to power in the deuteronomistic history, the statement that Yhwh had given David rest also appears to be out of its chronological place. The Chronicler duplicates virtually all of the elements of the plot from the opening scene of 2 Sam 7 (cf. 1 Chr 17:1–3), but omits the reference to Yhwh giving David rest, perhaps because 2 Sam 8's catalogue of David's wars makes it clear that David is not at this time enjoying rest from

[6] Shimon Bar-Efrat, *Narrative Art in the Bible* (Sheffield: Almond, 1989), 64–65.

[7] Cf. Kenneth Craig, *A Poetics of Jonah: Art in the Service of Ideology* (2nd ed.; Macon, Ga.: Mercer University Press, 1999), 77–88.

his enemies. Thus, information conveyed in the initial verse of chapter 7 appears to be chronologically out of place on two counts, and this rearranging serves a distinct rhetorical purpose: the initial statement sets the stage for the characterization of God in charge (or at least able to look after David) that will be approached from multiple angles throughout the chapter.

The opening verse also functions at another level. It contains key words—בית "house," ישב "dwelling," כל "all"—that may be interpreted in the light of former events and that gain in rhetorical strength throughout the chapter. The report of David's living in security stands in sharp contrast to the time when he and his troops "wandered wherever they could go" in 1 Sam 23:13 (cf. God's words in 7:6–7). David's first quoted speech about his "dwelling" in a "house" in v 2 is reminiscent of the narrator's first words in v 1 (a form of ישב and בית is used by both David and the narrator), but David adds an important word: he now lives in a house of cedars (ארזים). A house of cedar would have been a well-constructed and impressive building fit for any king or queen. Tents, on the other hand, could be blown away or suffer the ravages of nature, and they were inhabited by nomads, members of a lower stratum of society. This repetition with variation on the word בית is but one clue among many that reveals the author as an artist. The word will be repeated a number of times in the chapter, and it will often carry a new shade of meaning. Characterization is achieved through this type of repetition. The contrast between a king residing in a strong house and God's ark residing in a transportable tent is striking. Now that God has given David rest from his enemies, what could be more natural than acknowledging the favor?

The considerations that prompt David to think of building a "house" (בית) for Yhwh are commendable, and they set an initial stage by establishing the king as grateful to Yhwh. David's desire in this context is certainly not unlike that of other kings of the ancient Near East. Michiko Ota describes the god-king-temple phenomenon:

> The relationship god-king-temple was clear. A king was a mediator between the divine and the human worlds and, as such, he carried an immense load of responsibilities in two directions: heavenward to assure the gods of the devotion of the people, and earthward to confirm the fertility thus resulting from the gods' pleasure. One of the most important of the royal duties was to build, rebuild, and repair the gods' earthly abodes—the temples—and to keep them and their functions

> in good condition. None of those activities, however, could be undertaken at a king's own will or whim. The sole authorizing power rested with gods.[8]

In a chapter where key words (בית "house," ישב "dwelling," כל "all") are often repeated, the reader may be struck by one word that is absent in v 2. In conversation with Nathan, David alludes to his desire to build a house (that is a temple) for Yhwh, but conveys his thought without uttering the word בית (temple).[9] Just as the narrator conveys two pieces of information in v 1 (David's rest/God's responsibility for it), David now conveys two facts in his speech to Nathan in v 2: the king lives in a cedar house; the ark of God resides in a tent. This second sequence is not causal, as in v 1, but contrastive. It is the comparison between David in a house and the ark in a tent that invites Nathan (and the audience) to infer David's desire. David's wish may be self-evident, yet he does not say the word בית when referring to the ark of God. Nathan also avoids the word in his prompt response to the king to do all that he has in mind. Thus this key term (בית, with the nuance of "temple") is not mentioned in this opening scene, but it will often appear in the subsequent recorded speech.[10] Such changes at the linguistic level lay the groundwork for the subsequent changes at the thematic level as David's desire is recast by God.

The implications of this phenomenon, which we might describe as a reversal situation (the key word בית is avoided [vv 1–3], but then often repeated [vv 5–16]), may be observed in a more pronounced and significant way by focusing on the prophet Nathan. Why does Nathan even appear in this context? Why doesn't David voice his thoughts directly to God (as he had on separate occasions as recently as 2:1 and 5:19)? And what are we to make of the prophet's poor advice in v 3? The series of events in the opening

[8] Michiko Ota, "A Note on 2 Sam 7," *A Light Unto My Path. OT Studies in Honor of J. M. Myers*, Gettysburg Theological Studies 4 (ed. H. N. Bream et al.; Philadelphia: Temple University Press, 1974), 404.

[9] David does use the word בית to refer to his house, but avoids it when referring to his thoughts about a temple. When translating from the Hebrew, the single word is conveyed by multiple English words ("house," "temple," "palace," "dynasty").

[10] Vv 5, 6, 7. Cf. also vv 1, 2, 11, 13, 16, 18, 19, 25, 26, 27, 29.

scene may cause us to conjecture that the prophet's appearance serves some kind of rhetorical purpose, but what is it? Nathan appears in David's court on three separate occasions (here, in 2 Sam 12, and in 1 Kgs 1), and we may find provisional answers to these questions by looking for clues when Nathan appears at the court.

David seeks advice of the prophet in 2 Sam 7, and this situation is rare. Robert Polzin has called attention to the different postures that Saul and David take with respect to prophets. On the one hand, Saul actively seeks a prophet when inquiring of God (cf. 1 Sam 9:9–10; 28:6, and 28:15). David, on the other hand, is more reluctant to take the initiative.[11] Thus in 2 Sam 12:1–15 Nathan appears, but unsummoned, to confront the king just after David lies with Bathsheba. Nathan appears on the scene having been "sent by Yhwh" (2 Sam 12:1), and David is obviously unsuspecting, as his harsh words about himself reveal ("As Yhwh lives, the man who has done this deserves to die" [v 5b]). On this occasion, the court prophet avoids the language of the court. The narrator describes Nathan's entrance in a neutral tone: "[Nathan] came to [David], and said to him" (12:1); "Nathan said to David" (vv 7, 13); "then Nathan went to his house" (v 15). Nowhere in the parable of the poor man's ewe lamb does Nathan adopt any of the titles or language of the court, as he will elsewhere.

In 1 Kgs 1:22–27 the prophet appears once again as an uninvited guest, but this time his speech is marked by a different tone; he addresses the king with words that follow the rules of court decorum. The narrator tells us that Nathan bows before the king with his face to the ground (v 23), and then addresses the king with the words "My lord the king" (v 24). The prophet subsequently refers to David's "servant Solomon" (v 26) and then refers to David as "my lord the king" (v 27). Nathan also refers to himself as one of the king's "servants" (v 27) and then again to David as "my lord the king" (v 27). In these two passages the correspondence between style and content reinforces the impact of the speeches.

It is in 2 Sam 7 that David makes the unusual move by initiating conversation with Nathan, and it is the one time that Nathan's words mislead *us*. The prophet's instruction, "Go, do all that you

[11] Robert Polzin, *Samuel and the Deuteronomist: A Literary Study of the Deuteronomic History (1 Samuel)* (New York: Harper & Row, 1989), 184.

have in mind; for Yhwh is with you" (v 3), is hardly surprising. As recently as 5:10, the narrator had reported that "Yhwh . . . was with [David]," and previous actions against the Philistines (5:17–25) would also appear to support Nathan's commendation. Yet in this rare instance, the prophet misspeaks. Even though Nathan appears only for a short while—virtually all of the description and quoted speech is given over to David and Yhwh in this chapter—his role in this scene is crucial in terms of the characterization of God. His presence and short speech create a reversal situation. This misdirection that David (and we) experience results from what seems to be a reasonable desire on David's part and the prophet's encouraging words. That very night (v 4) the word of Yhwh comes to Nathan. We learn with Nathan that the prophet has given David bad advice, which God will correct subsequently in an extensive fashion. Having hardly recovered from God's quick attempt that night to correct God's own prophet, the reader will learn next how David's wish is transformed in the specific words of the extended oracle (vv 5–16). The human initiative is negated, and our expectations are quashed as early as v 5. Even the prophet emerges as a fallible spokesperson in this context. Immediately, and in an extended fashion, God is portrayed as redirecting the course of human desires.

Thus the reader is set up in the opening scene by means of David's initiative and the prophet's blessing. God responds, beginning in v 5, with decisive words that alter the humans' situation. The prophet's complete submission to God—it is worth noting that Nathan's response to the oracle also characterizes God—is expressed subsequently in v 17, where we learn precisely how Yhwh's speech is conveyed to David: "in accordance with all these words and with all this vision" (ככל הדברים האלה וככל החזיון הזה). V 17 complements v 4 with a visual image (חזיון), and by the time of the report of Nathan's execution of Yhwh's command (v 17), the word כל ("all") is familiar: "all [David's] enemies" (v 1); "go, do all" (v 3); "I have cut off all your enemies" (v 9); "I will give you rest from all your enemies" (v 11). The doubling of ככל in v 17, however, emphasizes the point that Nathan passes on God's words to David verbatim. Thus God is characterized before God speaks (vv 1–4), in the extended oracle itself (vv 5–16), and by the narrator's report of God's words revealed to David via Nathan (v 17).

God's Questions and the Oracle

As mentioned above, the narrator frequently reports action in the Hebrew Bible (as we observed in 2 Sam 6 and 8), but in 2 Sam 7 the narrator's role diminishes. The narrator does report that the "king was settled" (v 1); that "the word of Yhwh came to Nathan" (v 4); that "in accordance with all these words . . . Nathan spoke" (v 17); and that "David went in and sat before Yhwh" (v 18). But virtually all of the characterization in this chapter is accomplished by the speaking characters themselves. When God delivers the first major speech in the oracle of vv 5–16, language and syntax continue to play an important role in characterization. Yhwh's first words to Nathan, "Go and tell" (לך ואמרת) in v 5, are reminiscent of the prophet's instructions to David reported outside the oracle itself in v 3: "go, do" (לך עשה). Nathan offers David a green light: "Go, do all that you have in mind." Yhwh, on the other hand, redirects Nathan (who later re-directs David) with the words "Go and tell . . . 'Are you the one to build me a house to live in?'" Such a shift in tone affects characterization. Nathan's initial words to David, "Go, do all," help the reader establish a first impression; however, Yhwh's first words to Nathan quickly dispel the view that David is the one in charge here: it is Yhwh who offers a great surprise through the spoken word and in so doing quickly makes clear Yhwh's desire to control the action. The similarity in speech—Nathan's first word is the same as Yhwh's—is not a coincidence. Neither is the difference reflected in the change of the second imperative (from "do" to "tell"), which anticipates the characterization that will be accomplished from this point forward by the speech of characters ("tell") rather than the narrator's report of action ("do").

Clues other than the large units of quoted direct speech suggest that the spoken word plays an important role in this chapter. For example, Yhwh's words in vv 5–16 are actually reported as Yhwh's speech. The narrator could have indicated initially that Nathan received words and a vision from Yhwh, that Nathan approached David, and then that Nathan shared Yhwh's words with the king and with us simultaneously. When Nathan approaches the king on a separate occasion (2 Sam 12), the account of Yhwh's speech is recorded through Nathan's voice: "Nathan said to David, 'You are the man! Thus says Yhwh, the God of Israel: I anointed you king over Israel, and I rescued you from the hand of Saul . . .'" (v 7).

And Nathan continues, "Thus says Yhwh: I will raise up trouble against you from within your own house . . ." (v 11). God is characterized by means of direct speech, but Nathan's speech—not God's—characterizes God in 2 Sam 12. With respect to the Nathan passages,[12] Yhwh's first-degree speech appears only in 2 Sam 7.

Speech itself is also highlighted in 2 Sam 7 by means of embedded markers. First, God alludes to the absence of speech: "[in the past,] Did I ever speak a word with any of the tribal leaders of Israel . . . saying, 'Why have you not built me a house of cedar?'" (v 7). Second, David, in his response to the oracle, quotes God: "For you, O Yhwh of hosts, the God of Israel, have made this revelation to your servant, saying, 'I will build you a house'" (v 27). Third, God's extended speech in 2 Sam 7:5–16 falls into three parts. The three segments of the oracle (vv 5–7, 8–11a, 11b–16) are marked off in slightly different fashions (in vv 5a, 8a, 11b), but in each case an embedded speech pattern allows the addressee and the audience to refocus attention on the material within the three layers[13] of the oracle itself. The specific rhetorical function of each layer will be considered below, but first the introductions to these narrative blocks may be isolated:

1. Go and tell my servant David: Thus says Yhwh: [First layer of the oracle]
   לך ואמרת עבדי אל דוד כה אמר יהוה. . . (v 5a)
2. Now therefore thus you shall say to my servant David: Thus says Yhwh of hosts: [Second layer of the oracle]
   ועתה כה תאמר לעבדי לדוד כה אמר יהוה צבאות. . . (v 8a)

[12] In the third and only other passage where Nathan appears before the king (1 Kings 1), the prophet does not invoke Yhwh's name. He advises Bathsheba that she should "go in at once to King David and say to him, 'Did you not, my lord the king, swear to your servant, saying: Your son Solomon shall succeed me as king, and he shall sit on my throne? Why then is Adonijah king?'" (v 13). Bathsheba follows Nathan's advice but changes his words. She invokes Yhwh's name. She approaches David and says, "My lord, you swore to your servant by Yhwh your God, saying: Your son Solomon shall succeed me as king, and he shall sit on my throne. But now suddenly Adonijah has become king, though you, my lord the king, do not know it" (vv 17–18). In similar fashion, David responds, "As Yhwh lives, who has saved my life from every adversity, as I swore to you by Yhwh, the God of Israel" (vv 29–30).

[13] While the term "layers" has source-critical connotations, I use it here to denote integrated segments.

3. Moreover Yhwh declares to you that Yhwh will make you a house: [Third layer of the oracle]
   והגיד לך יהוה כי בית יעשה לך יהוה... (v 11b)

At each of these points of the oracle, the author introduces what appears to be the narrator's, as opposed to God's, words. If a report of direct speech is one of the most dramatic means of conveying characters' psychological and ideological points of view, the momentary blending of perspectives accentuates the spoken word. It is the combined viewpoints that allow us to sense the drama of Nathan's nocturnal encounter with God, and, ironically, the blending of points of view proves to be a fine rhetorical tool for conveying the author's view of God's place in Israel's history. At precisely these three points in the oracle (vv 5a, 8a, 11b), two speech events are combined: that of the reporter (i.e., narrator) and that of the reportee (in this case, God). I call these places where another point of view enters the narrative *combined viewpoint markers*.

The First Layer of the Oracle (vv 5–7)

The first portion of the oracle is introduced with a double phrase. The conventional declaration "thus says Yhwh" is here preceded by the imperatives "go and tell my servant David." God's initial words to Nathan reinforce the type of relationship that exists between God and David: David is God's servant. An association had of course already been suggested by the narrator, who described David's security as the result of Yhwh's gift of rest from his enemies (v 1). In the much broader context of the deuteronomistic history, the word עבדי ("my servant") is especially forceful because it is so seldom conferred by God.[14] God applies the title only to Moses (Josh 1:2 and 1:7; 2 Kgs 21:8) and David (2 Sam 3:18; 7:5, 7:8; 1 Kgs 11:13, 32, 34, 36, 38, and 14:8; 2 Kgs 19:34 and 20:6) in the deuteronomistic history. By inviting a comparison with Moses, the author calls attention to the importance of God's speech even before the oracle is delivered. Like Moses, David plays a vital role in Israel's history; yet both leaders stand in a subordinate relationship to Yhwh.

[14] J. P. Fokkelman, *Narrative Art and Poetry in the Books of Samuel: A Full Interpretation Based on Stylistic and Structural Analyses* (Throne & City: II Sam. 2–8 & 21–24), vol. 3. Studia semitica neerlandica 27; Assen/Maastricht: Van Gorcum, 1990) 214.

Yhwh and David invoke several questions in 2 Sam 7. Both use rhetorical questions to introduce their speeches. The important rhetorical function of questions in this chapter is emphasized when we recall that one central thought is on David's mind: may I build a temple for Yhwh? Yet this thought is not expressed as an interrogative. The question David has on his mind is expressed as a declarative suggestion: A is the case; therefore B should follow. This discrepancy between thought (should I build?) vs. speech (I should build) is revealing. David wishes to build, and by avoiding the interrogative in speech he is able to suggest that his desire should be realized. The important rhetorical function that questions play in 2 Sam 7 is also evident when we observe that the Chronicler, who follows the text of 2 Sam 7 closely, changes the initial rhetorical question that Yhwh speaks to Nathan from "Are you the one to build me a house to live in?" (v 5) to a statement, "You shall not build me a house to live in" (1 Chr 17:4).

The first layer of the oracle contains two questions that Yhwh addresses to Nathan, which Nathan in turn addresses to David (v 17). These questions serve a foundational role in the characterization of God. The first is "Are (ה) you the one to build me a house to live in?" (v 5). And the second is "Wherever I have moved about among all the people of Israel, did (ה) I ever speak a word with any of the tribal leaders of Israel, whom I commanded to shepherd my people Israel, saying, "'Why (למה) have you not built me a house of cedar?'" (v 7).

The characterization of God is achieved in part through these rhetorical questions because the asking itself suggests divine indignation (GKC: §150d). All of the questions that God, an omniscient, asks are rhetorical rather than information-seeking. Indeed, God has a virtual monopoly on thoughts and performative utterances. Characterization is achieved not only through these rhetorical questions, but also by their answers. By definition, answers to rhetorical questions are implied, but here Yhwh actually supplies an answer to make the point: "[No,] I have not lived in a house since the day I brought up the people of Israel from Egypt" (v 6). God appears to reject dwelling in a temple, but the refusal is provisional as suggested by the emphatic pronouns in the Hebrew, which may be rendered: "Do *you* want to build a house for *me*?" God's denial concerns the person of David and not the temple itself as the emphatic position of the pronoun האתה ("Do you?") makes clear. More of the answer to the question is found in the second layer of the oracle ("He shall build a house for my name," v 13a), and emphasis is made in v 13, where the emphatic הוא יבנה ("he shall build") parallels the forceful denial of v 5. By answering the rhetorical question God emerges early as the one in charge; the choice of the builder is God's to make.

The two questions form a frame in this first layer of the oracle, and they both contain key words: "you" (sg. and pl.), "build," and בית ("house"/"temple"). In the second rhetorical question of the frame, the singular "you" of v 5 merges into the plural "you"—the leaders of Israel, who thus far have never built a dwelling place for Yhwh (v 7). David, the individual, fades from view and is replaced by a collective human partner, the Israelites. An important word, "build," that we conjecture David considers but does not utter in conversation with Nathan, also appears in both questions. What has been alluded to previously (v 2) is now made clear, and it is God who leaves no doubt when expressing an opinion on David's plan about building. Just as God now takes the initiative in speaking, God will also take the initiative in building. God contrasts the past with the present by means of the word בית (vv 5–6): "A house for me to live in" (בית לשבתי) in v 5 is paralleled by the negative, "I have never lived in a house" (כי לא ישבתי בבית) in v 6. God has not commanded the construction of the temple to any of Israel's past leaders, nor to David himself.

These two questions call the reader's attention to the material inside the frame: to history, the period between the exodus and the monarchy. The focus of God's interest in the welfare of the nation becomes obvious as Israel is mentioned as many as four times in vv 6–7: "I have not lived in a house since the day I brought up the people of Israel from Egypt. . . . Wherever I have moved about among all the people of Israel, did I ever speak a word with any of the tribal leaders of Israel, whom I commanded to shepherd my people Israel?" (v 6). A contrast is suggested between David's residing (ישב) in a house of v 1 and now God's "moving about" (מתהלך) in a tent and a tabernacle in v 6. The contrast continues in v 7 as God refers to "moving about" (התהלכתי) among the Israelites. God's existence is really not analogous to that of the well-intentioned David. The king suggested through analogy (v 2) that God should have what David has, but God rejects the same sort of living quarters as the king. This opposition between the human and divine realms will be carried further in the second layer of the oracle, and the contrast will reach its highest expression in the final layer. In each layer of the oracle one finds an expression of the ideologically significant view that Yhwh is not bound to one place but can choose a dwelling anywhere. By means of repetition throughout God's speech, a central concept is emphasized: God's ways contrast with the habits and customs of mortals.

The Second Layer of the Oracle (vv 8–11a)

The second layer of the oracle highlights one family and establishes David as the founder of a dynasty. Throughout this layer God emphasizes leadership by means of chosen individuals (David, the judges). While the divine promise to David has already been mentioned (by David himself in 2 Sam 6:21), the view now emerges in a broader sense. The intimate relationship that God has had with the people, emphasized in the first layer, is concentrated in the blessing of an individual in vv 8–9. God led the Israelites up from Egypt (v 6) and then delegated authority to the judges to "shepherd" the people of Israel (v 7). Now the delegation of authority is transferred to the shepherd David who is "to be prince over [God's] people Israel" (v 8).

At the beginning of the second layer of the oracle proper, one finds the independent pronoun "I" (אני), which in the Hebrew is unnecessary since the pronominal suffix is attached to the verbal form לקחתיך ("I took you"). This emphasis highlights God's initiative, while the single word לקחתיך suggests an "I-you" relationship: David ("you") is presented as the beneficiary of Yhwh's ("I") action. לקחתיך also reinforces the reference to "my servant" that stands at the beginning of the oracle (v 5). In addition, the phrase "I have been with you" (ואהיה עמך) in v 9 is reminiscent of the prophet's words to David, "Yhwh is with you" (יהוה עמך) in v 3.

We noted earlier that the narrator does not describe a great deal of action in 2 Sam 7. However, action is revealed in the words of the characters throughout much of the chapter. This phenomenon of characterization through speech is particularly evident in the second layer of the oracle. Shlomith Rimmon-Kenan discusses the relationship between action and characterization, and concludes that "a trait may be implied both by one-time (or non-routine) actions [or] . . . by contrast, habitual actions [that] tend to reveal the character's unchanging or static aspect."[15] Yhwh describes such "habitual actions" and thus reveals an "unchanging or static aspect" of character in this layer of the oracle. The specific guidance and care that David knows firsthand is recounted: "I took you . . . I have been with you" (vv 8–9). It is the previous experience of God's care both for David and the people Israel that now provides a vision and foundation of hope for the future: "I will make for you a great name . . . I will appoint a place for my people Israel" (vv 9–10). At the end of v 10 Yhwh appeals "to the very beginning" (בראשונה), a temporal designation that may cause the reader to think of the bondage in Egypt alluded to in the first layer of the oracle (v 6). Again, the positive acts of God, appointing and planting (v 10), are given meaning based on the past. This image of Israel, "planted" and secure—like David who is "settled" (ישב) in his house (v 1)—calls attention to the author's attempt to highlight a difference between God and humans.

In this second layer of the oracle, the portrayal of God is also accomplished by God's words about the people of Israel. In vv 9c–11b Israel becomes the direct object of God's concern. Promise of "a house" includes "a great name" for David in v 9 as well as a place for the people of Israel "that they may dwell in their own place, and be disturbed no more" (v 10). In the introduction (vv 1–4), no attention was given to the people. Our thoughts were drawn instead to the aspirations and advice of David and Nathan. In each of the layers of the oracle, on the other hand, God highlights the people of Israel (vv 6–7, 8, 10–11, 12, 16). God's initiative will ensure that the kingdom provides security and justice for all Israel (v 10). The "dynasty" (בית) is not an end in itself; it ensures God's proper, just rule of the people.

The Third Layer of the Oracle (vv 11b–16)

We meet once again a combined viewpoint marker embedded within Yhwh's own speech that signals a new layer of the oracle. This third speech marker (v 11b) serves as a type of headline or announcement, which the third layer proper of the oracle (vv 12–16) develops. The marker is followed by a series of "I" statements that punctuate the final part of the oracle: "I will raise up . . . I will estab-

[15] Rimmon-Kenan, *Narrative Fiction*, 61.

lish his kingdom . . . I will establish the throne . . . I will be a father to him . . . I will punish him . . . I will not take my steadfast love . . . as I took it from Saul, whom I put away" (vv 12–15). The author emphasizes in this passage that God is the causal agent.

The first combined viewpoint markers (vv 5a, 8a) each contained two clauses, and once again this third layer of the oracle opens with two parts: "Moreover Yhwh declares to you / that Yhwh will make you a house." The first two markers each contained an introductory clause that called attention to speech: "go and tell" (אמרת) in v 5a; "thus you shall say" (תאמר) in v 8a. Both markers also incorporated a subsequent clause, the traditional prophetic formula, that reinforced the impulse of speech: "Thus says (אמר) Yhwh" (vv 5a, 8a). The third marker (v 11b) is the first to open with a verbal form, in this case הגיד ("declare"), that accentuates the speech phenomenon. Again, unlike the first two markers, the second clause of v 11b does not contain the expected "thus says Yhwh" formula (found in vv 5a and 8a). Instead, David learns (v 17) that Yhwh will make him a בית ("dynasty"). God's character is now drawn in this third layer by means of a new theme organized around a familiar word. In effect, David discovers that he will not build a בית ("house") for God; God will build a בית ("dynasty") for him. Yhwh's initiative involves a pun on two meanings of the word "house": the former requires building materials (a dwelling); the second requires people (a dynasty). David considers building a בית ("house") for Yhwh in v 2, and now that Yhwh vows to build a בית ("dynasty") for David (vv 11, 16), we are confronted with the main point of attack on David's plan to build a temple: if God requires a בית it will follow God's own plan. The human impulse to build a shrine is transposed to a new key through speech, as David is promised a new kind of בית. It is not a building that matters when it comes to the exercise of God's plan, but a human line that will serve as a conduit of divine care (vv 12, 15–16).

Yhwh does reveal that David's offspring will be allowed to build an edifice, but the building will not be a place of dwelling (ישב)—at least not in the same sense that the king "dwells" (ישב) in his house (v 1). This בית will eventually be built, God announces, "for my name," and by the person God chooses (v 13). In the rhetorically charged opening question, Yhwh had asked David if he is the one to build Yhwh a house to dwell in (v 5). The change from בית לשבתי ("house to dwell in") in v 5 to בית לשמי ("house for my name") in v 13—the initial לש and final י sounds are similar—calls attention to God's uniqueness. This aspect of God's character is reinforced in this final portion of the speech when God indicates that nomadic life presents no real problem. In fact, God can do without the permanent security of residence that David now enjoys (v 1). The contrast between God and David was suggested in the previous layer of the oracle and applied also to the people of Israel: "I will appoint a place for my people Israel and will plant them, so that they may live in their own place" (v 10). The circuitous manner by which David expresses himself at the beginning of this story—David's thought is "May I build?" while his spoken words are "I am living in a house of cedar, but the ark of God stays in a tent"—now gains its true rhetorical strength: a nomadic existence (the ark in a tent) presents no problem for God at this moment in history.

Key words are repeated, once again, in the concluding portion of the oracle. God promises that David's בית ("dynasty") and kingdom "shall be made secure forever" (עד עולם) and that his "throne shall be established forever" (עד עולם; v 16). The temporal phrase is duplicated in the short narrative space of a single verse, and it is the final word of God's speech. The author has attempted throughout to portray God as the one in charge of history: the rest that David now enjoys is the direct result of God's action (v 1); Yhwh speaks to Nathan that very night (v 4) after David expresses his thoughts to Nathan; God refers to events both past and projected throughout the oracle (vv 6–15); and, at the end, God emphasizes that David's בית ("dynasty"), kingdom, and throne will be established עד עולם ("forever"). Vv 15b and 16a end with the same word, לפניך ("from before you"). Again the author uses events of the past to imply that God's words have implications that transcend the present moment. David is reminded that "Saul was previously put away from before you" (לפניך; v 15b) and is then told: "Your house and your kingdom shall be made sure forever before you" (לפניך; v 16a).

In retrospect, we discover that God never tells Nathan why David is not allowed to construct the temple. A specific reason will be given in 1 Chr 22:8. According to the Chronicler, it is not David who, with bloodstained hands from many wars, is allowed to build the temple, but the one whose name, Shelomoh (שלמה, "Solomon"), is a reminder of *shalom* (שלום, "peace") who is granted permission to build. Even David in his prayer recorded in vv 18b–29 does not allude to any reason why he is denied the opportunity to build God's בית ("house"). This lack of specificity also characterizes God. David is not allowed to build solely because of God's desire expressed in the context of 2 Sam 7. The main issue is that the initiative for building the temple and the choice of that builder shall come from God and not from the individual king. Thus 2 Sam 7 blends four points of view (the narrator's, Nathan's, God's, and David's) to present the author's view of God transforming human initiative.

In sum, characterization is achieved in 2 Sam 7 through the invocation of questions and a preponderance of dialogue. By paying attention to the contours of speech one gains insight into characterization in this passage, which is neither "dreary prose" nor "a mire of unintelligible verbiage." Dialogue often sheds light on both the speaker and addressee, and a number of words show that speech serves distinct rhetorical purposes. Combined points of view appear in vv 5a, 8a, and 11b. At precisely these three points in the oracle, two speech events are combined: that of the reporter and that of the reportee. Verses 1–17 blend several points of view while presenting God as a causal agent who transforms David's desire to build a temple. The human impulse to build a shrine is modified through speech as David learns that he will not build a בית ("house" or "temple") for God; God will build a בית ("dynasty") for him. Direct speech thus provides a dramatic means for conveying God's psychological and ideological points of view.

CHAPTER TEN

THE DUPLICITOUS QUESTION (1 KINGS 1:11–31)

Introduction

Leonhard Rost's influential book, first published in 1926, caused readers to view the content of 2 Sam 9–20 and 1 Kgs 1–2 as a unified literary unit. This succession narrative, Rost argued, answers the question, Who will next sit on David's throne? Rost stressed the importance of the first two chapters of 1 Kings for they are the key to understanding the entire document, 2 Sam 9 through 1 Kgs 2.[1] Within the large court history narrative we find stories about political life in Israel during the precarious moments of the beginning of the monarchy. These stories prove to be more about the inner workings of the royal family, of sibling rivalry and rape, of bad blood and spilled blood, of plotting and avenging than of unadorned details of succession. The beginning of a deception-and-subversion chain of events might be traced to David who, after sending messengers "to get" Bathsheba, "lies with her" (2 Sam 11:4). Their child, conceived as husband Uriah and "all Israel" fight the Ammonites, dies seven days after he is born. The tragedy is presented by the Historian as the result of divine action: "And Yhwh struck the child that the wife of Uriah bore to David" (12:15). By way of contrast, the second child born to Bathsheba and David in Jerusalem is Solomon, also called Jedidiah, "Beloved of Yhwh." First Kings 1–2 tells the story of how this son inherits the throne as two of the principals from 2 Sam 11–12—Bathsheba and Nathan—reenter the picture.

Between these two narrative points of birth and enthronement is a story of a dysfunctional family, as intense in tone and as complicated in breadth as the sibling, parent-child, and various in-law rivalry stories of the first families (Gen 3–4 and 12–50). In the book of Samuel, between the account of Solomon's birth and enthronement,

[1] Leonhard Rost, *Überlieferung von der Thronnachfolge Davids*, BWANT 3/6 (Stuttgart: Kohlhammer, 1926).

we read of another of David's sons raping his half-sister; he himself is murdered by an avenging half-brother who subsequently seizes the throne (momentarily). This half-brother, Absalom, dies tragically, hanging from a tree as he is bludgeoned three times in the heart. And in the midst of the rivalry, greed, deceit, and bloodshed, we witness the personal and private dimensions of a father's grief: "And the king grieved, and he went up to the chamber over the gate. And he wept. And he said as he went: O my son Absalom. My son, my son Absalom. Would that I had died instead of you. O Absalom, my son, my son" (19:1).

1 Kings 1

As David's health declines, son Adonijah threatens another son, Solomon, as he vies for the prize of the crown (1 Kgs 1). The elder Adonijah is aggressive; the younger Solomon appears initially as a quiet pawn whose future at court depends upon the success of an alliance that brings Bathsheba and the court prophet Nathan together in a counterplot. David's days are waning. First Kings 1:11–31 features an interchange among three people at court: the ailing King David, his wife Bathsheba, and the court prophet Nathan. Duplicity reigns. In an effort to guarantee Solomon's place on the throne, Nathan devises a plan whereby the old king will take action that will circumvent the maneuverings of Adonijah and his supporters. This plot unfolds through dialogue seasoned with interrogatives, which Nathan intends Bathsheba to invoke in the king's presence. Scholars are divided on the matter of whether or not Nathan asks Bathsheba to lie to her husband. If we assume that no lies are told—and it does not give the argument away to say that this is a grand supposition—there is no doubt that Nathan's words and questions are intended to trick David into action so that Solomon's new throne would be secure. Nathan invokes no less than five questions in two of the four scenes, which may be abbreviated as follows:

> Scene i: Have you not heard? Did you not swear? Why is Adonijah reigning?
> Scene iii: Have you said? Has my lord brought this about?

These questions, enhanced by dialogue that surrounds them, develop from the plot sequence conveyed in the previous scene (vv 5–10).

The very handsome Adonijah—the attention to physical appearance may or may not bode well[2]—has exalted himself and proclaimed that he will be king! The announcement is made with considerable fanfare: chariots, horsemen, and fifty men run before him. He confers with Joab, commander of the army, and Abiathar, the priest. He sacrifices oxen, fatted cattle, and sheep, and invites "all" his brothers (but not Solomon) and the royal officials of Judah. Spoiled by his father (v 6) and now supported by Joab and Abiathar, this handsome son is not unopposed in his claim to the throne. Trouble brews below the surface; many people are not with Adonijah: Zadok, Nathan, Shimei, Rei, Benaiah, David's warriors, and brother Solomon (v 10).

Who is Adonijah? He is David's fourth (2 Sam 3:4) and eldest surviving son.[3] (We know of the deaths of Amnon and Absalom from 2 Sam 13:28 and 18:15. Chileab's death is not mentioned in the Bible). When the narrator describes Adonijah "exalting himself, saying, I will be king," we might think of Absalom, whose matching words (and actions) plunged Israel into civil strife (2 Sam 15:10; 16:15–17:14). Additional details point to an analogy. We are told that both brothers get chariots with horses and fifty runners (2 Sam 15:1; 1 Kgs 1:5). Like Absalom, Adonijah is very handsome (2 Sam 14:25; 1 Kgs 1:6). With analogies drawn, all that remains is for details of Adonijah's fall to be worked out.

Tension develops around contours of the plot. Will old David, unwarmed by clothes and impotent beside the youthful virgin Abishag (vv 1, 4), be able to summon enough command in a time of crisis to wield influence on the matter of succession? He is no longer capable of dealing with the affairs of government, and he was unable to manage the ploys of his own family even during more virile days. We know of his physical incapacity, but what about his mental disposition? Will he become a pawn in the hands of those who know how to manipulate? By contrast, we have seen young David quite able to assume control of his affairs and quite capable of working

[2] Cf. 1 Sam 10:23–24 and 16:12 with 2 Sam 14:25.

[3] David Howard expresses this view when he writes, "Presumably he [Chileab] had died, along with David's first- and third-born sons, Amnon and Absalom, when David's fourth son Adonijah attempted to seize the throne" (*ABD* 1. 907). And the NRSV critical note to 1 Kgs 1:5–10 indicates that "Chileab seems to have died young."

at the helm of government: his return to Jerusalem after Absalom's revolt (19:10–19a; 42–44), his swiftness in suppressing Sheba's rebellion (20:1–22), his expiation for the Gibeonites (21:1–9) leave no doubt that he has never shown a desire to surrender the throne.

In this chapter, versions of Adonijah's ploy to succeed David is narrated four times: by the narrator (vv 5–10), by Nathan to Bathsheba (v 11), by Bathsheba to David (18–19), and by Nathan to David (vv 25–26). The narrator's version, twice retold by Nathan and once recounted by Bathsheba, undergoes a series of modifications, and, upon arriving at the end in the king's presence with Bathsheba (v 28), one learns of yet another account of succession, this one, the most consequential of them all, projected in the king's own voice.

(a) prelude	narrator's report (vv 5–10)
(b) dialogue scene i	Nathan speaks to Bathsheba (vv 11–14)
(c) dialogue scene ii	Bathsheba speaks to David (vv 15–21)
(d) dialogue scene iii	Nathan speaks to David (vv 22–27)
(e) dialogue scene iv	David speaks to Bathsheba (vv 28–31)

A central question propels our reading as the author pits voices against one another: How (or will) David react to Adonijah's plot and the double-pronged wife-prophet counterplot?

Scene i

> 11And Nathan said to Bathsheba, mother of Solomon, Did you not (הלא) hear that Adonijah, son of Haggith, has become king, and our lord David doesn't know about it? 12And now (ועתה), come, let me advise you so that you may save your life and the life of your son Solomon. 13Go quickly to King David and say to him, Did you not (הלא), my lord the king, swear to your maidservant saying: Indeed,[4] Solomon your son shall reign after me, and he shall sit upon my throne? So why (מדוע) is Adonijah reigning? 14All of a sudden (הנה), while you are still speaking with the king, I will come in after you and confirm your words.

The scene consists almost entirely of Nathan's speech, which shows a scheming man's mind at work. The cunning man hopes to catch the king unawares. The prophet initiates—but, we will soon discover,

[4] The Hebrew word כי may serve to introduce speech. It here follows לאמר which functions to indicate so-called direct discourse. In this case כי functions as a strong asservative, "indeed" or "surely."

does not control—this drama. Nathan works here behind the scenes. The prophet is a shrewd political man, critical at times, pleasing on other occasions: "You are the man!" he once reprimanded David, but later said, "Go, do all you have in mind, for Yhwh is with you" (2 Sam 7:3), only to be redirected that night by Yhwh. He will work with whatever means necessary, in heaven or on earth, to accomplish the task at hand.

His initiative in the opening chapter of 1 Kings contrasts with his other two appearances at court. In the first instance (2 Sam 7 = 1 Chr 17), Nathan is portrayed as eager to support David's initiative to build the temple, but redirects David after receiving word from Yhwh: Yhwh will build David a dynasty (בית); David will not build Yhwh a house (בית). On the other occasion (2 Sam 12), Nathan, having been sent by Yhwh, rebukes David in the parable of the poor man's ewe lamb. But now in 1 Kgs 1, *Nathan* initiates a ploy. The difference is so striking that Johannes Hempel proposed that two men share the same name.[5]

Early in the scene the men are introduced as sons of their mothers: Solomon is Bathsheba's son; Adonijah is the son of Haggith. Such introductions are usually made by way of the father.[6] The mothers are mentioned because their names serve a connotative purpose relevant to the plot. Double puns are reflected in both names. Adonijah, away at a festive coronation ceremony, is son of Haggith (חגית). The name is derived from חג and denotes eating and drinking on a holiday or special occasion (1 Sam 30:16). By contrast, Solomon is the son of Bathsheba, or "daughter of an oath." The solemn nature of the occasion that unfolds in 1 Kgs 1 is underscored by frequent oaths: Nathan advises Bathsheba to remind David that the king once swore that Solomon would reign next; in David's presence Bathsheba embellishes the command—he swore by Yhwh his God, Bathsheba says. The effort is not lost on the king who, at

---

[5] Johannes Hempel, *Geschichte und Geschichten im Alten Testament bis zum persischen Zeitalter* (Gütersloh: Gütersloher – G. Mohn, 1964), 131.

[6] 1 Sam 1:1; 8:2; 10:11; 13:16; 14:3, 50, 51; 16:18; 17:12; 22:9, 20; 23:6; 25:44; 26:5, 6; 27:2; 30:7; 2 Sam 2:13; 3:15, 23, 25; 4:8; 8:3, 12, 16, 17, 18; 9:4, 5, 6; 10:2; 11:3, 21; 13:37; 14:1; 15:27; 16:5; 17:27; 18:2, 22; 19:17, 22; 20:2, 23, 24; 21:19; 23:9, 11, 18, 29, 33, 34, 36, 37. Though cf. 1 Sam 9:1. When step-children are born, the names of mothers are sometimes included (2 Sam 3:3–4; 21:8).

the end, "swears" as he "swore" before. In 2:19–25, Bathsheba has a "small request" of King Solomon—that Abishag be given to Adonijah as his wife. The proposal angers Solomon. She evokes an oath from him who "swears by Yhwh" that Adonijah shall be put to death.

In the first dialogue scene, the action is conveyed through Nathan's singular speech, though his discourse is manifest at three levels:

Nathan's First-level Speech to Bathsheba (a + a′ = Frame 1):

> (a) Did you not hear that Adonijah, son of Haggith, has become king, and our lord David doesn't know about it? And now, come, let me advise you so that you may save your life and the life of your son Solomon. Go quickly to King David and say to him
>
> (a') All of a sudden, while you are still speaking with the king, I will come in after you and confirm your words.

Nathan's Projection of Bathsheba's Speech to David (b + b′ = Frame 2):

> (b) Did you not, my lord the king, swear to your maidservant saying
>
> (b') So why is Adonijah reigning?

Nathan's Projected Retrospective Speech of David (Centerpiece)

> (c) Indeed, Solomon your son shall reign after me, and he shall sit upon my throne.

The key word מלך ("king," "reign") appears in each component part of Nathan's opening speech: a (2x), b (1x), c (1x), b' (1x), a' (1x).

Nathan's First-level Speech to Bathsheba (Opening the a Frame)

In the first level of speech (frame 1), the verbal form מלך modifies Adonijah; in the second and third instances, it references David. Its twin purpose highlights a double concern: If David is not able to function as king, will Adonijah replace him? Born next after Absalom and a very handsome man (v 6), he may be the heir apparent. Indeed, David's older sons are all dead (see above). But the Bible has been challenging the notion of primogeniture from the beginning—second born Abel's sacrifice is preferred over first-born Cain's; Isaac, Jacob, and Joseph are all second or subsequent children. But there are also other clues that hint at tension below the surface. Zadok,

Shimei, Rei, and David's warriors have not sided with Adonijah, and the Historian has already made clear that Solomon is the only son born in Jerusalem.[7] He is also called Jedidiah, "beloved of Yhwh." Nathan says, "Adonijah has become king, and our lord does not know about it."

מלך אדניהו
ואדנינו לא ידע

At the intersection of these parallel lines are words which share the common root "lord." Adonijah's name means "Yh(wh) is my Lord," and David is frequently addressed with the honorific title in this passage.[8] The lines underscore the problems surrounding the situation. What are the implications of "Beloved of Yhwh" being opposed by "Yhwh is my Lord?" And furthermore, what are the implications of "lord" David "not knowing" that "Yhwh is my Lord" has proclaimed himself king? Who is in charge? Who will command Israel?

The prophet's introductory words are phrased in the form of an interrogative—Have you not heard? Nathan here intends to make Bathsheba receptive to learning (ידע), to involve her in the struggle for power, to put her in a defensive posture. The consequences will be colossal, he tells her, if she remains inactive: she and her son will lose their lives. His reference to Solomon as "your son" is, of course, unnecessary in her hearing. This citation will also be duplicated in Nathan's projected retrospective speech of David. These "superfluous" words carry great psychological weight.[9]

The dire circumstances are underscored by the frequent verbal forms that Nathan employs in a brief narrative space:

Have you not heard?
Adonijah has become king.
Come.
Let me advise you.
Save your life and Solomon's life.
Go quickly (lit. "go" and "come").
Say to him.

[7] Most of David's sons were born at Hebron.
[8] 1:11, 13, 31, 37, 43, 47.
[9] Cf. also the "unnecessary" but psychologically shaded family language in Genesis 22 and passim.

Nathan's Projection of Bathsheba's Speech to David (Opening the b Frame)

Nathan intends for Bathsheba to speak to her husband, and he projects her words in the b + b' frame. A and a' surround "her" words. Speech surrounds speech. She is to open with an interrogative: Did you not, my lord the king, swear? The question is intended to hold David responsible, and its format corresponds to Nathan's first level of speech to Bathsheba: Did you not hear? But the first words of (b) differ from their (a) frame counterpart in two important ways: hearing becomes swearing, and she is to draw David to action by the polite reminder: Did you not, *my lord the king*, swear to *your maidservant.* (Such attention to inequity in position is a hallmark of the Bible's bargaining scenes. Abraham, eager to buy land as a burial ground from the Hittites, reminds the landowners that he is a "stranger" and "alien." Responding in dialogue with him, they call him "lord" and "mighty prince.")[10] Deferential talk may bode well in the hearing of the king, but the reader, like Bathsheba, knows that these words are only projected speech. The Bible displays a myriad of messages transformed in delivery. The content of the oath appears at the heart of Nathan's discourse in yet another level of projected speech.

Nathan's Projected Retrospective Speech of David (Centerpiece)

Now we arrive at the heart of the matter. The oath appears as speech within speech within speech: Nathan speaks to Bathsheba, who is to speak to David about a promise made long ago. Is Bathsheba to remind David of this promise? Or is she introducing an idea that serves the new extemporaneous goals of Nathan-Bathsheba? Nowhere in 2 Samuel does the narrator record David making such a promise to his wife, and though the alleged oath is unverifiable, commentators have not been deterred from speculating on whether or not David once spoke the words. Three positions, represented by the quotations below, are discernible: the oath is (a) contrived or (b) genuine, or (c) the matter is unresolvable.

---

[10] Gen 23:4–6. And at the price of 400 shekels of silver (v 15), Ephron proposes an outlay that only a royal figure could afford! David will pay Araunah the Jebusite only 50 shekels for property, which includes cattle for sacrifice (2 Sam 24:24). Jeremiah will buy his cousin's field at Anatot for a mere 17 shekels (Jer 32:9).

(a) The oath is contrived

> Since this is the first notice of an oath on the elevation of Solomon, this is probably a case of auto-suggestion, Nathan exploiting the dotage of the king.[11]

> When Bathsheba says: "And now, my lord the king, the eyes of all Israel are upon you, to tell them who shall sit on the throne of my lord the king after him" (1:20), and Nathan adds: "You have not told your servants who should sit on the throne of my lord the king after him" (1:27), their words betray that David's pledge to Solomon was a fabrication. Evidently, there was neither pledge nor designation, but the indecision of a senile king who was vaguely expecting that the eldest son would be designated as his successor. If Solomon's supporters had stood idle, Adonijah would have been king. The narrative clearly tells us that the one who changed the current was not Adonijah but Solomon. In other words, Solomon gained his designation as David's successor by challenging the existing order supported by the regime, whose nominal ruler was doting David, and whose strong-man was Joab, commander-in-chief of the army.[12]

> The question is, *did* he so swear? And, as various critics have noted, there are good indications in the narrative that the claim is to be seen as fabricated for the occasion.
>
> Certainly it is remarkable that any other reference to thus [*sic*] crucial promise is missing from the story. Moreover the manner of its introduction here seems calculated to raise our suspicions. Nathan's opening words to Bathsheba, obviously designed to galvanize her into taking desperate measures, are not (as far as we can judge in terms of the narrative) strictly true; despite a rather ominous (and teasing) parallel with the circumstances of Absalom's rebellion (and the murder of Amnon), Adonijah's feast at En-Rogel is not in fact a coronation feast, at least not yet. Then it is noticeable that it is Nathan who puts the words of the alleged promise in Bathsheba's mouth.... And finally the way in which he stage manages an apparently independent confirmation appears highly contrived.
>
> The strong possibility exists, therefore, that we are witnessing an act of deliberate deception, an ingenious ploy by the Solomonic party.[13]

---

[11] John Gray, *I & II Kings*, 88.

[12] Tomoo Ishida, "Solomon's Succession to the Throne of David—A Political Analysis," *Studies in the Period of David and Solomon and Other Essays*, ed. Tomoo Ishida (Winona Lake, IN: Eisenbrauns, 1982), 179.

[13] David M. Gunn, *The Story of King David: Genre and Interpretation*, JSOTSup 6 (Sheffield: Sheffield Academic Press, 1989 reprint), 105–6.

(b) The oath is genuine

> The likelihood is, however, that he expected the reader to assume the oath. Why must everything be directly stated? In this case, if Nathan and Bathsheba and David were all so clear that David had indeed made such an oath, it should go without saying that it had actually occurred. [John] Gray . . . suggests that Nathan wants Bathsheba to practice auto-suggestion on a senile King David, getting him to think he has given such an oath even though he never did; such subtle psychologizing has to be beyond the naïve art [*sic*] of the narrator.[14]

(c) The matter is unresolvable

> One of the intriguing aspects of this whole story . . . is that we have no way of knowing whether David in fact made such a pledge in favor of Solomon or whether it is a pious (?) fraud that Nathan and Bathsheba are foisting on the old and failing king, who hardly seems to know at this point what is happening around him.[15]

> The present story is easily stamped as that of a court cabal to influence the king in his dotage with the impromptu invention of such a promise. . . . However the present case is not without analogy in the ancient world, where queens themselves were masterful persons. . . . David's choice of Solomon as successor may well have been the result of Bathsheba's influence on her old husband. But it may have coincided with his own judgment.[16]

What are we to make of these disparate views? The narrator never resolves the question of whether or not David swore to Bathsheba, but instead provides enough clues to tempt us to believe that it is possible—and this is as precise as we should be—that the oath is nothing more than language engineered by the king's prophet and spoken in execution by the king's wife. To argue for or against the authenticity of the oath is to rob the text of its rich ambiguity. The narrator has made (vv 1–4) and will make (v 15) enough of David's infirmity to allow for the possibility that both prophet and wife are opportunists. Even David's own subsequent attestation (v 30) remains suspect, but ultimately the narrator keeps us in the dark throughout.

---

[14] Simon J. de Vries, *I Kings*, WBC (Waco: Word Books, 1985), 10, 15.

[15] Alter, *Art of Biblical Narrative*, 98.

[16] James A. Montgomery, *A Critical and Exegetical Commentary on the Books of Kings*, ICC (Edinburgh: T. & T. Clark, 1951), 74–75.

J. P. Fokkelman, who also finds it unnecessary to resolve the matter, notes:

> I value this abstruseness as a literary asset and find it unnecessary to seek a "solution." How strange that the work itself never mentions David's promise to Bathsheba! We could have expected its notation, for example, at the end of II Sam. 12, in which Solomon's nickname, Jedidiah, subtly anticipates his future importance. This is yet more curious if the work were truly a Thronfolgegeschichte in which the concluding section is meant to legitimize Solomon's succession, as Whybray et al. suppose. The oath might have played a part in the Absalom affair as well.[17]

What is more certain is that old David is both forgetful and likely to believe (or too proud to admit) that he could forget. These real possibilities propel their actions. They must convince and/or remind David that he spoke the oath, but even more, they must persuade him to act upon it now.

Nathan's Projection of Bathsheba's Speech to David (Closing b' Frame)

After projecting the king's words within the projected speech of Bathsheba, Nathan frames "her" speech. What the prophet proposes is a simple three-word question: So-why-is Adonijah reigning? She is to ask it just after "reminding" David of his oath. It may prompt the king to action.

Nathan's First-Level Speech to Bathsheba (Closing a' Frame)

Nathan's plan has two parts, which he explains in the opening frame and in the conclusion to the frame. Bathsheba will "remind" David of his oath, then Nathan will enter the king's presence and immediately verify her assertion. In the opening (a) frame of his first-level speech, Nathan spoke of "our lord David." But in (a') the plural reference is manifest as a "you-I-you" sequence: while you are speaking I will come in after you. They remain united in their common goal, even as they work individually. With the speech-within-speech-within-speech design outlined in the opening scene, misquotation is an ostensible possibility, and Nathan's plan of entering the room to confirm her words also carries certain risks. What if he does not

[17] Fokkelman *Narrative Art*, vol. 1, 354.

hear her talk to the king? Given the ailing monarch's infirmity, will he confirm or confound her words? If his entrance is not well timed, David might confuse the projected confirmation. Potential problems propel our reading.

Scene ii

> [15]And Bathsheba went to the king in his room. And the king was very old, and Abishag the Shunammite was attending the king. [16]And Bathsheba bowed and made obeisance to the king, and the king said, What (מה) ails you? [17]And she said to him, My lord you swore by Yhwh your God to your maidservant that Solomon your son shall reign after me, and he shall sit upon my throne. [18]And now (ועתה), all of a sudden (הנה), Adonijah is king, and now (ועתה) my lord the king you don't know about it. [19]And he has sacrificed oxen, fatted cattle, and sheep in abundance, and he has invited all the sons of the king, Abiathar the priest, and Joab the commander of the army—but Solomon your servant he did not invite. [20]And you my lord the king—the eyes of all Israel are upon you to tell them who shall sit on the throne of my lord the king after him. [21]And it may be that, when my lord the king sleeps with his ancestors, I and my son Solomon will be considered offenders.

We are not informed of Bathsheba's reaction to Nathan's proposal. We might infer that she likes it. The narrator presents her departing quickly from Nathan. She immediately *goes to* the king and is *in* his room. Her movement toward David is not unique to the chapter. Another woman, Abishag, had also been brought to the king's room. In this new scene, the narrator assumes a more prominent role in the telling of the story (vv 15–16a), but a significant portion of the scene is given over once again to a speaking character (vv 16b–21). Indeed, after the king speaks one word (what-ails-you) the major portion of the drama develops as the long quoted speech of Bathsheba.

But the narrator does depart from conveying the story momentarily to recount descriptions that precede the Nathan-Bathsheba ploy: David, we are reminded, is very old and attended by Abishag the Shunammite woman (cf. vv 1–4). Why this duplication? The fact that David the king is situated in his bedroom where Abishag has joined him, coupled with the reminder of his old age, convey, the image of a man tottering and confined to his room. The visual image is reinforced through speech. He utters one word to Bathsheba. He does not wish, is perhaps too enervated, to speak at length. His simple question aims at the central issue at hand: "ma-lak" (מה־לך)

points to Adonijah reigning, "malak" (מלך).[18] Indeed, the word מלך appears five times in the narrator's brief introduction to scene ii. Impotent, shivering, old—the image is of a king roused from a shivering torpor no longer able to conduct the business of state affairs. The Nathan-Bathsheba plan may fail.

Bathsheba bows *and* makes obeisance to the king. Why does a laconic narrator stress this image? The repetition pattern mirrors her speech: six times in her single speech she refers to David as "my lord." This bowing and obeisance also provide her time to collect her thoughts as she transforms the few words that Nathan had given her into a speech four times longer and considerably more persuasive than what he had projected.

Nathan's projected retrospective speech of David was highlighted in scene i by its central place in the a-b-c-b'-a' discourse pattern. Bathsheba highlights this important speech by duplicating it exactly. She recalls Nathan's words to the letter: Solomon your son shall reign after me, and he shall sit upon my throne. Bathsheba quotes what she is projecting as David's speech as *he* would have spoken the words to her: Solomon your son [i.e., Bathsheba's son] shall reign after me [Solomon] and he shall sit upon my [Solomon's] throne.

While the center of Nathan's projected speech (c) is faithfully duplicated, Bathsheba transforms both frames in numerous ways. The reader's intuition that her bowing and obeisance shows her outward deference while simultaneously giving her time to think is immediately confirmed through her quoted speech. She begins, My lord you swore by Yhwh your God to your maidservant. Nathan's rather inoffensive, information-seeking lead question, Did you not swear, is now an audacious statement of fact: You swore. The address of respect, my lord, now introduces this statement, and the supporting title which Nathan projected, the king, is dropped altogether. Nathan had the king swearing to Bathsheba, but in the execution Bathsheba represents David swearing to Yhwh, his God. Her modification hints at the seriousness of the matter. Any alteration of the oath, she would have him believe, violates the promise to Yhwh.

In the forecast, Nathan projected Bathsheba's speech as a simple

---

[18] Ibid., p. 355.

three-word question to be spoken after the oath: So-why is-Adonijah reigning. In David's presence, Bathsheba transforms the simple question into a full-fledged discourse that highlights Adonijah's coronation ceremony (past), the "eyes of Israel" on David (present), and the likely fate that she and "her" son will soon suffer (future) if preemptive measures are not taken. The speech is delivered with alacrity. In this expanded version she says nothing that is factually incorrect, but says everything with heavy psychological shading.

After duplicating the "old" oath, Bathsheba moves to the present. She offers an explosive הנה variation of what Nathan had proposed, and double-barreled עתה and עתה points: (a) And now, all of a sudden, Adonijah is king. (b) And now, my lord the king, you know nothing about this.

The conflation of time present with time past highlights the problem: Adonijah is now king, and David confined to his room, knows nothing about the recent defections of Abiathar and Joab and the feast of Adonijah at En Rogel. The modification from what Bathsheba heard (כי מלך אדניהו) to what she says (הנה אדניה מלך) can be captured in the translations: that Adonijah has become king is transformed into the wording, all of a sudden, Adonijah is king. She now includes the full address which she had heard from Nathan as she calls him "my lord the king" for the first time (cf. vv 17 and 18). Adonijah is king, but my king you don't know of it. Such doubletalk calls attention to the problem at hand: who is king—David, Adonijah, Solomon?

The reference to lack of knowledge is found in scene i, but the words were not part of the projected speech that David was to hear. Nathan told Bathsheba that David did not know, but he did not present the thought as projected speech. While it is Bathsheba who "has not heard," David, we twice learn, "does not know." The repetition highlights David's decline in both physical and political terms. The reference is followed by Bathsheba's account of what must be well known in the public sphere: her surprising revelation of sacrificed oxen, cattle, and sheep can be confirmed by the narrator's report in v 9.[19] To the narrator's account she adds that the sacrifice has

[19] The meat from the sacrifices would serve as the coronation meal (Hugo Gressmann, *Narrative and Novella in Samuel: Studies by Hugo Gressmann and Other Scholars*, trans. David E. Orton, ed. David M. Gunn, JSOTSup 116/HTIBS 9 (Sheffield: Almond, 1991), 54.

been "in abundance," and we discover that Bathsheba has "heard" (v 11) this news before Nathan spoke to her. He did not mention the sacrifices. The psychological drama continues as she discloses the invitation list. She first says that "all" the king's sons are with Adonijah. Even the priest Abiathar has joined the forces, and the accomplished and politically astute Joab has deserted David as well.[20] A comparison with the narrator's report reveals that she does not mention the measured show of force among the party faithful who still support David: the priest Zadok, Benaiah son of Jehoiada, the prophet Nathan, Shimei, Rei, and David's warriors. If we assume that she is aware of these details, the conclusion that Bathsheba is a political figure in her own right is easy to draw; she increases the severity of the dilemma by omitting these names. She then qualifies her statement by saving to the end the news that one son, "Solomon your servant," has not been invited to the celebration. The word "servant" has appeared before, but not as a modifier of Solomon. Nathan used it to refer to Bathsheba when he spoke to her, and she duplicated that reference in David's presence. By linking herself with Solomon (servant*s*) she plays on David's sympathy while playing with the truth: your wife and one loyal son remain while everyone else has joined forces with the conspirators. David must not think that Solomon has support equal in size to Adonijah's. She modifies verifiable facts as she puts psychological pressure on her husband. The picture is drawn of an oath to Yhwh and enduring family faithfulness (David, Bathsheba, Solomon).

After presenting the image in bleak terms (conspiracy), she quickly reminds David that he is commander. He is "my lord and king"—the modifiers couch the point in personal and national terms—who still holds power. The eyes of all (כל) Israel eagerly look for his decision. Make no mistake: the situation is potentially calamitous, but time remains, if only you will tell the nation who will next sit on the throne of "my lord the king" (her repetition). Her lord whom she previously said knew nothing (about the insurrection) is now her lord who can tell everyone who will reign next. She began on a personal front: you swore to your maidservant concerning your son. She has the good sense to embellish the truth with good rhetoric.

[20] See esp. 2 Sam 2:12–32; 3:22–30; 10:9–14; 11:1, 6, 11, 14–25; 14:1–33; 18:1–23; 19:1–8; 20:7–26; 24:1–9.

This is no small family matter; it is in the nation's interest that you end the civil strife and settle the matter of succession.

In her final petition she returns to the familiar image as she addresses him as "my lord the king," invoking the double title for the fourth time. The words אחריו and אבתיו ("after him" and "his ancestors") are closely linked in sound: David, positioned between children and ancestors, can determine, if he has fortitude, the political landscape. And with yet another new thought, David, she projects, may not be the only one at death's door. She speaks of familial death in personal, contrasting terms. To sleep with one's ancestors is a euphemism denoting a rather peaceful death, whereas she and her son will likely suffer the fate of "offenders."[21]

After Bathsheba delivers her impassioned speech—an appeal much broader in scope and more persuasive in tone than what Nathan had proposed—the court prophet appears. His entrance is introduced with the key word הנה, which also appeared in the forecast immediately after Nathan projected Bathsheba's speech. The word appears twice in the introduction to scene iii. In the second instance, they tell the king: here is (הנה) Nathan. The unusual, unexpected duplication of the word reminds us that David, old and infirm, may have trouble perceiving that Nathan is in his presence.

Scene iii

> [22]And all of a sudden (הנה) as she was still speaking with the king, Nathan the prophet came in. [23]And they told the king, Here is (הנה) Nathan the prophet. And he came before the king and he bowed before the king with his face to the ground. [24]And Nathan said, My lord the king, have you said (אתה אמרת[22]) Adonijah shall reign after me, and he shall sit upon my throne? [25]For he has gone down today and sacrificed oxen, fatted cattle, and sheep in abundance, and he has invited all the sons of the king and the commanders of the army and Abiathar the priest. And all of a sudden (והנה) they are eating and

[21] The original core meaning of the word חטא is "missing the mark" (or: "sinning"). In various contexts, the word reflects shades in meaning. Bathsheba is here projecting that she and Solomon would be treated as offenders in a political rather than a theological sense. This relational and political meaning of the word would put Bathsheba and Solomon "on the wrong side."

[22] No interrogative particle is attached to the initial word אתה. Cf. chapter 7, n. 1.

> drinking before him and saying, Long live King Adonijah. [26]But I your servant, Zadok the priest, Benaiah son of Jehoiada, and Solomon your servant he did not invite. [27]Has (אם)[23] my lord the king brought this thing about and not made it known to your servants who should sit upon the throne of my lord the king after him?

True to his word, Nathan the prophet enters as Bathsheba is "still speaking" with the king. The mention of his court title lends authority to his words. He enters, as Bathsheba before him, bowing. His face is to the ground. The ceremonial bowing—underscored by double reference—gives the prophet time to think, and it contrasts with his straight-up entrance on the two other occasions when he approached the king (2 Sam 7 and 12).

The length of his address to the king approximates the speech of Bathsheba in the previous scene, and his words are actually closer to hers (v 19) than what he had originally projected for himself (v 13). He opens with the address he first uttered in Bathsheba's presence and which she echoed four times in scene ii (my lord the king), and follows it with a question. The repetition of the deferential address links the two plotters, and in invoking a question he returns to a form he had originally proposed to Bathsheba (v 13), which she rejected. Both the content of what he had projected in scene i and the words she spoke in scene ii now undergo considerable transformation by the speech engineer.

In the presence of David, Nathan expands his original projected speech (scene i). While some words mirror Bathsheba's recent speech, he departs in significant ways at times. His first words signal the change as his "confirmation" (v 14) of Bathsheba's words from scene ii take a provocative form. He introduces the idea that David may have previously proclaimed *Adonijah* successor! He has calculated (i.e., in the expansive bowing) that David will "correct" the words he now hears based upon the words he has just heard from Bathsheba. Nathan's bold move is accompanied by a number of strategies that become apparent to the audience (but not to the unsuspecting David) when his new speech is compared to the projected speech of scene i and the speech which David first hears in scene ii.

Nathan misquotes himself. At the center of his original double-framed speech (c, from scene i) we find: Solomon your son shall

[23] Cf. GKC §150f.

reign after me, and he shall sit upon my throne? (Nathan, scene i). These words are duplicated in the first retelling (scene ii) and modified in the next instance (scene iii): Solomon your son shall reign after me, and he shall sit upon my throne (Bathsheba, scene ii); and Adonijah shall reign after me, and he shall sit upon my throne? (Nathan, scene iii)

Why is it the case that after Bathsheba quotes the center of Nathan's projected speech verbatim, Nathan proceeds to modify *his* original speech? The answer is found in part when we remember that Bathsheba recently introduced Adonijah's name: all of a sudden Adonijah is king, and you don't know about it! With seeds of doubt concerning Adonijah's actions planted in David's mind, Nathan now modifies his original plan, quite possibly because he has just heard Bathsheba's words to the king. Yet, with persuasion on his mind, Nathan cleverly omits any reference to Adonijah as David's son. Indeed, in Nathan's discourse Adonijah's name is spoken without any embellishment, an important fact when viewed against Nathan's fondness for uttering names and titles in David's presence: (my lord the king, Abiathar the priest, Zadok the priest, Benaiah son of Jehoiada, Solomon your servant, my lord the king, my lord the king).

Nathan also introduces his words to the king differently than he had projected. He originally said (scene i): Did you not, my lord the king, swear to your maidservant? The words are transformed twice: Bathsheba (scene ii): My lord, you swore by Yhwh your God to your maidservant. Nathan (scene iii): My lord the king, have you said? The change is striking when we realize that Bathsheba did preserve the performative verb "swore" (שבע). Why Nathan's change to "say" at this late stage? The departure in delivery might be explained by the risky introduction of Adonijah's name. No need to project David swearing to that!

Nathan duplicates Bathsheba's reference to sacrifice, the list of animals, and the invitation to all the king's sons, but he enlarges the crisis: not only Joab, but all the commanders have joined Adonijah's celebration. In her speech the "all of a sudden (הנה)" reference was followed by "Adonijah is king!" In Nathan's speech the keyword הנה appears again but is followed by a description of them "eating and drinking before the king." This allusion is Nathan's invention. It never appeared in scenes i or ii, or in the narrator's initial description (vv 5–10). In similar fashion, Nathan's report of an acclamation,

Long live King Adonijah!, is new to the story. Nathan exaggerates to stir the king to action.

In David's presence, both Bathsheba and Nathan inform the king that supporters of Adonijah have been invited to a coronation ceremony. (We have seen Nathan exploiting the image.) Both speakers also indicate that some people have not been invited. Nathan did not mention these lists in his original speech. A comparison of the two invitation and noninvitation sequences presented to David reveals interesting details. Nathan begins by amplifying Bathsheba's remarks. Why does he project Adonijah going down "today" to offer sacrifices? It may be the case that the prophet adds to Bathsheba's speech for the purpose of implying that Adonijah's movement has not (yet!) gained momentum. Both speakers tell the king that Adonijah is offering sacrifices "in abundance," a point Nathan has apparently just heard for the first time from Bathsheba. Nathan tells David that the commander*s* of the army are with Adonijah at this sacrifice ceremony. In fact, it is Joab the commander who is there, according to both Bathsheba and the narrator.

In view of the objective (convince David to intervene), it is hardly surprising that neither wife nor prophet mention that "all the royal officials of Judah" were invited (v 9). Bathsheba concluded the sequence by noting that Solomon (only) was not invited. Nathan "corrects" (cf. v 10) her point: "I your servant, Zadok the priest, Benaiah son of Jehoiada, and Solomon your servant he did not invite." In addition to supplying names that Bathsheba did not mention, Nathan also repeats a word that was not included in the narrator's account. Bathsheba might have left the impression that a countermove on David's part would be risky—Solomon is alone! But Nathan provides a balanced picture framed by references to those loyal to the king. From Nathan's angle, attention shifts to the "manageable" size of Adonijah's opposition and loyalty to David as both Nathan and Solomon remain the king's "servants."

Bathsheba concluded her appeal to David by stressing the dire consequences that she and her son face as a result of Adonijah's actions. Nathan concludes his speech differently. He opened his petition with a brazen question of the king. He now frames it with a second one that once again boldly puts the matter before David: Have you done this thing? The question is posed shrewdly with no less than three (additional) references to loyalty at both the personal and national levels: Has *my lord* the king brought this thing about and not made it known to *your servants* who should sit upon the throne of *my lord* the king after him? She focused on the consequences to Solomon; he hints that all this has come about because the plan has been withheld from the servants. The implication of this double effort leads tacitly to one conclusion: David has conspired against Solomon, "beloved of Yhwh!"[24]

The issue of who knows and who does not know is central to this story; it is a matter of concern in each of the first three scenes. In scene i Bathsheba does not know (lit. has not heard) what Adonijah has done, and David does not know (ידע) about the conspiracy. In scene ii Bathsheba accuses David of not knowing (ידע). Now in scene iii the tottering king is implicated: Have you done this, but not made it known (ידע)? Nathan cleverly leaves the whole issue open with an interrogative, Have you brought this about?[25]

After a persuasive appeal, Nathan brings the whole issue into focus: who will next sit on the throne? To David, he has recently mentioned "Solomon your servant," duplicated words first spoken by Bathsheba in scene ii. It is significant, and no accident on the part of the narrator, that these words are heard only as the wife of David and prophet to David speak to the king; they were not uttered by Nathan when he projected speech in scene i. Will Bathsheba and Nathan succeed in their interweaving rhetoric of manipulation?

Scene iv

> [28]And King David answered and said, Summon to me Bathsheba. And she came before the king and stood before the king. [29]And the king swore and said, As Yhwh lives who has redeemed my life from every adversity, [30]as I swore to you by Yhwh the God of Israel saying, Solomon your son shall reign after me, and he shall sit upon my throne in my place—so I will do it today. [31]And Bathsheba bowed her face to the ground and made obeisance to the king and said, May my lord King David live forever.

Though having just heard from Nathan, David wishes to speak to Bathsheba. His command to summon her indicates that he perceives

[24] Named Jedidiah in 2 Sam 12:25.
[25] Cf. n. 21 above.

that she withdrew from his room, or that she stands behind Nathan. But has she withdrawn? We know (or suspect) the following: David, ailing and cold, may be unable to see. As partners, Nathan and Bathsheba plot against the king. They stand figuratively, and perhaps literally, side by side. The narrator never indicates that she withdraws from David's room after speaking to him. Indeed, she first comes *into* the king's room (v 15), but, summoned, she comes and stands *before* the king. Feeble David fails to perceive what we know: the actions and words of Nathan and Bathsheba are contrived. Bathsheba, previously bowing and buying time like Nathan, now stands before her husband. No longer the supplicant, no longer the plotter, she awaits his decision.

From the vantage point of Nathan and Bathsheba, the narrator's introduction of David's speech is encouraging: the king swears (שבע, as Bathsheba told him he had previously) and says (אמר, as Nathan intimated he had). The king's words enhance this initial view: he says it is Yhwh who has redeemed him from all adversity. It was to Yhwh that Bathsheba implied that David had sworn. "As I swore to you," David continues, "by Yhwh the God of Israel." While the title is unique to the four scenes, the words were uttered at different moments in Bathsheba's long speech. She had David swearing "to Yhwh your God" and "the eyes of all Israel are upon you." Thus, for both husband and wife, this intensely personal issue is presented in the light of national importance above all else. And these early hints that Nathan and Bathsheba have succeeded are sustained as David re-presents the oath that the prophet and his wife had both quoted to David. He quotes it—now the third time for the reader—to the letter: "Solomon your son shall reign after me, and he shall sit upon my throne." The old tottering king has not only heard the words of his alleged oath and repeated those words; he is able to add to them. For the prophet-wife team, it is icing on the cake: he shall sit upon my throne, in my place, so I will do it today! What was spoken before is actualized this day through performative speech.

David's swearing about earlier promises still leaves open the possibility that the speech Nathan projected in scene i was a ruse. It is quite possible that David yields to the persuasive, though invented, speech of Nathan and Bathsheba. Perhaps David believes himself incapable of remembering when he "once" swore again that Solomon would reign next. The oath (c), real or invented, that appears as a central concern in each of the scenes, has become an effective political tool for the dialogists Nathan and Bathsheba.

Having heard the words, Bathsheba bows her head, and with her face to the ground makes obeisance to the king. The narrator's description of this bow is marked by an amplification in words. Previously she "bowed and made obeisance to the king" (v 16), and Nathan earlier "bowed to the king with his face to the ground" (v 23). Now she "bows her face to the ground and makes obeisance to the king." Mission accomplished, attention to the show of deference increases. In her brief and concluding remark of five Hebrew words, she reconfirms David's authority ("king" and "my lord") as she expresses hope that his proclamation will have enduring validity. To the dying king, she expresses the thought with a brushstroke of irony that David will live forever in the person of Solomon and his offspring. The prospect of Solomon's success soon becomes reality. Adonijah's supporter Abiathar the priest is expelled (2:26–27) and his ally Joab is killed (2:34). Language once used in the coronation of Adonijah scene is supplemented by David's subsequent pledge and instructions: make my son Solomon ride upon my mule; anoint him; blow the trumpet; he shall come and sit upon my throne and he shall be king in my place; for I have appointed him to be ruler over Israel and over Judah (1:32–35). Nathan and Bathsheba succeed. Duplicitious questions have persuaded the king.

CHAPTER ELEVEN

QUESTIONS AS LITERARY THREADS (HAGGAI TO ZECHARIAH 1–8)

Introduction: Haggai, Zechariah, and the Twelve

The subject of coherence and the book of the twelve (Hosea–Malachi) has been explored in at least three ways: unity of a single book that has often been fragmented in scholarly circles,[1] unity of a few books among the twelve,[2] or unity of all twelve prophetic books.[3] In this chapter I propose to support, indirectly, the unity-of-the-twelve thesis while looking at the unity question and two of the twelve books, Haggai and Zechariah.

The Hebrew Bible is, of course, one big book, but it does not require us to read it sequentially—from Genesis to Malachi (or Chronicles)—in quite the way the novel genre does. Indeed, its translators have different ideas on how to arrange the books, and there is no universal agreement on what to put in and what to leave out. A question we confront implicitly each time we read is where to begin and where to end. Scenes, chapters, but perhaps most often the books themselves serve as boundaries. I will argue that literary textual clues suggest that there is no reason to imagine a reading boundary between Haggai and Zechariah as I address these questions: Does the frequent invocation of interrogatives in these two books suggest literary affinity? Do these interrogatives reflect a distinct rhetorical pattern, and is there a typological scheme to the questions invoked along the text continuum from Hag 1:4 to Zech 8:6? I will

---

[1] Kenneth Craig, *A Poetics of Jonah: Art in the Service of Ideology* (2d ed.; Macon, Ga.: Mercer University Press, 1999), 89–110.

[2] Ronald W. Pierce, "Literary Connectors and a Haggai/Zechariah/Malachi Corpus," *JETS* 27 (1984), 277–89; also Ronald W. Pierce, "A Thematic Development of the Haggai/Zechariah/Malachi Corpus," *JETS* 27 (1984), 401–411.

[3] Paul House, *The Unity of the Twelve*, JSOTSup 77 (Sheffield: Sheffield Academic Press, 1990); also Dale Allen Schneider, *The Unity of the Book of the Twelve*, Yale University, Ph.D. dissertation, 1979.

comment on the interrogatives while analyzing their literary function. Because the biblical authors had the option of telling the story straight—what happens, to whom, for what reason, and so forth—the invocation of a question represents a special literary phenomenon. And these two books are loaded with interrogatives.

The books of Haggai and Zechariah can be linked on historical grounds. Both prophets find themselves confronting unfamiliar circumstances at the time of Darius I's reign, and together they give prophetic authority in support of the reestablished province of Yehud (Judah). They are concerned with reestablishing institutions during a period of restoration, and the same set of characters appears in the books: the high priest Joshua, the governor Zerubbabel, the priests, and the citizenry (or representatives). But despite obvious similarities in context and content, not to mention shifting currents in biblical studies, discussions about so-called primary and secondary (or "original" and "additional") material continue.[4] Apart from the obvious overlap in context, are there textual clues suggesting that Haggai and Zechariah are a composite work? Carol Meyers and Eric Meyers have argued for an envelope construction of language and content that ties together Haggai 1–2 with Zechariah 7–8,[5] and Ronald Pierce has explored some implications of the interrogative material in Haggai, Zechariah, and Malachi.[6]

---

[4] Paul Redditt, "Zerubbabel, Joshua, and the Night Visions of Zechariah," *CBQ* 54 (1992), 249–59; Paul Redditt, *Haggai, Zechariah, and Malachi*, NCBC (Grand Rapids: Eerdmans, 1995), and Yehuda Radday and Dieter Wickmann, "The Unity of Zechariah Examined in the Light of Statistical Linguistics," *ZAW* 87 (1975), 54.

[5] Carol Meyers and Eric Meyers, *Haggai, Zechariah 1–8*, AB 25B (New York: Doubleday, 1987), xlix.

[6] Pierce focuses more on patterns broken by narrative interludes than on the rhetorical impact of the questions themselves in "Literary Connectors" and "Thematic Development." He notes that interrogatives appear as a consistent element both before and after Zechariah 9–14, and his analysis leads him to place Zechariah 9–14 as the thematic centerpiece of the Haggai Zechariah Malachi corpus. The abrupt shift before and after Zechariah 9–14 helps the reader draw the vivid picture of a flock doomed for slaughter in this focal point. Burke O. Long ("Two Question and Answer Schemata in the Prophets," *JBL* 90 [1971], 129–39) has discussed a question-answer schemata in Jeremiah. He finds two types: A (in Jer 22:8 and parallels) and B (in Jer 5:19 and parallels).

Four Interrogative Types in Haggai-Zechariah

No less than four types of questions appear in the book of Haggai: rhetorical questions, sequential questions, questions that function primarily to advance the plot, and questions that increase the number of characters in a given scene. (Some interrogatives can be placed in more than one of these categories.) While Zechariah is a larger corpus, the questions that appear in this prophetic book also fall into one of these four categories. Indeed, all four types found in Haggai also appear in Zechariah.

The Rhetorical Question

The first question in Haggai is rhetorical: Is-it-time[7] for-you yourselves to-live in-your-finished[8] houses, and-this house is-desolate? (Hag 1:4).

No answer is recorded. It is apparent: No, this is not the time for the Yehudites to dwell, content and secure in their homes, while the house of Yhwh remains unfinished and desolate. The question consists of two parts. The first part contains six words; the second only half as many. The emphasis falls on the houses of the people. The duplication of the pronouns (you, yourselves, and your finished houses) in the first part highlights the lack of responsibility and inactivity of the Yehudites, and the repetition drives home the contrast between "their houses" and the neglected "this house." The people do have time for themselves and their projects (you, your, yourselves). Their houses, well-built and decorated, contrast with "this house," a temple in ruins.

The people had argued that now was not the time for rebuilding

[7] In this chapter I have attempted to maintain both the Hebrew syntax and the original number of words while translating (hence the somewhat awkward English constructions). Single Hebrew words often require more than one English word in translation, and in such instances I use hyphens to join the English words that convey the one Hebrew word. (I attach the word "and" to the subject, even when the *vav* is conjoined to the Hebrew verb.) Phyllis Trible recommends this scheme in *Rhetorical Criticism: Context, Method and the Book of Jonah* (Minneapolis: Fortress, 1994).

[8] Meyers and Meyers, *Haggai, Zechariah 1–8*, 3, 23. The word סְפוּנִים has been variously rendered as "panelled" (P. R. Ackroyd, *Exile and Restoration*, OTL [London: SCM, 1968], 155) and "ceiled" (H. G. Mitchell, *A Critical and Exegetical Commentary on Haggai, Zechariah, Malachi, and Jonah*, ICC [Edinburgh: T. & T. Clark, 1912], 45).

the house of Yhwh (v 2). The rhetorical question in v 4 highlights their indifference and lack of fervor in rebuilding the temple. The issue is not lack of time; priorities are skewed. Their living (lit., "to sit") in v 4 contrasts with "their running" in v 9, a verse that also contains a question that reinforces the theme of misplaced priorities. Yhwh's house is overlooked amidst the hustle and bustle of daily life. All their activity, at home or away, is undertaken for their own benefit, while religious obligations, epitomized by the temple, are neglected. The near duplication in language, "this house is desolate" in v 4 with "my house is desolate" in v 9, links the two verses, and the use of double interrogatives reinforces the theme of misplaced priorities. The rhetorical questions are thus woven into the thematic pattern of individual productivity achieved at the expense of communal responsibility.

The initial interrogative in Zechariah—Your-ancestors, where-are-they? (Zech 1:5a)—is also a rhetorical question. It is followed by two additional rhetorical questions in 1:5b and 1:6a.

> And-the-prophets, do-they-live forever? (Zech 1:5b).
>
> But my-words and-my-statutes, which I-commanded my-servants the-prophets, did-they-not overtake your-ancestors? And-they-repented and-they-said, Whenever Yahweh-of hosts purposed to-deal with-us according-to-our-ways and-our-deeds, thus he-dealt with-us (Zech 1:6).

The answers to questions on the whereabouts of ancestors and prophets are easily supplied: the ancestors have died and of course the prophets do not live forever. The point is accentuated as the prophets are linked here not with God or God's word but with "the ancestors" in their mortality. The first two rhetorical questions highlight the vanishing nature of human life and the third conveys the lessons of history on the minds of the audience. The overall rhetorical charge of these three questions contrasts dead ancestors and prophets with enduring statutes that had been commanded by these now dead prophets. The words "overtook" these very ancestors (v 6).

In v 6a, the rhetorical question asks, Did not my words and my statutes overtake your ancestors? The Hebrew word הִשִּׂיגוּ, "overtake," is a hunting term. Zechariah's question to the hearers is intended to make clear by contrast that God's "words and statutes" are enduring, unlike one's ancestors or the prophets. The ancestors were overtaken and they "repented" (שׁוב), a key word that appears now for the fourth time in a short narrative space (1:3, 3, 4, 6).

The word of Yhwh is manifest to Zechariah in a series of eight night visions (1:8–17, 1:18–21, 2:1–5, 3:1–10, 4:1–14, 5:1–4, 5:5–11, 6:1–8), and the three rhetorical questions in 1:5–6 rekindle the prophecies of old and also generate these new visions which were anticipated in the "former" prophecies (Zech 1:4). For example, the prophecies of the seventy years' captivity in Zech 1:12 has a parallel in Jer 25:11 and 29:10; the man with a measuring line in Zech 2:5 (Ev 2:1) has a parallel in Ezek 40:3, and the branch in Zech 3:8 and 6:12 has a parallel in Jeremiah's righteous Branch (23:5 and 33:15).

The words about the past are put in the form of a question: Did this not happen? A few persons alive just after the return to Israel could remember the history of 597–587 BCE. The exile had been foretold, and even though the prophets died, the words they spoke lived on and would be known even by those not alive at the time of the exile. These words "overtook" the ancestors. Such words and statutes are portrayed as the overpowering covenant of God with Israel.

Zechariah 3:2 ends with another rhetorical question: And-Yahweh said to-ha-satan, may-Yahweh rebuke you, O-ha-satan! And-may-Yahweh rebuke you who-has-chosen Jerusalem! Is-this not a-brand plucked from-fire? (Zech 3:2). The word used for "fire" here is אש, and the image is reminiscent of Amos 4:11's reference to the northern kingdom as "a brand plucked out of the fire" (משרפה). The brand is a charred piece of wood, but snatched from the fire it is spared from destruction. Joshua, the high priest, has been plucked from the exile. His appearance is not unlike the appearance of the wood snatched from the fire. Both are dirty. Joshua is wearing "filthy clothes" (Zech 3:3), and the filth may represent the sins of the priest and the people. The angel commands those standing before Joshua to undress him (v 4). Then they crown him with "a clean turban" and dress him with "festal apparel" (vv 4–5). This change of clothes has a symbolic function: the new, clean appearance symbolizes ritual purity and heralds the advent of the messianic age.

Sequential Questions (or the "Pile-up" Phenomenon)

As the name implies, sequential questions are invoked one after another while the addressee is denied the opportunity of answering. These interrogatives are similar to the rhetorical type, and indeed the two types sometimes overlap—the three questions in Zech 1:5–6, for example, discussed above. With sequential questions, the rhetorical effect is always heightened. Three questions, one after another, are found in Hag 2:3: Who among-you is-left who saw this-house in-its-former glory? And-how are-you seeing it now? Is-it-not as nothing in-your-sight?

The temple burned down in 587 and the year is now 520. With this set of three queries Haggai compares the pre-exilic temple with its present state. The combination functions as a rhetorical device for involving all of Haggai's audience in the continuity-discontinuity tension that characterized the restoration period. A small group of eyewitnesses old enough to remember Solomon's temple are now seventy or seventy-five years old. According to Peter Verhoef, some scholars (Mitchell, Koole, Van der Woude) conclude that no one would have attained the age of seventy at this time due to the circumstances of the exile. The question would therefore be addressed to those who had memories of the temple based on the literature such as Psalm 137 or by means of oral tradition. But Verhoef has argued convincingly that such an assumption is unlikely.[9]

These three questions all contain second-person plural references—who among you, how are you, in your sight—and are intended to capture the attention of the audience. The temple is also referred to in each question. The interrogatives are thus conjoined by similar vocabulary and a single image, but they also work independently at the rhetorical level: the first question challenges the oldest members of the returnees, the ones who remember Solomon's temple; the second inquires about the present state of affairs; the third asks about consequences.

The whole affair is defined in terms of "glory," a word that is ambiguous. The temple may house Yhwh's glory, Yhwh's indwelling holy presence, but the word can also signify physical splendor, such as the beautiful temple described in 1 Kgs 6–7 with its ornamentation and precious metal before it was demolished by Nebuchadnezzar II in 587 BCE. The "glory" of Solomon's temple is associated with wealth, and the term also carries economic and political meaning.

The work on rebuilding has just begun and seems to have stalled.

---

[9] Peter Verhoef, *The Books of Haggai and Malachi*, NICOT (Grand Rapids: Eerdmans, 1987), 95–96 and n. 19.

The second question creates an antithesis in the minds of the audience between the "former" (הראשון) and the "now" (עתה). But the issue at hand revolves not around two temples, but one: the temple before destruction and the temple at this present moment which the people had been admonished to rebuild. The interrogative particle מה is usually translated as the interrogative "what," but is used here in the sense of "how" (cf. Gen 44:16).

The final "is not" question (הלא) moves the audience to the inevitable affirming response and its rhetorical impact is increased by the two questions that precede it. As the present ruins are compared with the former "glory," the present ruins are as "nothing" at all. A formulation such as this third question would have forced an affirming response from those in the community dissatisfied with the present state of affairs because the interrogative ה followed by the negative particle suggests a positive answer. Haggai aligns himself with the older generation. Though the building operations are underway, this "new temple" suffers by comparison with Solomon's magnificent building. The comparative particle כ twice refers to the same object: the present state of the temple. It intensifies the comparison between present desolation and previous glory.

Questions are invoked once again in sequence in Zechariah 7:5–7.

> Say to-all-the-people-of the-land and-to-the-priests, saying: When-you-fasted and-mourned in-the-fifth and-in-the-seventh (months), and-this seventy years, fasting, was-it-for-me?[10] (Zech 7:5).
>
> And-when you-eat and-when you-drink, do-you not eat and-drink only-for-yourselves? (Zech 7:6).
>
> Are-not (these) the-words that Yahweh proclaimed by-the-hand-of the-earlier prophets, when Jerusalem was-inhabited and-in-prosperity, and-her-cities around-her, and-the-Negeb and-the-Shephelah were-inhabited? (Zech 7:7).

A delegation from Bethel included Sharezer, Regem-melech, and others. Consistent with the interrogative style of Hag 2:3, the author formulates the oracular response in the form of sequential questions.

---

[10] On the "strongest way of asking," see the comments of Ralph Smith, *Micah-Malachi*, WBC (Waco, Tex.: Word, 1984), 221 n. 5a. Cf. also the comments on this elevated discourse in Meyers and Meyers, *Haggai, Zechariah 1–8*, 389.

The question in v 3 originates with the delegation, but the answer is addressed to "all the people of the land and the priests" (v 5). The delegation arrived to entreat Yhwh and to ask the priests and prophets if the custom of fasting and mourning in the fifth month should continue. The reference is to the practice of fasting on the anniversary of the temple, which took place on the fifth month (2 Kgs 25:8–9). (The commemoration of this date by means of a fast is nowhere mentioned in the Bible.) The first oracular response (7:4–7) to the question in v 3 takes the form of three sequential questions (vv 5, 6, 7). The lead question—when you fasted and mourned, was it for me?—appears to be a rhetorical question, one that stimulates further reflection because the answer is obvious. But one may allow for the possibility that fasts were not undertaken primarily for the benefit of Yhwh. Saul fasted in an effort to help himself communicate with God in 1 Sam 28:23. The juxtaposition of vv 5 and 6 in chapter 7 of Zechariah appears to imply that just as eating and drinking benefits the individual, fasting likewise affects the one who abstains. The implied answer to the rhetorical question is: No, it was not for Yhwh.

Eating and drinking (v 6) are of course necessary to sustain life, but they are also part of festal activity, and the reference to priests here along with the people of the land may suggest cultic meals. In sum, vv 5 and 6 work together to show that the people and the priests do not give proper consideration to God, and v 7's question confirms that the former prophets did indeed speak in a fashion consistent with the questions articulated in the previous two verses.

Questions that Function Primarily to Advance the Plot

In the dialogue between the prophet and interpreting angel—the angel is a major literary figure in Zechariah's visions—the question-answer format often serves the plot by presenting the vision's subject matter and then its meaning. Take, for example, Haggai 1:9:

> You-have-looked for-much, and-behold, only-little; and-when-you-brought-it to-the-house, I-blew it away. On-account-of what? An-utterance-of Yahweh-of hosts. On-account-of my-house which-is desolate. And-you-are running each-of-you to-his-house.

A two-word question, יען מה (on-account-of what?), appears at the center of this verse. Donald Gowan has observed that the יען sentence signals divine speech, spoken either by God or a messenger.[11] Here Yhwh utters both the question and answer, and the response includes an "on account of my house which is desolate" answer. The questions, admonitions, and curse-fulfillment sayings of the previous verses are now replaced by this tight question—answer framework, and the duplication of יען at the beginning of the answer highlights the point that the temple is still in ruins because of the misplaced fervor of the people who "run" in their eagerness to build and build up their own houses. As in v 4, Haggai contrasts "my house" (Yhwh's house) with "his house" (the houses of the people). The people have time, energy, and the inclination to build, but their energy is misdirected.

The answer duplicates ideas already expressed. After repeating the first word of the interrogative sentence, "on-account-of," the prophet continues by repeating what has already been conveyed: Yhwh's house is in ruins; words from v 4 appear again ("house" and "desolate"); and the formula "Yhwh of hosts" concludes the clause in vv 4–5 and precedes it in v 9. A form of the second masculine plural pronoun also appears multiple times in vv 4 and 9, and the contrast is, as in v 4, between the houses of the Judahites and the house of Yhwh. But "the house" of v 4 has become more personalized. It is now "my house."

In Zechariah an intermediary figure, the interpreting angel, emerges. In contrast to the visions in Amos where the prophet has direct verbal and visual associations with Yhwh, the interpreter guides, influences, and even assumes the traditional prophetic prerogatives of intercession and proclamation in Zechariah. Each of the eight night visions is colored by the use of a question-answer schema in the dialogue between prophet and interpreting angel. Sometimes the prophet asks the angel about details of the vision (1:9; 2:2[1:19), 2:4[1:21], 2:6[2:2]; 4:4, 11, 12; 5:6, 10; 6:4), while on other occasions the angel inquires of the prophet (3:2; 4:2, 5, 7, 13; 5:2). Both formats are used to draw the reader into the experience of the prophet. A question that advances the plot is voiced in the opening night vision by the prophet.

> And-I-said, What-are-these, my-lord? And-to-me the-angel said, the-one-who-speaks with me, I myself-will-show-you what-they are (Zech 1:9).

[11] Donald Gowan, "The Use of *ya'an* in Biblical Hebrew," *VT* 21 (1971), 177.

Many of the questions that Zechariah invokes throughout the night visions serve ultimately to advance the plot, to unfold the meaning of the visions themselves. The book opens with a chronological formula (1:1), and the cycle of night visions, which begins at 1:7, is also introduced by a similar expression. But the night vision formula is more precise. It specifies the day and the name of the month taken from the Babylonian calendar. The first vision (1:8–17) opens with a description of a man riding a red horse with horses of other colors behind him. This interpreting angel appears on stage without introduction in v 9 and offers to show Zechariah "what they are." By offering to show—but not to tell—what they are, the interpreting angel projects Zechariah back into the visionary world. But it is the man who rides the red horse who actually answers Zechariah's question in v 10: "they are those whom Yhwh has sent to walk to and fro over the whole earth" gathering information to report to God or God's angel (v 11). This man stands (vv 8, 10) among the myrtle trees, evergreens whose branches were used in building booths for the Feast of Tabernacles (Neh 8:15). According to Isa 41:19 and 55:13, these trees will flourish in the prosperity of the messianic age. Figures from the heavenly counsel do range over the face of the earth and report to God about the conditions of human affairs as in Job 1:6 and 2:1–2. The patrol is inclusive ("all the earth"), and the report is that the earth is dwelling peacefully.

But the image of cosmic peace changes at v 12 when the angel of Yhwh asks, "How long will you withhold mercy from Jerusalem, and the cities of Judah with which you have been angry these seventy years?" Zechariah uses this question to elicit a response from God and to call attention to the temple complex in ruins. The first oracle concludes with a message of hope. God will return to Jerusalem with compassion; the temple will be rebuilt and "a measuring line" will be stretched over the city. God's cities will also be rebuilt, and they "shall again overflow with prosperity" (v 17) as Yhwh comforts Zion.

The second night vision continues the thought of the first, and, at the literary level, is linked by the duplication of the interrogative form.

> And-I-said to-the-angel, the-one-who-speaks with-me, What-are-these? And-he-said to-me, These-are the-horns that have-scattered Judah, Israel, and-Jerusalem (Zech 2:2[1:19]).

Once again and with one word, Zechariah asks the interpreting angel "What-are-these?" On this occasion the interpreting angel answers Zechariah's question. The prophet sees four horns and learns from the answer to his question that advances the plot that these four horns "have scattered Judah, Israel, and Jerusalem." The interpretation is geopolitical. "Scattering" is an important theme of this vision, and the horns have brought destruction on Judah and Israel. The vision continues in 2:3[1:20] as Yhwh shows Zechariah four smiths or artisans.[12] The messenger interprets the horns metaphorically. These horns that have "scattered" Judah, Israel, and Jerusalem are political-military entities.

In the second stage of this second vision, the question pattern is altered.

> And-I-said, What-are these coming to-do? And-he-said, saying, These-are the-horns that-scattered Judah, so-that-one could-not-raise one's-head. And-these (smiths) have-come to-terrify them, to-strike-down the-horns-of the-nations that-lifted-up horn(s) against-the-land-of Judah to-scatter it (Zech 2:4[1:21]).

The active participle "coming" suggests motion, and Zechariah now asks about the significance ("to-do") of these smiths. This question is the only interrogative in the visions that asks about the purpose of the visionary figures. Elsewhere the questioner asks only about the identity of a figure—such as the horses in vision 1, the lampstand and trees in vision 4, the scroll in vision 5, the ephah in vision 6, the horse and chariots in vision 7—or, as in vision 3, about the place where a figure is going. The departure from the questioning pattern in vision 2 highlights the activity of the workers themselves and draws attention to the smiths' role as direct agents of Yhwh's action.

But as attention turns to Judah alone the interpreting angel's response in 2:4 focuses more on the "horns" than the "smiths." These horns, political-military entities, have scattered Judah so that no head can be raised. This metaphor suggests total destruction, and the language derives from the battlefield. This metaphor is used in the Bible (Judg 8:28) and in a number of ancient Near Eastern reliefs where a king's foot is pictured on the head of the defeated

---

[12] The term חרשים can designate any craftsperson who works with stone, metal, or wood.

enemy. After disclosing that the horns had signified military conquest and total destruction for Judah, Zechariah learns at the end of 2:4 that these "horns" will "strike down the horns of the nations that lifted up their horns against the land of Judah to scatter its people." The horns of destruction have become symbols of protection and restoration: "but these have come to terrify them." By means of the interrogative the author points to a coming political reordering, and God is portrayed as one who liberates the people.

In the fifth vision the questioning becomes intensive. When the scene opens, the interpreting angel reappears and stirs Zechariah "as one is wakened from sleep." The angel asks, "What do you see?" (Zech 4:1). This question is the first in a series of seven that will appear in this vision. Once again, we observe that the plot advances as a string of interrogatives are invoked.

> And-he-said to-me, What-do you see? And-I-said,[13] I-see, and-behold, a-lampstand-of gold all-of-it, with-a-bowl on-top-of-it and-seven lamps on-it, with-seven spouts[14] on-each-of the-lamps that are-on-top-of-it (Zech 4:2).
>
> And-I-answered and-I-said to-the-angel, the-one-who-speaks with-me, saying, What-are-these, my-lord? (Zech 4:4).
>
> And the angel answered, the-one-who-speaks with-me and-he-said to-me, Do-you-not know what-they are? And-I-said, No, my-lord (Zech 4:5).
>
> Who-are-you, great-mountain? Before Zerubbabel, a-plain. And-he-shall-bring-out the-top stone amid-shouts-of grace, grace to-it![15] (Zech 4:7).

In this vision the interpreting angel initiates conversation before Zechariah indicates that he has seen something. In the earlier visions Zechariah had spoken first: I saw a man (1:8); I saw four horns (2:1); I saw a man (2:5), he showed me Joshua (3:1). Now in chapter 4 it appears that the angel is attempting to cause Zechariah to continue the visionary experience. Zechariah reveals that he sees a golden

[13] MT reads "and he said I see." I follow qere and versions that read first-person imperfect, "and-I-said."

[14] Following Meyers and Meyers, *Haggai, Zechariah 1–8*, 227, 235–238.

[15] Translation of the Hebrew is difficult. Cf. the translation of Smith, *Micah-Malachi*, 203, and the comments of Meyers and Meyers, *Haggai, Zechariah 1–8*, 249.

menorah with a bowl on top. The menorah holds seven lamps with seven lips for the wicks. Beside the lampstand are two olive trees, one on the right and the other on the left. The problems and possible interpretations of the gold menorah and two olive trees have been discussed by David Petersen and need not be rehearsed here.[16] Verses 4 and 12 are the only two instances where Zechariah's questions are answered with a question, and as Zechariah and the interpreting angel converse in this vision, the prophet twice confesses that he does not know what the vision means (vv 5 and 13).

Zechariah continues the dialogue in v 4 by asking, "What-are-these, my-lord?" and he utters the word "my-lord" on three other occasions when speaking to the angel (1:9, 4:5, and 4:13). Such language suggests familiarity between the dialogists, and the fact that three of the four occurrences are found in this fifth vision suggests that it is thematically significant. The sentence is conveyed by two Hebrew words and for the first time Zechariah receives from the interpreting angel a reprimand in the form of a question: "Do you not know what they are?" This counter question is a rebuke and appears only in the fifth vision (here and in 4:13). In 2:2 Zechariah had asked, "What are these?" and was immediately told, "the horns that have scattered Judah, Israel, and Jerusalem." In the fifth vision, immediately after Zechariah admits his lack of knowledge, the author records two answers spoken by the interpreting angel to Zechariah. The first is a double-pronged oracle that enhances the status of Zerubbabel (4:6d–7 and 4:8–10a) and then a more explicit response to the question at hand in v 10b. It becomes apparent in this question-answer sequence that more work remains to be done despite the encouraging tone of the first four visions. In the course of the oracle Zerubbabel is depicted as a temple builder par excellence. It is he who is the "great mountain" (v 7). A new Solomon, he is the one whose elevation has come not by his own might or power but by Yhwh's spirit (v 6b). Zerubbabel's elevation is similar to that of Joshua in the previous vision, and their portraits reflect the importance of the dyarchic structure of governor and high priest approved by the Persian authorities.

Two individuals are introduced in the oracle. Zerubbabel receives an endorsement amid shouts of approbation, in contrast to the

[16] David Petersen, *Haggai and Zechariah 1–8*, OTL (Philadelphia: Westminster, 1984), 217–24.

unnamed "you" in v 7 ("Who are you?"). The identity of "you" remains unsolved.[17] The contrasting imagery of v 7 is, however, clear: Zerubbabel is the mountain and someone else is the plain. Zerubbabel is the one who shall succeed: "he shall bring out the top stone (to be used in the reconstruction of the temple) amid shouts of "grace, grace to it!" (v 7).

Zechariah asks next about the two olive trees, and this question is followed by two additional interrogatives:

> And-I-answered and-I-said to-him, What-are-these two olive-trees on-the-right-of the-lampstand and-on-its-left? (Zech 4:11).

> And-I-answered a-second-time and-I-said to-him, What-are-the-two branches-of the-olive-trees, which-are in-the-hand-of the-two pipes-of gold pouring-out from-upon-them the-gold (Zech 4:12).

> And-he-said to-me, saying, Do-you-not know what-these-are? And-I-said, No, my-lord (Zech 4:13).

The two questions of the interpreting angel in the first part of the fifth vision are now balanced by the two questions that the prophet asks in the second part of the vision (vv 11, 12). At v 12 Zechariah asks a question similar to the one invoked in v 11. The second question is more specific. In this follow-up he asks about the "two branches" of the olive trees that pour gold through the golden pipes. The two branches have not been previously mentioned. Again the interpreting angel expresses dismay at Zechariah's ignorance and answers Zechariah's question with a question: "Do you not know what these are?" As before, Zechariah must admit that he lacks knowledge and again the angel interprets: the two trees are the sons of the oil who stand next to the Lord of the entire earth. In this fifth vision, more than in any other, the frequent use of the interrogative allows new information to be added to the primary vision.

After the comparatively large number of questions that appear in the fifth vision (4:1–14), one finds only an occasional question in the next three visions. In the sixth vision (5:1–4) the only interrogative appears in 5:2. In the seventh vision (5:5–11) interrogatives are found at 5:6 and 5:10. In the eighth and final vision (6:1–8) the only interrogative appears in 6:4.

[17] Paul Redditt summarizes the lack of scholarly consensus in *Haggai, Zechariah, and Malachi*, 69.

> And-he-said to-me, What-do you see? And-I-said, I see a-flying scroll; its-length-is twenty cubits, and-its-width ten cubits (Zech 5:2).

> And-I-said, What-is-it? And-he-said, This-is the-ephah that-goes-forth. And-he-said, This-is its-iniquity[18] in-all-the-earth (Zech 5:6).

> And-I-said to-the-angel, the-one-who-speaks with-me, Where-are they-taking the-ephah? (Zech 5:10).

> And-I-answered and-I-said to-the-angel, the-one-who-speaks with-me, What-are-these, my-lord? (Zech 6:4).

Each of these questions serves to advance the plot. The fifth vision opens with the narrator's description of Zechariah looking up and seeing a flying scroll. Thereupon the interpreting angel asks him what he sees. Only in the fifth and sixth visions does the interpreting angel initiate conversation with this question. In all other visions, the prophet asks the angel "what are," "where are," "what is" questions. The departure in the sixth vision allows the author to emphasize the narrator's report of the "flying scroll," and to embellish it with a description of its dimensions: it is twenty cubits (approximately thirty feet) wide and ten cubits (approximately fifteen feet) tall. A scroll of twenty cubits in length was not uncommon, but scrolls were usually less than a cubit in height. One ten cubits high would have been unmanageable.[19] This unwieldy scroll corresponds to the vast number of thieves and perjurers (vv 4–5) and suggests the extent of God's judgment upon them.

At the beginning of the seventh vision Zechariah is instructed to lift his eyes and see what is coming out. He obeys and immediately asks, "What is it?" (5:6) This opening question is similar to others Zechariah asks—in the first, second, third, and eighth visions (1:8, 2:2, 2:6, and 6:4)—but it is set apart by the follow-up question in v 10: "Where are they taking the ephah?" At the rhetorical level the opening questions serve to elicit a description of the object, and the interpretation of the object follows after it is identified: "this (ephah) is their iniquity in all the earth." After a description of the women with wings who carry the ephah between earth and sky (v 9), the visionary asks about the destination of the ephah. The inter-

---

[18] Following LXX and Syriac. The slight emendation of MT (י to ו) creates a parallel with "wickedness" in v 7. But cf. the comments of Meyers and Meyers, *Haggai, Zechariah 1–8*, 297–98.

[19] Redditt, *Haggai, Zechariah, and Malachi*, 72.

preting angel answers the question, then supplies more information: "to the land of Shinar to build a house for it; and when this is prepared, they will set the ephah down there on its base." This "where" question accentuates movement of the ephah from Palestine to Shinar, i.e., the land of Babylon.[20] Their "iniquity" (v 6) will be sent to the land from which the Judeans have recently been freed under the edict of Cyrus, and the building of a house for a deity in Shinar (v 11) balances the restoration of Yhwh's house in Jerusalem. Zechariah's eighth and final vision begins at 6:1. He sees four chariots driven by vividly colored horses coming out between two bronze mountains. His "what are these" question in v 4 is a request for interpretation; the details of the vision he already knows (vv 1–3). The interpreting angel immediately responds: "these are the four winds of heaven going out, after presenting themselves before Yhwh of all the earth" (v 5). This image encompasses a vast geographic range for the four winds represent the four compass directions, and the explanation in vv 5–8 creates a sense of confidence in the restored world order under Yhwh's universal realm.

Questions that Increase the Number of Characters in a Given Scene

In another dialogic situation whereby prophetic utterances unfold, the number of characters in a scene increases as questions are invoked. On the twenty-fourth day of the ninth month, in the second year of Darius, Yhwh asks for a ruling of the priests.

> If[21] one-carries consecrated-meat in-the-fold-of one's-garment, and-touches with-the-fold the-bread, or-the-stew, or-the-wine, or-oil, or-any-kind-of-food, does-it-become-holy? And-the-priests answered and-they-said, No (Hag 2:12).

Dialogic situations involving three parties (prophet, priests, and Yhwh in this instance) are quite rare in biblical Hebrew narrative. This questioner asks if holiness can be transmitted by accidental contact with a person carrying meat (lit., "holy flesh") in the fold of one's garment. This meat in question is dedicated to the altar for the purpose of sacrifice. The prophet is thus commissioned to ask whether

---

[20] The LXX, Syriac, and Targum substitute "Babylon" for "Shinar."

[21] For this translation of הֵן, see the comments of Hans Walter Wolff, *Haggai: A Commentary* (Minneapolis: Augsburg, 1988), 88, n. 12a; and Verhoef, *Books of Haggai and Malachi*, 116–17.

an object becomes holy through indirect contact with holy sacrificial meat (cf. Lev 6:18). If the fold touches something else, is the sanctity of the holy meat transmitted to the common object? The priests answer in the negative. Indirect contact with the sacred does not make holy what is profane. By means of this question Haggai brings to the attention of his audience a pragmatic issue and follows with another question, this time about defilement:

> And-Haggai said, If-one-touches an-unclean-corpse[22] with-any-of-these, does-it-become-unclean? And-the-priests answered, and-said, it-does-become-unclean (Hag 2:13).

In this second hypothetical case before the priests, Haggai asks about a person who touches a corpse and then contacts the articles of food mentioned in v 12. Do they become unclean? The priests affirm that the food would indeed be unclean. Such impurity is contagious. The corpse's uncleanness has infecting power and any person who touches it can contaminate food. Any such person who has not been made pure by cleansing rituals "defiles the tabernacle of Yhwh and that person shall be cut off from Israel" (Num 19:13). Anything connected with death has no place before Yhwh.

Holiness, therefore, is not contagious in the way that uncleanness is contagious. The Samaritans were eager to participate in sacrifices and to assist the Jews in rebuilding the temple.[23] The prophet rejects such a coalition on the grounds that the people must trust in Yhwh's assistance and not in any help from the Samaritans (1:13; 2:4b, 2:5b; cf. 2 Kgs 17:29–41; Ezra 4:2). From this double question-answer scheme, Haggai draws the conclusion: "so it is with this people, and with this nation before me, says Yhwh: and so with every work with their hands; and what they offer there is unclean" (v 14).

In his discourse on laying the foundation of the temple, Haggai continues to expand the number of characters by referring to "this people" and "this nation before me" (2:14). He asks and answers a question in 2:16:

> How-did-you-fare?[24] When-one-came to-a-heap-of-twenty-(measures), there-were-but ten; when-one-came to-the-winevat to-draw fifty measures, there-were-but twenty.

---

[22] For the translation of נפש as "corpse," see the comments of Smith, *Micah-Malachi*, 159, n. 13a.

[23] Verhoef, *Books of Haggai and Malachi*, 119.

[24] LXX. On the "incomprehensible" MT's third-person plural suffix, see Wolff, *Haggai*, 58, n. 16a–a. Cf. also Meyers and Meyers, *Haggai, Zechariah 1–8*, 60, n. 16.

The "how did you fare?" question refers to the time before the temple was ritually purified and before rebuilding began. The question underscores the plight of the people before work on the temple was begun, and by asking *and* answering the question Haggai exhorts the people to remember their previous distress. The answer is given in two parallel sentences. The previous occasions have been marked by disappointment: when one came looking for a heap of twenty measures, there were only ten, and the person wanting to draw fifty measures from the vat could draw only twenty. Before mentioning the projected day of blessing (v 19), Haggai first of all reminds the people of their past circumstances. In this question-answer sequence Haggai thus constructs an antithesis between the negligence of the people in the past with the projected blessing of Yhwh.

The interrogative form of Hag 2:16 resumes at 2:19.

> Is-yet the-seed in-the-granary? And-is-it-yet-that-the-vine, and-the-fig-tree, and-the-pomegranate, and-the-olive tree do-not produce?[25] From-this day-on I-will-bless-you.

With these questions we perceive what Hans Walter Wolff calls "Haggai's own, familiar, spoken, dialogue."[26] The prophet again announces an abrupt turn, a new blessing from this day forward. Grapes, wine, figs, pomegranate, and olives—the very staples of Israelite diet—will once again be plentiful. These new images of seed in the granary and fruit on the vine enhance the agricultural picture conveyed by verses 16–17.

In the midst of Zechariah's first vision, the interpreting angel also increases the number of characters with a question addressed to Yhwh.

> And-the-angel-of-Yhwh answered and-said, Yahweh-of hosts, how-long-will you have-no-mercy on-Jerusalem and the-cities-of Judah, with-which you-have-been-angry these seventy years? (Zech 1:12)

The interrogative word עד־מתי ("how-long") is often found at the beginning of the individual or communal lament Psalms. By invoking this question, the angel hopes to elicit a response and to call

[25] The interrogative particle is found with the first question, but is not repeated in the second instance. The particle applies, however, to both sentences in the העוד . . . ועד construction.

[26] Wolff, *Haggai*, 66.

attention to the incomplete temple complex.[27] Rather than record the words of God's response, the narrator reports that Yhwh's response was gracious and comforting (v 13). Deprived of the words, the audience can only infer their content from the oracles conveyed by the interpreting angel in vv 14–17. With the city and temple in ruins, it appeared that God had failed to show mercy on Jerusalem, and with this question the petitioner addresses a compelling thought directly to God: the time to act has arrived. The question is actually a protest against continued intolerable existence, and in this instance it is the interpreting angel, not the prophet, who utters the impassioned plea.

Just before a series of questions in 7:5–7 (discussed above under "the sequential questions") an interrogative is voiced about fasting over the destruction of the temple:

> to-say to-the-priests who-were of-the-house-of-Yahweh-of hosts and-to-the-prophets, saying, Should-I-weep in-the-fifth month, restricting-myself,[28] as I-have-done this many years? (Zech 7:3).

In a fashion similar to the examples above, the invocation of this question increases the number of characters. After the question about mourning and fasting is posed, Yhwh appears manifest in the form of a voice. The question originates with the people of Bethel, who are sent as a delegation to ask the priests whether people should continue observing the fast as the temple is being rebuilt. The question is framed in the first person, presumably by one who represents the group and the community who sent them. The petitioner asks if this lamentable period of destruction, punishment, and exile has ended. What sort of rights and attitudes are appropriate for a community that is rebuilding, and at a time when Jerusalem barely exists? Is this a time of grief or hope? This question also provokes a series of sayings on the present spiritual condition of the community, the divine judgment on the ancestors, and a declaration of God's promises for future blessings.

[27] Direct answers to such questions addressed to God are not usually found with this type of lament.

[28] Following Meyers and Meyers, *Haggai, Zechariah 1–8*, 386–87.

Conclusion

Interrogatives function as literary threads in Haggai-Zechariah. Four different types can be discerned: rhetorical questions, sequential questions, questions that function primarily to advance the plot, and questions that increase the number of characters in a given scene. A sense of unity is heightened in the two books by means of this vivid rhetorical style. The frequent and varied use of interrogatives anticipates the protean forms of interrogatives that pepper certain dialectic forms of instruction evident in rabbinical discourses and are reminiscent of the multiple forms found in the Socratic dialogues.[29]

While one discovers an obvious literary connection among the interrogatives in Haggai-Zechariah 1–8, the pattern does not extend to Zechariah 9–14. The night visions conclude at Zech 6:8 and the remainder of proto-Zechariah (6:9–8:23) is composed of oracles. When reading chapters 9–14, sometimes called second (chs. 9–11) and third (chs. 12–14) Zechariah, one cannot help but be struck by a change in style. More than thirty questions are invoked in the Haggai-Zechariah 1–8 corpus, but only one interrogative appears in Zechariah 9–14 (i.e., at 13:6). This shift at the literary level is matched by other changes: Zechariah is never mentioned in the last six chapters; no identifiable person or event is mentioned; the new temple exists in chapters 9–14 (9:8, 11:13, 14:16–21), whereas before it was anticipated; and no visions are reported in chapters 9–14 in marked contrast to the opening chapters. While such discontinuity does suggest a different rhetorical strategy beginning with Zechariah 9, it does not necessarily imply disunity between the two works. However, if one wishes to argue for the unity of Haggai and the fourteen chapters of Zechariah, clues other than the author's predilection for the interrogative must be found.[30]

---

[29] Kenneth Craig, *Reading Esther: A Case for the Literary Carnivalesque*, Literary Currents in Biblical Interpretation (Louisville: Westminster/John Knox, 1995), 22, 36–41, 50.

[30] Radday and Wickmann ("Unity of Zechariah") explore this topic from the standpoint of statistical linguistics. Rex Mason ("The Relation of Zech 9–14 to Proto-Zechariah," *ZAW* 88 [1976], 227–239) discusses unity as he focuses exclusively on the oracular material in the fourteen chapters of Zechariah. But cf. esp. the discussion at n. 4 above and the articles by Ronald Pierce ("Literary Connectors" and "Thematic Development"). In a subsequent study, one might ask if the many interrogative forms in Malachi fit into the distinct typological scheme of Haggai-Zechariah 1–8.

BIBLIOGRAPHY

Ackroyd, Peter R. *Exile and Restoration.* OTL. London: SCM, 1968.

——. *The Second Book of Samuel.* CBC. Cambridge: Cambridge University Press, 1977.

Alter, Robert. *The Art of Biblical Narrative.* New York: Basic Books, 1981.

Andersen, Francis I., and David Noel Freedman. *Hosea: A New Translation with Introduction and Commentary.* AB 24. Garden City, N.Y.: Doubleday, 1980.

Anderson, A. A. *2 Samuel.* WBC 11. Dallas: Word, 1989.

Auerbach, Erich. *Mimesis: The Representation of Reality in Western Literature.* Willard R. Trask, trans. Princeton: Princeton University Press, 1953.

Bakhtin, Mikhail. *Problems of Dostoevsky's Poetics.* Theory and History of Literature, 8. Caryl Emerson, trans. and ed. Minneapolis: University of Minnesota Press, 1984.

Bakon, Shimon. "Jonathan." *JBQ* 23 (1995): 147–48.

Ball, E. "The Co-Regency of David and Solomon (1 Kings 1)." *VT* 27 (1977): 268–79.

Bar-Efrat, Shimon. *Narrative Art in the Bible.* Sheffield: Almond, 1989.

Ben-Barak, Zafrira. "Succession to the Throne in Israel and in Assyria." *OLP* 17 (1986): 85–100.

Berlin, Adele. *Poetics and Interpretation of Biblical Narrative.* Sheffield: Almond, 1983.

Bussche, Henri. "Le texte de la prophétie de Nathan sur la dynastie davidique." *ETL* 24 (1948): 354–94.

Cassuto, Umberto. *A Commentary on the Book of Genesis: Part 1, From Adam to Noah (Genesis 1–6:8).* Israel Abrahams, trans. Jerusalem: Magnes, 1961.

Chang, Suk-Jin. "Non-Standard Questions: Polarity and Contrast." *Language Research* 18 (1982): 157–70.

Cohen, Felix. "What Is a Question?" *The Monist* 39 (1929): 350–64.

Craig Jr., Kenneth M. "The Character(ization) of God in 2 Samuel 7:1–17." *Sem* 63 (1993): 159–76.

——. *A Poetics of Jonah: Art in the Service of Ideology.* 2nd ed. Macon, Ga.: Mercer University Press, 1999.

——. "Questions Outside Eden (Genesis 4:1–16): Yhwh, Cain, and their Rhetorical Interchange." *JSOT* 86 (1999): 107–28.

——. *Reading Esther: A Case for the Literary Carnivalesque.* Literary Currents in Biblical Interpretation. Louisville: Westminster/John Knox, 1995.

——. "Rhetorical Aspects of Questions Answered with Silence in 1 Samuel 14:37 and 28:6." *CBQ* 56 (1994): 221–39.

Cryer, Frederick H. "David's Rise to Power and the Death of Abner: An Analysis of 1 Samuel xxvi 14–16 and its Redactional-Critical Implications." *VT* 35 (1985): 385–94.

Daube, David. "Direct and Indirect Causation in Biblical Law." *VT* 11 (1961): 246–69.

Ewen, Joseph. *Character in Narrative* (Hebrew). Tel Aviv: Sifriyat Po'alim, 1980.

——. "The Theory of Character in Narrative Fiction" (Hebrew). *Hasifrut* 3 (1971): 1–30.

Flanagan, James W. "Court History or Succession Document? A Study of 2 Samuel 9–20 and 1 Kings 1–2." *JBL* 91 (1972): 172–81.

Fokkelman, J. P. *Narrative Art and Poetry in the Books of Samuel: A Full Interpretation Based on Stylistic and Structural Analyses (The Crossing Fates, I Sam. 13–31 & II Sam. 1)*, vol. 2. Studia semitica neerlandica 23. Assen/Maastricht: van Gorcum, 1986.

——. *Narrative Art and Poetry in the Books of Samuel: A Full Interpretation Based on Stylistic and Structural Analyses (King David, II Sam. 9–20 & I Kings 1–2)*, vol. 1. Studia semitica neerlandica 20. Assen: van Gorcum, 1981.

——. *Narrative Art and Poetry in the Books of Samuel: A Full Interpretation Based on Stylistic and Structural Analyses (Throne & City: II Sam. 2–8 & 21–24)*, vol. 3. Studia semitica neerlandica 27. Assen/Maastricht: van Gorcum, 1990.

Frank, Jane. "You Call that a Question?" *Journal of Pragmatics* 14 (1990): 723–738.

Garsiel, Moshe. "Puns upon Names as a Literary Device in 1 Kings 1–2." *Bib* 72 (1991): 379–86.

Gordis, Robert. "A Rhetorical Use of Interrogative Sentences in Biblical Hebrew." *AJSL* 49 (1933): 212–17.

——. *The Word and the Book: Studies in Biblical Language and Literature*. New York: Ktav, 1976.

Gowan, Donald. "The Use of *yaʿan* in Biblical Hebrew." *VT* 21 (1971): 168–85.

Gray, John. *Joshua, Judges, Ruth*. NCBC. Grand Rapids: Eerdmans, 1986.

——. *I & II Kings: A Commentary*. OTL. 2nd ed. Philadelphia: Westminster, 1964.

Gressmann, Hugo. *Narrative and Novella in Samuel: Studies by Hugo Gressmann and Other Scholars (1906–1923)*. JSOTSup 116/HTIBS 9. David E. Orton, trans., and David M. Gunn, ed. Sheffield: Almond, 1991.

Grønbaek, Jakob H. *Die Geschechte vom Aufstieg Davids (1 Sam. 15–2 Sam. 5): Tradition und Komposition*. Copenhagen: Munksgaard, 1971.

Gunkel, Hermann. *Genesis*. 8th ed. Göttingen: Vandenhoeck & Ruprecht, 1969.

Gunn, David M. *The Story of King David: Genre and Interpretation*, JSOTSup 6. Sheffield: Sheffield Academic Press, 1978.

Hamilton, Victor P. *The Book of Genesis: Chapters 1–17*. NICOT. Grand Rapids, Mich.: Eerdmans, 1990.

Hauser, Alan Jon. "Genesis 2–3: The Theme of Intimacy and Alienation." In *Art and Meaning: Rhetoric in Biblical Literature*. JSOTSup 19. David J. A. Clines, David Gunn, and Alan J. Hauser, eds. Sheffield: Sheffield Academic Press, 1982. Pp. 20–36.

——. "Linguistic and Thematic Links between Genesis 4:1–16 and Genesis 2–3." *JETS* 23 (1980): 297–305.

Heidegger, Martin. *Being and Time*, John McQuarrie and Edward Robinson, trans. New York: Harper, 1962.

Held, Moshe. "Rhetorical Questions in Ugaritic and Biblical Hebrew." *EI* 9 (1969): 71–79.

Hempel, Johannes. *Geschichte und Geschichten im Alten Testament bis zum persischen Zeitalter*. Gütersloh: Gütersloher Verlagshaus G. Mohn, 1964.

Hertzberg, Hans Wilhelm. *I & II Samuel: A Commentary*. OTL. 4th ed. Philadelphia: Westminster, 1976.

House, Paul. *The Unity of the Twelve*. JSOTSup 77. Sheffield: Sheffield Academic Press, 1990.

Hurowitz, Victor. *I Have Built You an Exalted House: Temple Building in the Bible in Light of Mesopotamian and Northwest Semitic Writings*. JSOTSup 115; JSOT/ASOR Monograph Series 5. Sheffield: Sheffield Academic Press, 1992.

Hyman, Ronald T. "Fielding 'Why' Questions in Genesis." *HAR* 11 (1987): 173–83.

——. "Questions and the Book of Ruth." *HS* 24 (1983): 17–25.

Ishida, Tomoo. "Adonijah the Son of Haggith and His Supporters: An Inquiry into Problems about History and Historiography." In *The Future of Biblical Studies*. Richard Elliott Friedman and H. G. M. Williamson, eds. Atlanta: Scholars, 1987. Pp. 165–87.

——. "Solomon's Succession to the Throne of David—A Political Analysis." In *Studies in the Period of David and Solomon and Other Essays*. Tomoo Ishida, ed. Winona Lake, IN: Eisenbrauns, 1982. Pp. 175–87.

Japhet, Sara. *I & II Chronicles: A Commentary*. OTL. Louisville: Westminster/John Knox, 1993.

Klein, Ralph. *1 Samuel*. WBC 10. Waco: Word, 1983.

Koops, Robert. "Rhetorical Questions and Implied Meaning in the Book of Job." *BTrans* 39 (1988): 415–23.

Kruse, Heinz. "David's Covenant." *VT* 35 (1985): 139–64.

Landy, Francis. "Humour as a Tool for Biblical Exegesis." In *On Humour and the Comic in the Hebrew Bible*. Bible and Literature Series, 23. Y. T. Radday and A. Brenner, eds. Sheffield: Almond, 1990. Pp. 99–115.

Lasine, Stuart. "Judicial Narratives and the Ethics of Reading: The Reader as Judge of the Dispute between Mephibosheth and Ziba." *HS* 30 (1989): 49–69.

Lawton, Robert B. "Saul, Jonathan, and the 'Son of Jesse.'" *JSOT* 58 (1993): 35–46.

Lewis, Jack P. "The Offering of Abel (Gen 4:4): A History of Interpretation." *JETS* 37 (1994): 481–96.

Long, Burke O. "A Darkness between Brothers: Solomon and Adonijah." *JSOT* 19 (1981): 79–94.

——. "Two Question and Answer Schemata in the Prophets." *JBL* 90 (1971): 129–39.

Louis, Kenneth R. R. Gros. "The Garden of Eden." In *Literary Interpretations of Biblical Narratives*. Kenneth R. R. Gros Louis, ed. Nashville: Abingdon, 1974. Pp. 52–58.

——. "Genesis 1–2." In *Literary Interpretations of Biblical Narratives*. Kenneth R. R. Gros Louis, ed. Nashville: Abingdon, 1974. Pp. 41–51.

Malamat, Abraham. "A Mari Prophecy and Nathan's Dynastic Oracle." In *Prophecy: Essays Presented to Georg Fohrer on his Sixty-fifth Birthday*. J. A. Emerton, ed. New York: Walter de Gruyter, 1980. Pp. 68–82.

—— "Prophetic Revelations in New Documents from Mari and the Bible." VTSup 15 (1966): 207–27.

Mason, Rex. "The Relation of Zech 9–14 to Proto-Zechariah." *ZAW* 88 (1976): 227–39.

McCarter Jr., P. Kyle. "'Plot, True or False': The Succession Narrative as Court Apologetic." *Int* 35 (1982): 355–67.

——. *I Samuel*. AB 8. Garden City, N.Y.: Doubleday, 1980.

——. *II Samuel: A New Translation with Introduction, Notes, and Commentary*. AB 9. Garden City, N.Y.: Doubleday, 1984.

McHale, Brian. "Free Indirect Discourse: A Survey of Recent Accounts." *Poetics and the Theory of Literature: A Journal for Descriptive Poetics and Theory of Literature* 3 (1978): 249–87.

McKenzie, John L. "The Literary Characteristics of Genesis 2–3." *TS* 15 (1954): 541–72.

Mettinger, Tryggve N. D. *King and Messiah: The Civil and Sacral Legitimation of the Israelite Kings*. Lund: G. W. K. Gleerup, 1976.

Meyers, Carol, and Eric Meyers. *Haggai, Zechariah 1–8*. AB 25B. New York: Doubleday, 1987.

Miscall, Peter. *1 Samuel: A Literary Reading*. Bloomington: Indiana University Press, 1986.

——. *The Working of Old Testament Narrative*. Philadelphia: Fortress/Chico, Calif.: Scholars, 1983.

Mitchell, H. G. *A Critical and Exegetical Commentary on Haggai, Zechariah, Malachi, and Jonah*. ICC. Edinburgh: T. & T. Clark, 1912.

Moberly, R. Walter L. "Did the Serpent Get it Right?" *JTS* 39 (1988): 1–27.
Montgomery, James A. *A Critical and Exegetical Commentary on the Books of Kings*. ICC. Edinburgh: T. & T. Clark, 1951.
Myers, J. M. *II Chronicles*. AB 13. Garden City, N.Y.: Doubleday, 1965.
Nelson, Richard D. *First and Second Kings*. Atlanta: John Knox Press, 1987.
Noort, Edward. "Eine weitere Kurzbemerkung zu 1. Samuel XIV 41." *VT* 21 (1971): 112–16.
Noth, Martin. "David and Israel in II Samuel VII." In *The Laws in the Pentateuch and Other Studies*. Martin Noth, ed. London: SCM, 1966. Pp. 250–59.
Olyan, Saul M. "Honor, Shame, and Covenant Relations in Ancient Israel and its Environment." *JBL* 115 (1996): 201–18.
Ota, Michiko. "A Note on 2 Sam 7." In *A Light Unto My Path. OT Studies in Honor of J. M. Myers*. H. N. Bream et al., eds. Gettysburg Theological Studies 4. Philadelphia: Temple University Press, 1974. Pp. 403–7.
Petersen, David. *Haggai and Zechariah 1–8*. OTL. Philadelphia: Westminster, 1984.
Pfeiffer, Robert. *Introduction to the Old Testament*. New York: Harper & Brothers, 1941.
Pierce, Ronald W. "Literary Connectors and a Haggai/Zechariah/Malachi Corpus." *JETS* 27 (1984): 277–89.
——. "A Thematic Development of the Haggai/Zechariah/Malachi Corpus." *JETS* 27 (1984): 401–11.
Polzin, Robert. *David and the Deuteronomist: A Literary Study of the Deuteronomic History, Part Three (2 Samuel)*. Bloomington and Indianapolis: Indiana University Press, 1993.
——. *Samuel and the Deuteronomist: A Literary Study of the Deuteronomic History, Part Two (1 Samuel)*. San Francisco: Harper and Row, 1989.
von Rad, Gerhard. *Genesis: A Commentary*. OTL. Philadelphia: Westminster, 1972.
——. *Old Testament Theology*, vol. 1. D. M. G. Stalker, trans. New York: Harper & Row, 1962.
Radday, Yehuda T., and Dieter Wickmann. "The Unity of Zechariah Examined in the Light of Statistical Linguistics." *ZAW* 87 (1975): 30–55.
Ramaroson, Léonard. "A propos de Gn 4,7." *Bib* 49 (1968): 233–37.
Rebera, Basil A. "He Got Up—Or Did He? (1 Samuel 20:25)." *BTrans* 40 (1989): 212–18.
Redditt, Paul. *Haggai, Zechariah, and Malachi*. NCBC. Grand Rapids: Eerdmans, 1995.
——. "Zerubbabel, Joshua, and the Night Visions of Zechariah." *CBQ* 54 (1992): 249–59.
Riemann, Paul A. "Am I My Brother's Keeper?" *Int* 24 (1970): 482–91.
Rimmon-Kenan, Shlomith. *Narrative Fiction: Contemporary Poetics*. London and New York: Methuen, 1983.
Rosenberg, Joel. "The Garden Story Forward and Backward: The Non-Narrative Dimension of Gen 2–3." *Proof* 1 (1981): 1–27.
Rost, Leonhard. *Überlieferung von der Thronnachfolge Davids*. BWANT 3/6. Stuttgart: Kohlhammer, 1926.
Rouillard, Hedwige. "Les feintes questions divines dans la Bible." *VT* 34 (1984): 237–42.
Savran, George W. *Telling and Retelling: Quotation in Biblical Narrative*. Bloomington and Indianapolis: Indiana University Press, 1988.
Schneider, Dale Allen. *The Unity of the Book of the Twelve*, Yale University, Ph.D. dissertation, 1979.
Schulz, Alfons. "Narrative Art in the Books of Samuel." In *Narrative and Novella in Samuel: Studies by Hugo Gressmann and Other Scholars (1906–1923)*. JSOTSup 116/HTIBS 9. David E. Orton, trans., and David M. Gunn, ed. Sheffield: Almond, 1991. Pp. 119–72.
Simon, Marcel. "La prophétie de Nathan et le Temple: Remarques sur II Sam. 7." *RHPR* 32 (1952): 41–58.

Simon, Uriel. "A Balanced Story: The Stern Prophet and the Kind Witch." *Proof* 8 (1988): 159–71.
Simpson, Cuthbert. A. "The Book of Genesis." In *The Interpreter's Bible*, vol. 1. George Buttrick, ed. Nashville: Abingdon, 1952. Pp. 438–829.
Skinner, J. A. *A Critical and Exegetical Commentary on the Book of Genesis*. ICC. 2nd ed. Edinburgh: T. & T. Clark, 1930.
Smith, Ralph. *Micah-Malachi*. WBC 32. Waco: Word, 1984.
Soggin, J. Alberto. *Judges: A Commentary*. OTL. Philadelphia: Westminster, 1981.
Speiser, E. A. *Genesis*. AB 1. Garden City, N.Y.: Doubleday, 1964.
Sternberg, Meir. *The Poetics of Biblical Narrative: Ideological Literature and the Drama of Reading*. Bloomington: Indiana University Press, 1985.
——. "Point of View and the Indirections of Direct Speech." *Language and Style* 15 (1982): 67–117.
——. "Time and Space in Biblical (Hi)story Telling: The Grand Chronology." In *The Book and the Text and Literary Theory*. Regina Schwartz, ed. Oxford: Basil Blackwell, 1990. Pp. 81–145.
Tate, Marvin E. *Psalms 51–100*. WBC 20. Dallas: Word, 1990.
Thompson, John A. "The Significance of the Verb *Love* in the David-Jonathan Narratives in 1 Samuel." *VT* 24 (1974): 334–38.
Trible, Phyllis. *God and the Rhetoric of Sexuality*. Philadelphia: Fortress, 1978.
——. *Rhetorical Criticism: Context, Method and the Book of Jonah*. Minneapolis: Fortress, 1994.
Tsevat, Matitiahu. "The House of David in Nathan's Prophecy." *Bib* 46 (1965): 353–56.
——. "What was David Promised in II Sam. 7:11b–16?" *HUCA* 34 (1963): 71–82.
Verhoef, Peter *The Books of Haggai and Malachi*. NICOT. Grand Rapids: Eerdmans, 1987.
Vorster, Willem S. "Readings, Readers and the Succession Narrative: An Essay on Reception." *ZAW* 98 (1986): 351–62.
de Vries, Simon J. *1 Kings*. WBC 12. Waco: Word, 1985.
Walsh, Jerome T. "Genesis 2:4b–3:24: A Synchronic Approach." *JBL* 96 (1977): 161–77.
Weiss, Meir. "Einiges über die Bauformen des Erzählens in der Bibel." *VT* 13 (1963): 456–75.
Wenham, Gordon J. *Genesis 1–15*. WBC 1. Waco: Word, 1987.
Wénin, André. "Le discours de Jonathan à David (1 S 20, 12–16) et autres notes (2,20; 9,24; 15,9)." *Bib* 64 (1983): 1–19.
Westermann, Claus. *Genesis 1–11: A Commentary*. Minneapolis: Augsburg, 1984.
White, Hugh. "Direct and Third Person Discourse in the Narrative of the 'Fall.'" *Sem* 18 (1980): 91–106.
——. *Narration and Discourse in the Book of Genesis*. Cambridge: Cambridge University Press, 1991.
Williams, Jay G. "Genesis 3." *Int* 35 (1981): 274–79.
van Wolde, Ellen. "The Story of Cain and Abel: A Narrative Study." *JSOT* 52 (1991) 25–41.
Wolff, Hans Walter. *Haggai: A Commentary*. Minneapolis: Augsburg, 1988.
Yee, Gale A. "The Book of Hosea: Introduction, Commentary, and Reflections." In *The New Interpreter's Bible*, vol. 7. Leander E. Keck, ed. Nashville: Abingdon, 1996. Pp. 195–297.

INDEX OF MODERN AUTHORS

INDEX OF BIBLICAL TEXTS CITED